STATIONS
OF THE BANQUET

Faith Foundations for Food Justice

Cathy C. Campbell

To: VAL
all the blessings of
the banquet ✝

APRIL 1 '04

LITURGICAL PRESS
Collegeville, Minnesota

www.litpress.org

Design by David Manahan, O.S.B. Cover illustration: *Wedding Feast at Cana,* courtesy of Christ the Saviour Orthodox Church, Harrisburg, Pennsylvania.

Scripture quotations are taken from New Revised Standard Version Bible, Catholic edition, © 1989 by the Division of Christian Education of the National Council of the Churches of Christ in the U.S.A. Used by permission. All rights reserved.

1	2	3	4	5	6	7

Library of Congress Control Number: 2003109554

ISBN 0-8146-2938-5

Stations of the Banquet

To all involved in food ministries—
at home, at church,
in the field, factory, or laboratory,
in restaurants or grocery stores,
in community and non-governmental organizations,
in government and international agencies.

On that day . . . every cooking pot [and perhaps most especially 'cooking pots'] *in Jerusalem and Judah shall be sacred to the* LORD *of hosts* (Zech 14:20a, 21a).

CONTENTS

INTRODUCTION

Food is essential to our lives. Indeed, we become what we eat both physically and spiritually. Food and the ways we produce, distribute, and consume it have always been central to the story of life. It shapes our relationships to the land, to each other, to ourselves, and to the Sacred. It can lead to life abundant for all or scarcity and deprivation, to wholeness and health or disease and fractured community, to celebration and joy or desperation and violence. Food and food ways are inseparable from an understanding of justice and the fullness of the reign of God.

From the beginning, food has been central to the Christian faith. It is no surprise then that virtually every church event is a food event. When we gather for Bible study, meetings, work, or worship, we share coffee, tea, and often a taste of something. We share food with others through meal programs, food pantries, food drives, community kitchens or gardens. We share bread and wine whenever we celebrate the Eucharist. Appreciating the place of food in our faith reveals much about our Christian story of salvation. Yet this dimension of our faith is little explored.

In fact, the busy, practical, physical nature of food has often been considered antithetical, or at least peripheral, to a life of faith. Food activities are often relegated to the basements or invisible margins of our life together. The activist Martha, busy preparing supper in the kitchen for Christ, has all too often been set in opposition to her sister, the contemplative Mary, who sits quietly listening to Christ's word. This book is an invitation to explore the fundamental relationship between these two sisters. It examines the relationship of our experience with the Holy and our struggle for justice or right relationship with each other and creation. It retells the story of salvation with a food-justice lens that we might see it anew and be transformed. For whether written large in the stories of our nations or in the fine calligraphy of our daily lives, our salvation is encountered, negotiated, lived in the dance between the sisters. This book is for all who yearn to be re-freshed, nourished, and challenged at the table of the one who came as the Bread of Life to invite us all to the fullness of the banquet.

INTENTION OF *STATIONS OF THE BANQUET*

Stations of the Banquet emerges from the internal conversation of a person of faith, priest of the Anglican Church of Canada, and a food activist, frequent cook, and community organizer. I've spent twenty-five years up-to-my-elbows in the kitchen sinks of such contemporary food questions as:

- Why are so many people hungry or food insecure in both develop-ing and industrialized countries?

- Why do our agricultural system and food processing and trans-portation practices threaten the integrity of the very ecosystems on which we rely for life?

- Why, with more wealth, information, and technological capacity than ever before, are these issues so intractable?

- Why do we seem unable to mobilize our collective will to act con-structively on these issues?

In the struggle to answer these questions, a host of economic, eco-logical, political, sociological, and psychological factors emerge. Some argue that there is also a profound epistemological dimension to these interwoven issues. The simultaneous developments labeled "globaliza-tion" and "postmodernism" also significantly complicate any collective action on these issues. It is clear that these food and agriculture issues are but one knot of symptoms in the tangled yarn of our life together on the planet.

In the face of these realities, I began to suspect that there is a deep spiritual dimension to the food and agriculture issues we are facing. It is clear that any substantial reorientation of the trajectory we are on as a planet will require a fundamental conversion of commitment, priori-ties, and worldview. It will require deeply rooted, creative action with many others, both close at home and around the globe, who differ markedly from us. The nourishment to sustain and inspire such work, whose outcome may only be seen well after our lifetimes, is the spiritual territory explored in this book.

The thesis of *Stations of the Banquet* is that serious reflection on the faith dimension of our lives reshapes our deepest commitments, our ways of being, doing, and thinking about ourselves and the world around us. Without engagement at this spiritual core, our struggle to reshape our lives together as a planet is likely to be limited in its effectiveness. *Stations of the Banquet* is not, therefore, a recipe book of solutions for our current food and agriculture issues. It does not provide prescriptions for the improvement or redesign of our food programs, or advice on how to be a better food consumer. It neither analyzes the nature of these issues, nor offers a detailed action plan. Much fine work has already been done on these issues. Appendix II provides a short overview and listing of websites for organizations working creatively on these issues.

Rather, *Stations of the Banquet* addresses such questions as:

- What are the faith resources that our Christian tradition offers to us who, in the practical details of our everyday life and work, struggle for life abundant for all (John 10:10)?

- What are the seeds that the Spirit has planted deep in the soil of our lives that can bear a thirty-, sixty-, or hundred-fold harvest (Mark 4:8)?

- What is the nature of the hope to which we have been called (1 Pet 3:15)?

- What is the sustenance, the bread, offered by the Word of life?

- What are the spiritual challenges that our faith calls us to address in our time and place?

- What are some of the practical ways we engage these faith challenges?

I believe that it is at this level of reflection that we learn to sing wholeheartedly the song of the Heart and Wisdom of the Universe revealed to us in Jesus Christ. And I believe that this song is transformative.

Stations of the Banquet is written in the language of faith, and more specifically the Christian language of faith. This approach is not a nostalgic turn to a pre-modern world of certainty and comfort. Nor does it suggest that this is the only language of faith. Rather, its agenda is to recover the Christian language of faith for those who are struggling with contemporary issues of food security, justice, and abundant life for all. In this arena, the language of faith is largely considered a private, individualistic matter. It is often silenced out of an appropriate respect for the differences of belief in our diverse communities and the potential of those differences to engender passionate dissension. Nonetheless, from a stance of faith, its power to inspire and transform commitments, to reshape imaginations and sustain constructive action, lies in its truth. The language of faith is much more than another marketing language. Its value is not in its usefulness to move hearts. Its truth cannot be bought, used, or manipulated without distortion and diminishment. Its power and meaning can only be accessed by deep engagement in its reality. To ignore it in secular contexts, or to trivialize it as happens too often in church outreach programs, is to miss a critical dimension of reality. *Stations of the Banquet* is an invitation to deepen our engagement with faith.

USE AND STRUCTURE OF THE BOOK

Consciously or not, gracefully or with angst, we engage the challenges and blessings of being a person of faith in our particular place and time. The dance between our faith and day-to-day practice is dynamic. It is unscripted and new each day. I hope that, read on its own or in a group, *Stations of the Banquet* will create the critical distance needed to consider the familiar elements in this dance anew, to bring what has become invisible into the light, and to refresh the meaning of our actions and our faith.

The implications of such reflection for either "the way we do things" or "the way we understand things" come into view in conversation with the practical details and relationships of our local situation. The Spiritual Challenge, Spiritual Practice, and Litany in each station provide starting points for a conversation about the ways the Voices of Our Tradition address our personal lives, work lives, or the life and work of a program or congregation. The litanies or prayers at the end of each station are included as a conscious invitation for God to enter into that conversation. They are written for group use and corporate prayer, as all conversation is infinitely enriched in community. It is my hope that *Stations of the Banquet* will bring some of the extraordinary riches of our tradition into that conversation and will deepen the connections between our faith and our practice. I hope that it will enliven and sustain our resourcefulness to meet the challenges of our particular time and place with courage, imagination, dignity, and deep faith.[1]

Each station considers a different dimension of the Christian story of salvation. The sequence of the stations creates a narrative from the creation of the universe (Station 1) to its unfolding renewal as the new creation (Station 14). Station 1 is a prose poem snapshot of our whole context: the glory of creation. Stations 2 and 3 acknowledge the diminishment and distortion of the fullness of creation, but do not linger in that place of disintegration and oppression. The eleven subsequent stations address the ever-widening circles of Christ's presence in history. The center of the journey of the banquet, Stations 4 through 8 consider aspects of Christ's presence in our midst and his claim on us. The widening horizons of our hope are explored in the final stations, 9 through 13. Station 14 returns to survey the whole journey as the eighth day of creation. Taken together, the stations tell the Christian story of salvation. Although shaped into a schematic framework, the stations make no claim to being systematic or comprehensive. The aim is rather to animate conversation and spiritual refreshment that individually and together we may be more fully salt, leaven, mustard seeds in a world crying for God's love and liberation.

Stations of the Banquet is also intended to be a basis for communal prayer like the traditional Stations of the Cross. The litanies of each station, with Stations 1 and 14 in their entirety, form a *Stations of the Banquet*, analogous to the fourteen Stations of the Cross. Appendix I elaborates ways the stations can be used for such communal prayer. Traditionally Stations of the Cross invite us to deepen our lenten journey with Christ to his death and thereby open us to the full joy of Easter. *Stations of the Banquet* invites us to root deeply in the fertile soil of the Easter and Pentecost components of our tradition. As a

---

[1] Kathryn Tanner, "Theological Reflection and Christian Practices," *Practicing Theology: Beliefs and Practices in Christian Life*, ed. Miroslav Volf and Dorothy C. Bass (Grand Rapids, Mich.: Eerdmans, 2002) 232, 233.

parish study resource, it can appropriately span the lenten and Easter seasons of the Church year and begin to draw those different seasons more closely together. As a resource for corporate prayer, it can also help to draw the mission and liturgical life of a congregation into conversation. It is easy for the activist and contemplative sisters, Martha and Mary, to become separated. *Stations of the Banquet* is an opportunity for them to dance together.

A WORD ABOUT LANGUAGE

First, in our post-modern world where the very capacity of words and images to communicate is contested, a comment about language may be useful for readers living and working in different situations. In the Pentecost experience, people with very different languages understood themselves to be addressed by the one Spirit. In hope of such broad comprehensibility, I use multiple ways of referring to the same reality. A variety of names for that ineffable reality we call God are used. At times, there are sequences or lists of related ways of referring to an experience, event, or concept. These are used to initiate or spark thought and discussion, as well as to offer alternatives to those for whom the traditional words of our faith no longer point to the rich meaning they once conveyed. This diversity of expression is not intended as a deconstruction of cherished words, but rather as a constructive exploration of possibilities for a more inclusive communion of understanding.

Second, the Christian Scriptures lie at the heart of *Stations of the Banquet*. This is rooted in a deep belief that "the unfolding of your word gives light" (Ps 119:130), that we meet Christ in and through the text, and that the Bible is indeed a revelatory text for us.[2] It is our common ground. The Scriptures are approached with the question: What is the Spirit saying to the churches through the Word (Rev 2:29; 3:6, 13, 22)? This question engages all levels of Scripture to discern its meaning for us in our time and place as a community of faith. I have taken seriously the work of contemporary biblical scholars on questions of what exactly the Scriptures say [in their original languages,

---

[2] Sandra M. Schneiders, *The Revelatory Text: Interpreting the New Testament as Sacred Scripture* (San Francisco: Harper SanFrancisco, 1991).

worldviews, historical context, etc.] and how they say it [literary devices, structure, etc.]. However, the main focus of this project is the question of its meaning for us: our appropriation of the text and its transformation of us. Sandra Schneiders describes such a project as "the work of theology and spirituality integrating the encounter with Jesus as the Christ in and through the revelatory text within the existential horizon of the individual and the community."[3] This process bears fruit as we enter into the world of the text, address it, and allow it to address us.

To facilitate our participation with the text, Scripture is extensively incorporated into each station. The Scripture passages are direct quotations, although sometimes limited for conciseness. They have not been adapted to make them gender inclusive. This choice is based on the conviction that

> dialogue [between ourselves and Scripture] cannot be called off because of limitations in either the text's mediation of its subject matter or the capacities of the interpreter. Rather, it must be pursued with relentless love by those who believe that this text, thoroughly human as Jesus himself, is yet a privileged mediator of the encounter between God and humanity.[4]

In this encounter is our deepest hope.

THE BACKGROUND OF *STATIONS OF THE BANQUET*

Contemporary scholarship has made us aware of the ways that our context, experiences, and social location affect the way we see the world as well as the way we read and understand texts and Scripture more specifically. *Stations of the Banquet* is written for people immersed in the North American experience of privilege and the great and growing gap between those with enough [and often more than enough], and those without even the basics for life with dignity. This has been my life context and *Stations of the Banquet* is profoundly shaped by that reality. *Stations of the Banquet* emerges out of a Christian journey of faith. It is my conviction that by rooting deeply in one's

[3] Ibid., 154.
[4] Ibid., 177, 178.

tradition, the full riches of that tradition can bear fruit and that fruit can nourish the multi-faith communities in which we live in North America. Every work, even a book of faith, is also colored by a particular ideology or point of view. *Stations of the Banquet* is written to be genuine "good news to the poor" and liberation from the structures of oppression that diminish the lives of rich and poor alike. It is written in the hope that the plentitude of creation will be as rich and diverse for the seventh generation from now as it is for us. *Stations of the Banquet* is written to be an invitation to the path of abundant life for all. It is an invitation to the journey of the banquet.

More specifically, the seed for this book was planted at a national ecumenical conference of the Anglican Church of Canada in August 2000. The conference, "Food Ministries: A Taste of the Banquet?" was for people of faith involved in work on food issues in secular and church contexts. The participants were people involved in local meal programs, community kitchen and garden projects, church, municipal, and national food banks, and government, agriculture, and domestic and international voluntary sector organizations. It is a fine, energetic, stimulating, and largely unsung network of people that work on these issues. As the coordinator of this conference, I was able to identify many excellent secular resources to support this work, but relatively few faith-based resources. The creation of such a faith resource was the initial impetus for this project. The beautiful outdoor Stations of the Cross at the conference's retreat center inspired the idea of *Stations of the Banquet.* My thanks go to the sponsors of this conference, specifically the Eco-Justice Committee of the Anglican Church of Canada; to those who helped me plan and facilitate the event: Debbie Field, Kathleen Gibson, Maureen Hollins, Christopher Lind, Margaret Marquardt, Maylanne Maybee, Verna Otto, and Cynthia Patterson; and most especially to all those who participated. Their energy, enthusiasm, and commitment carried this project through its dry spells to completion.

The seed germinated with the support and encouragement of an amazing circle of friends and colleagues stretched across the continent but centered in Vancouver. Their voices and those of all the food program and research participants I have worked with over the years are the soil, fertilizer, rain, and sun from which this plant grew. A special thanks to Maureen Hollins for the music for the *Stations of the Banquet* [see Appendix I] and to Karen Settee Cook with help from her friends

Stan Rossowski and Diana Thorneycroft for the photographs for each station. Thanks also to all who contributed editorial suggestions: Brenda Berck, Bill Crockett, Ellen Desjardins, Patrick Henry, Debbie Lippoldt, Wendy McFeely, Mary Margaret Pazdan, Cyril and Marjorie Powles; to the circle who prayed the stations for the first time; and to Janice Guthrie for her meticulous, thoughtful reading and re-reading of this manuscript. It is amazing what another set of eyes can see. A nine-month sabbatical at the Institute for Ecumenical and Cultural Research in Collegeville, Minnesota, gave me the perfect environment in which to turn an idea into a book. With generous Benedictine hospitality, Saint John's Abbey offered a community of prayer without which this book would never have been born. St. John's also brought me to the Liturgical Press with special thanks to Linda Maloney.

To all my friends and colleagues, new and old, and especially to my husband Dennis, I extend tremendous thanks. To the extent the book lives and sings it is yours. Its flat spots are mine. May the journey of the banquet flourish and the circle of our friendship continue to expand.

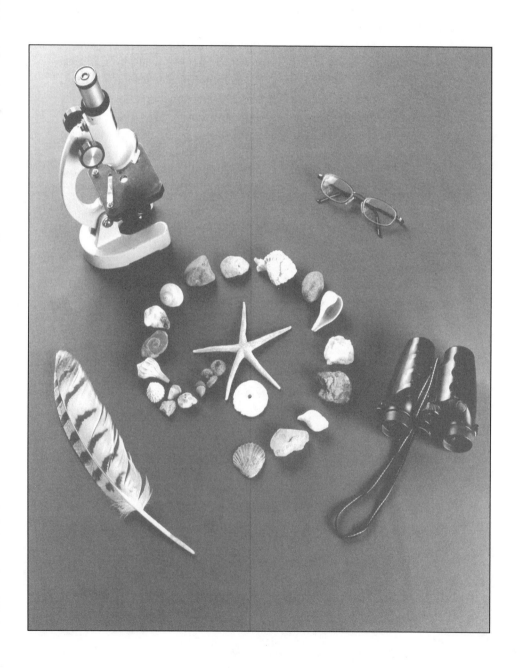

Station 1

PROLOGUE:
THE SONG OF THE UNIVERSE

Voice 1: From the earliest moments of creation,
     the farthest corners of our universe,
     the smallest particle of energy/matter,
  the seraphs can be heard singing:
  "Holy, holy, holy is the Lord of hosts;
     the whole earth is full of his glory" (Isa 6:3).

For indeed:
"The heavens are telling the glory of God;
  and the firmament proclaims his handiwork.
Day to day pours forth speech,
  and night to night declares knowledge.
There is no speech, nor are there words;
  their voice is not heard;
yet their voice goes out through all the earth,
  and their words to the end of the world" (Ps 19:1-4a).
The universe sings in glory, wonder, and awe of its Creator.

Voice 2: The best minds with the most sophisticated technology,
  probing the mysteries of the universe:
     its coherence,
     its exquisitely balancing forces,
     the precarious turns in its evolution,

all speak of the elegance and "immensely complex
    possibilities"[1]
of the ongoing unfolding of our cosmos.
The language of the scientists' song is filled with zeros:
    millions, billions, trillions—
    before & after the decimal point;
New words and names are coined at the drop of the hat.
Space and time, energy and matter, mind and language
    bend and merge
in contemplation of this extraordinary story
of beauty, power, destruction, and creation.

Can we recognize the artisan while paying heed to the
    artisan's works?
From the greatness and beauty of created things
comes a corresponding perception of their Creator.
If we have the power to know so much
that we can investigate the world
how can we fail to find sooner the Lord of these things
    (Wis 13:1, 5, 9)?
For surely, ever since the creation of the world
God's eternal power and divine nature, invisible though
    they are,
have been understood and seen through the things God
    has made (Rom 1:20).

Voice 3: Who will not take off their shoes before the great "I am"
    (Exod 3:5, 14)
who speaks from the whirlwind:
    "Where were you when I laid the foundation of the
      earth?"
    "Do you know the ordinances of the heavens?
      Can you establish their rule on the earth?"
    "Who has put wisdom in the inward parts,
      or given understanding to the mind?" (Job 38:4,
      33, 36).

---

[1] Brian Swimme and Thomas Berry, *The Universe Story: From the Primordial Flaring Forth to the Ecozoic Era, a Celebration of the Unfolding of the Cosmos* (New York: HarperCollins, 1992) 19.

Who will not stand in awe before the One
who creates "the luminous web" of all living things, with
    all its astonishing diversity:[2]
    Day 3's goodness: plants yielding seed, trees of every
        kind (Gen 1:12, 13);
    Day 5's gifts of birds and fish and sea monsters
        (Gen 1:22);
    And the blessings of the Day 6 creatures: cattle and
        creeping things and
        wild animals of every kind (Gen 1:24; see also
            Job 38:39–39:30);
        and, last but not least, humankind (Gen 1:26)?
Who will not acknowledge the One who knits us into a
    community of life—
    Who feeds us, helps us birth, thrive, and flourish,
    gives strength, freedom, and faithfulness,
    as well as quirkiness, wildness, and bloodthirstiness
        (Job 38:39–39:30)?
    Who remembers every sparrow,
    counts every hair on our heads (Luke 12:6, 7; parallel:
        Matt 10:29), and
    calls us each by name and claims us as precious, God's
        very own (Isa 43:1, 4, 7)?
And all this—
    layer after layer, of amazing form, difference,
        interconnectedness, and love,
Is only the back side of the glory of God (Exod 33:23)!

All: **We stand humbled, intrigued, delighted.**

Voice 4:   From the heart of this ongoing story of our cosmos,
        the psalmist's question remains:
        "When I look at your heavens, the work of your fingers,
          the moon and the stars that you have established;
        what are human beings that you are mindful of them,
          mortals that you care for them?" (Ps 8:3, 4).

---

  [2] Barbara Brown Taylor, *The Luminous Web: Essays on Science and Religion* (Cambridge, Mass.: Cowley Publications, 2000).

Who is this earth creature made in the image of God
(Gen 1:27);
made "a little lower than God, and crowned . . . with
glory and honor;
[and] . . . given dominion over the works of God's hands"
(Ps 8:5, 6a)?
Such power is in our hands—
the power to heal or destroy,
the power for life or death
for this beautiful web of life that clothes our globe in such
splendor.

All: We stand in fear and awe.

Voice 4:   Who are we humans—
We, creatures of the earth with the breath of God in
our nostrils;
We, day six creatures made in the image of God;
Fed with the bread of life and called to be bread for the
world?

All: What is our place in the universe story?

Visual focus: Images of nature's beauty, pictures of galaxies or the
evening sky, or a globe.

Station 2

IN THE BEGINNING . . . FOOD

The eyes of all look to you,
*   and you give them their food in due season.*
You open your hand,
*   satisfying the desire of every living thing.*

—Psalm 145:15-16

People have always told stories to answer big questions like: Who are we humans and what is our place in the universe story? The stories that we tell ourselves matter. They shape our thinking, direct our heart's attention, and move us to act. Stories are also the way that the wisdom of our ancestors comes to us. The journey of the banquet starts in such a story. It is set in the earliest of days, the time of creation, of first gestures and original people. Stories from the very beginning of the human journey swirl with ambiguity, paradox, unanswered questions, untidiness. Yet these tales of origins point obliquely to the fundamental dynamics of human existence in creation. In the language of story, they invite us to explore the truths of our life as creatures of the earth with the breath of God in our nostrils. Food, the politics of food, and the choices we make about food lie at the heart of this story.

THE VOICES OF THE TRADITION

Our Scriptures begin with a compact account of the birth of the universe (Gen 1:1–2:4a). Even in its condensed, abbreviated style, it conveys the grand sweep of events at the very beginning of time. All the elements of creation are introduced: the Creator and the creative power of the word of God, chaos and order, land and water, light and darkness, the heavens and the earth, the sun and moon for the night and day, creatures in the waters and birds to "fly across the dome of the sky," and the earth creatures: domesticated, creeping, and wild, with humans as one of these sixth-day creatures. This sweeping, almost breathtaking picture of our universe invites us to appreciate the beauty and goodness of this beloved creation of God, and to stand in awe before the power of its Creator.

Although contemporary cosmologies stop there, our scriptural account has scarcely begun. With the ease of the zoom lens of a camera, the focus shifts from the grand sweep of the creation to the intimacy of life in the garden (Gen 2:4b–3:24). It is a human-scale account of relationships between the Creator, plants, animals, humans, and the earth as the ever-present substrate of our common existence. The picture created in this tightly woven, but sadly abused, story depicts:

- a creation in process: dynamic, contingent, unfolding;

- humans as a curious combination of "dusty earth and divine breath . . . fragile ingredients, combined by God . . . whose life hangs on a breath that it does not control, indeed, that it does not breathe—for God is the breather";[1] and yet

- humans gifted with a garden filled with "every tree that is pleasant to the sight and good for food" (Gen 2:9b); a place of abundance and delight; a place with distinctions but without opposition; with dominion: "responsibilities" to till, to serve, and capacities to heal or harm, but without domination or oppression.[2]

In short, the garden is a place of original harmony and joy.

Over and over this garden is glimpsed in our Scriptures. The psalmist sings a hymn of praise to the Creator of such grace and fulfillment:

---

[1] Phyllis Trible, *God and the Rhetoric of Sexuality* (Philadelphia: Fortress Press, 1978) 80.

[2] Ibid., 85. Interestingly, it is almost impossible for us in our current context to even imagine dominion without domination.

The earth is satisfied with the fruit of your work.
You cause the grass to grow for the cattle,
    and plants for people to use,
to bring forth food from the earth,
    and wine to gladden the human heart,
oil to make the face shine,
    and bread to strengthen the human heart. . . .
O LORD, how manifold are your works!
    In wisdom you have made them all [e.g., the sea, creeping things,
    living things both small and great, ships, even the Leviathan].
These all look to you
    to give them their food in due season;
when you give to them, they gather it up;
    when you open your hand, they are filled with good things.
You renew the face of the ground (Ps 104:13b-15, 24, 27, 28, 30b).

The Hebrew people journey through the wilderness to the Promised Land—a garden of sorts:

a land flowing with milk and honey; . . . a land that the LORD your God looks after. The eyes of the LORD your God are always on it, from the beginning of the year to the end of the year.

You will gather in your grain, your wine, and your oil; and he will give grass in your fields for your livestock, and you will eat your fill. You shall eat there in the presence of the LORD your God, you and your households together, rejoicing in all the undertakings in which the LORD your God has blessed you (Deut 11:9b, 12, 14b, 15; 12:7).

The banquet is at the heart of the garden. The love poems of the Song of Solomon reveal the delight at the heart of the garden. There are the glimpses of the intended integrity and abundance of creation in Jesus' feeding and healing miracles.[3] The events of Pentecost celebrate the potential of mutual understanding in the midst of the diversity of God's creation, not in spite of it. And in John's picture of the New Jerusalem, we have a vision of the garden in the heart of the city with life renewed in all its wholeness and lived in intimacy with the Holy (Rev 21:1–22:5).[4] At the beginning, at the end, and in the heart of the story, the fullness of the garden is present.

[3] See Station 9.
[4] See Station 12.

In this place with everything a heart could desire, there is also choice. There is limitation. Out of the earth, the same earth from which the earliest human was formed:

> God made to grow every tree that is pleasant to the sight and good for food, the tree of life also in the midst of the garden, and the tree of the knowledge of good and evil. . . . And the LORD God commanded . . .: "You may freely eat of every tree of the garden; but of the tree of the knowledge of good and evil you shall not eat, for in the day that you eat of it you shall die" (Gen 2:9, 16, 17).

Phyllis Trible summarizes succinctly what is at stake in this matter:

> The forbidden tree spells limits to human dominion. Nature itself also has God-given independence. To eat and not to eat: permission and prohibition unite in a double command that is designed to preserve life. This command points up the opposites that can result from a single act. To eat is to live: "from every tree . . . you may surely eat," for the trees are "pleasant to see and good to eat." Yet to eat is to die: "for when you eat of it [the tree of the knowledge of good and evil] you will surely die." One act, eating, holds both life and death. The difference lies in obeying or disobeying the limits set by God.[5]

In the garden, dominion is not domination and differentiation is not alienation. Yet the potential for both domination and alienation is present. It is a matter of choice. Our choices matter.

The story continues with the creation of community: first, the animal kingdom and then human partnership. The stage is then fully set for the dynamic of human freedom within the blessedness of creation. In the condensed language of the dialogue with the serpent, "that wiliest of the wild animals," a space is created to break the harmony of the creation process. The conversation at the foot of the tree is about God, rather than with God. God as subject becomes God as object; the source of all goodness becomes a deceiver; the generous provider of abundance becomes a jealous guardian of prerogatives. The consequences of disobedience are renamed by the serpent: "You will not die; . . . your eyes will be opened, and you will be like God" (Gen 3:4b, 5).

---

[5] Trible, *God and the Rhetoric of Sexuality,* 87.

Whether it was the desire for nourishment ("the tree was good for food") or beauty ("it was a delight to the eyes") or wisdom ("the tree was to be desired to make one wise") or a combination of all three, the choice is made. The woman took, ate, and gave the forbidden fruit to the man and he ate (Gen 3:6b). The decision is made with Eve's initiative and Adam's acquiescence. Choices made, things done, actively or passively, become equivalent and decisive acts.[6]

The consequences are manifold. The life of harmony and joy with creation, with each other, and with God is fractured. It is true that the eyes of those original humans were opened. But the first thing they saw was their innocence, and the first thing they did was to hide it. To see became a not wanting to be seen. The unity of one flesh, which embraced all the differences of men and women as sources of life and joy, is broken asunder in blame, shame, and domination.[7] New life now comes only in pain. The work of the garden, tilling and cultivating (Gen 2:15), becomes alienated labor: "by the sweat of your face / you shall eat bread" (Gen 3:19). Relations with the land, the earth we come from and go to, become adversarial: "cursed is the ground because of you; . . . / thorns and thistles it shall bring forth for you" (Gen 3:17b, 18a). Enmity is born between humans and the creatures of the wild. Intimacy with God is lost. God, "walking in the garden at the time of the evening breeze," can only call: "Where are you?" and the human now responds in fear rather than love (Gen 3:8-10).

God, in compassion, makes sturdier clothes for this new world of insecurity, discord, oppression, pain, and loss. Clothed in the skins of our kindred day-six creatures, we leave the garden as exiles. Death, the clear limit, the limit we all share, the limit about which we have no choice, is now a nonnegotiable reality. We are both bounded and free. We are creatures of the earth with the breath of God in our nostrils, made both of earth and heaven. In this space between earth and heaven, we create in the freedom of our choices human history, culture, our place in the universe story. We stand always and forever at

---

[6] Ibid., 114.

[7] William Sloane Coffin writes: "Our sin is always and only that we put asunder what God has joined together. Human unity is not something we are called to create, only to recognize and make manifest." "Who Is There Big Enough to Love the Whole Planet," *The Future of Prophetic Christianity: Essays in Honor of Robert McAfee Brown,* ed. Denise Lardner Carmody and John Tully Carmody (Maryknoll, N.Y.: Orbis Books, 1993) 46. See also Station 6.

the foot of the tree of the knowledge of good and evil, both individually and collectively, and choose between the paths of life or death. The possibility of whole relationships between the earth, living plants and animals, humans, and the Creator remains, but is always contingent on our choices.

But the story, our story, does not end here. This account is but the opening rehearsal of the theme. In another beginning, right at the very start of Jesus' ministry, he too faces the tempter. He too faces the choices that lie at the heart of a human life turned toward or away from the Sacred. And the first choice he faces is also a food choice:

> He fasted forty days and forty nights, and afterwards he was famished. The tempter came and said to him, "If you are the Son of God, command these stones to become loaves of bread." But he answered, "It is written,
> 'One does not live by bread alone,
>   but by every word that comes from the mouth of God'"
>   (Matt 4:2-4; parallel Luke 4:2-4).[8]

Jesus rejects the tempter's encouragement to use his power to reach for food. But he was not turning his back on hunger. His choice is not the response of an ascetic or an acquiescence to deprivation. It is not the basis for a creed of coping with scarcity through sublimation of need into an otherworldly spiritualized reality. For Christ, the definition of the problem is not scarcity and abundance as the tempter intimates.[9] For Christ, the issue is always and only our connectedness with God.

Jesus knows God as the source, the creator of all the fullness, joy, harmony, and abundance of the garden.

> Consider the ravens: they neither sow nor reap, they have neither storehouse nor barn, and yet God feeds them. Consider the lilies, how they grow: they neither toil nor spin; yet I tell you, even Solomon in all his glory was not clothed like one of these. Do not keep striving for what you are to eat and what you are to drink, and do not keep worrying. For it is the nations of the world that strive after all these things, and your Father knows that you need them (Luke 12:24, 27, 29-30).

---

[8] See also Deuteronomy 8:3.
[9] See Stations 8 and 9.

Jesus knows God as his absolutely trustworthy, responsive parent.

> Is there anyone among you who, if your child asks for bread, will give a stone? Or if the child asks for a fish, will give a snake? If you then, who are evil, know how to give good gifts to your children, how much more will your Father in heaven give good things to those who ask him! (Matt 7:9-11; parallel Luke 11:11-13).

Jesus can say that we live by "every word that comes from the mouth of God" because that word has everything to do good things, with real nourishment for body and soul. With the eyes of faith, Christ comes to be known as that word, incarnate, embodied, the Word of God, present then and now. Christ is then the invitation, the way we have of re-creating that living relationship of intimacy with God that the original humans knew in the garden. Christ is our way to the tree of life. Christ is the path of abundant life for all.

For the other tree in the midst of the garden, the tree of life, remains although transplanted in John's vision to the New Jerusalem (Rev 22:2). Ironically, it is the tree of life, rather than the tree of the knowledge of good and evil, that came to be known as the path of wisdom.[10]

> Happy are those who find wisdom,
>   and those who get understanding,
> for her income is better than silver,
>   and her revenue better than gold.
> She is more precious than jewels,
>   and nothing you desire can compare with her.
> Long life is in her right hand;
>   in her left hand are riches and honor.
> Her ways are ways of pleasantness,
>   and all her paths are peace.
> She is a tree of life to those who lay hold of her;
>   those who hold her fast are called happy (Prov 3:13-18).

With God at the beginning of creation,[11] "She is a breath of the power of God, / and a pure emanation of the glory of the Almighty" (Wis 7:25).

---

[10] This is a later development in the history of Israel. The apocryphal books of Wisdom of Solomon, especially chapters 6–9, and Sirach 24 extend the discussion of wisdom in Proverbs and Ecclesiastes.

[11] Prov 8:22-31; Wis 9:9.

With us, in the midst of creation, the living Christ is: "the power of God and the wisdom of God. [For God] is the source of your life in Christ Jesus, who became for us wisdom from God, and righteousness and sanctification and redemption" (1 Cor 1:24b, 30).

Just as there are two trees in the garden, so there are two banquets: Wisdom's banquet and Folly's banquet (Prov 9:1-6, 13-18). One is a feast of life and the other a feast of death. Both Wisdom and Folly invite us to their banquets. It is our choice which invitation to accept. Our choice matters to God, to creation, to the human community, and to ourselves.

SPIRITUAL CHALLENGE: LIMITS

There are natural limits. The question is not why was the tree of the knowledge of good and evil present in the garden in the first place. Limits are part of God's good creation. In fact, creation itself can be thought of as God's self-limitation. God created a reality that is of God, but not God, and gifted it with real freedom. Dramatically, in the second creation story, God stood back, so to speak, to see what the original human would call the animals of the field and the birds of the air: "Whatever the man called every living creature, that was its name" (Gen 2:19).

Perhaps, to become "like God," as the serpent intimated, or to become fully who we are as children of God, is *not* to reach for more, but to ourselves learn to choose the path of self-limitation. Perhaps we too must learn to love creation with a love like that of God.

Just as in the original garden we continue to be entranced by the new, to reach for more even in situations of abundance and security. In practice, why would we or do we choose not to do something that is clearly good to do, to have, to consume, to reach for, or to admire? What trumps desire? Is it only a greater desire? How do we learn to "manage" our stomachs, still our "wanting minds," school our desires?

We live in a culture that fuels desire rather than schools desire. Entire industries exist to manufacture demand for commodities and services or to create desire. Advertising "begins by making you unhappy with what you currently have, or don't have. [It] widens the gap between what you have and what you want. Wanting to buy something then is a response to the feelings of dissatisfaction, envy, and craving."[12] Spending, owning, or consuming become the way to happiness or well-being and undergird our sense of identity, success, or worth. "When you build a system on a foundation of desire, dissatisfaction, envy and inadequacy, people buy things, yes; but it's no surprise that it happens at the expense of some damage to the psyche."[13] Who can say that the serpent in its current manifestation is not indeed the wiliest of the wild creatures?

In the domain of the psyche, the cycles of desire seem limitless. Yet we are creatures of the earth, dependent on the earth for our sustenance: air, water, and food; and this earth is not limitless. Yes, we are dust from the stars formed over a time scale that we can conceive but not really appreciated. And it is true we have been gifted with memory, reason, and skill, which has allowed such a flowering of technological genius that we fly to the moon and alter even the architectural plans for life itself seemingly at will. Yet, is this technological innovation limitless? Has not the potential of each technological innovation also brought a tremendous cost for creation? We have ballooning stockpiles of nuclear wastes, increasing cancer rates, and soaring demands for fertilizers, insecticides, and herbicides to sustain the green and now biotechnological agricultural revolutions. This can be good news for some, but very bad news for others. Just as in the garden, the same act can hold very divergent consequences. Sallie McFague's question is central to the challenges of our time: "What are the prospects of a people when they lose their sense of limits?"[14] The earth and the peoples of the earth are groaning under the illusion of limitlessness.

As in the garden, the easiest diversion from a focus on our desires is attributing blame: the original man blames the woman and the woman blames the serpent. But in our culture, blaming may be a futile trap. For, "we do not need to *deliberately* harm nature; we *will* do so simply by being favored players in Western culture. There are not 'green saviors' and 'evil exploiters' so much as *structures* that determine how

---

[12] Rick Poynor, "First Things Next," *Adbusters* (July/August 2001); quoting Jelly Helm.

[13] Ibid.

[14] Sallie McFague, *Life Abundant: Rethinking Theology and Economy for a Planet in Peril* (Minneapolis: Fortress Press, 2001) 71.

we all, willy-nilly, will act."[15] There is no easy way back into the innocence of the garden. In fact, in the poetry of our Scriptures God "placed
the cherubim and a sword flaming and turning to guard the way to the
tree of life" (Gen 3:24b). The way is not back to the garden, but into
the ongoing unfolding of God's good creation with our knowledge of
good and evil. The way is on toward the city with the Holy residing at
its very heart from whom flows "the river of the water of life . . .
through the middle of the street of the city. On either side of the river
is the tree of life" (Rev 22:1-2). The journey of the banquet includes
enrollment in a different school of desires than the one that wraps itself around us in all the messages of our culture.

It is not that desires are somehow not to be desired. They are part
of the very substance of life.[16] The question is what we desire and
whether our desires control us or simply inform us of options. Addic-
tions, in all their manifold manifestations, teach a lot about the challenges and approaches to schooling our desires. Gerald May names
addiction "as the sacred disease of the modern world."[17] He argues
that "nowhere else do issues of control and helplessness, mastery and
surrender, confront each other as brutally as in the battle between
mind and drug." As clever and powerful as we humans are, only the
Sacred can satisfy a hunger for life in its fullness. It is not a question of
willpower. Only the Holy can trump desire. The space in which we
make our choices at the foot of the trees in our lives is therefore critical. Creating a space big enough and sturdy enough for God to be fully
present in the choices we make is one of the central spiritual challenges
of the journey of the banquet.

---

[15] Ibid., 73. Emphasis in the original.

[16] Desire can be for both needs and wants. Even the language of need has become
conflated. Douglas Meeks writes: "We give to need the character of necessity. Need brings
together by association facts, nature, necessity and the centrality of the self. . . .
A world reduced to factual needs appears to make life simpler. Our life is governed by
a set of facts: need to work, needs of children, need for security. . . . Established
needs [at times] signify a right, a necessary claim to something and thus one can want
it without condemnation." *God the Economist: The Doctrine of God and Political Economy* (Minneapolis: Augsburg Fortress, 1989) 164, 165. The language of desire used here
keeps our choice-making clearly in focus and avoids the determinism inherent in some
writing about needs.

[17] Gerald May, *Will and Spirit: A Contemplative Psychology* (San Francisco: Harper &
Row, 1982) 40, 41. See also Station 10.

This journey is not a path of no's. It is not a path that denies the inherent goodness of the world or hates the body. By affirming God's goodness and centrality in our lives and choosing not to eat the forbidden, but desirable, fruit,

> it may seem that . . . we are turning our backs to the whole created world of the good, the true, and the beautiful. In fact, when we turn to God, we find that same world in God, sanctified and glorified. In God, in whom nothing worth preserving is lost, everything worth enjoying can be enjoyed.[18]

All the testimony of our ancestors in the faith suggest that Wisdom's banquet is indeed worth the journey. For:

> the fear of the LORD is pure,
>   enduring forever;
> the ordinances of the LORD are true
>   and righteous altogether.
> More to be desired are they than gold,
>   even much fine gold;
> sweeter also than honey,
>   and drippings of the honeycomb (Ps 19:9-10).

The apparent opposition between the material and spiritual agenda is false. They are bound inextricably together. At the heart of the school of desires, of learning limits, is life abundant—life abundant for all of creation.

SPIRITUAL PRACTICE: VOLUNTARY SIMPLICITY

How full is our time? How much stuff is there in our homes? How full are our minds? How full are our stomachs? How much room is there in our lives for God? The path of life abundant involves learning to have more by having less. It is a path of voluntary simplicity. It affirms our

---

[18] Miroslav Volf, "In the Cage of Vanities: Christian Faith and the Dynamics of Economic Progress," *Rethinking Materialism: Perspectives on the Spiritual Dimension of Economic Behavior*, ed. Robert Wuthnow (Grand Rapids, Mich.: Eerdmans, 1995) 191.

full freedom of choice and affirms the goodness of creation. It is not an attempt to willfully rid ourselves of the delight, beauty, and nourishment of the physical world. Nor is it an idealization of a life of deprivation. Choosing to simplify our lives is, however, a path of emptying and intentionally creating room for the Holy in our lives. Gerald May's image for this is the cultivation of spaciousness in the landscapes of our souls, calendars, and the physical spaces that we inhabit.

Traditionally the cultivation of simplicity has been through practices of fasting, renunciation, abstinence, silence, and various other ascetic regimes. Although there is much to be learned from these practices, approaches that strengthen our willpower can create a much deeper problem and/or are not sustainable. Spaciousness or simplicity is not something to be achieved, but something grown. It comes as we make real room for God in our everyday lives, as we attend to the gifts of grace that surround us each day, as we enter into emptiness rather than run from it in busyness, chatter, and the accumulation of stuff, status, accomplishments. God's goodness, love, and power are the active agents in the cultivation of spaciousness. We only will our consent to participate in God's agenda. There are, of course, a tremendous number of aids in this process, but the core movement is simple. The aids—the spiritual disciplines and practices—are only ever aids.

Wendell Berry offers an accessible example:

> Eating with the fullest pleasure—pleasure, that is, that does not depend on ignorance—is perhaps the profoundest enactment of our connection with the world. In this pleasure we experience and celebrate our dependence and our gratitude, for we are living from mystery, from creatures we did not make and powers we cannot comprehend.[19]

By taking the time to fully attend to the very basics of life with all of our mind (not in ignorance), body (pleasure), and spirit (celebration and gratitude), we encounter the mystery at the heart of creation as pure grace. Eating not only is an "enactment of our connection with the world" (in all its human and nonhuman dimensions), but it is a necessary connection. We are dependent for our health and well-being upon creation and the intricacies of all the processes that sustain life upon

---

[19] Wendell Berry, "The Pleasures of Eating," *Simpler Living, Compassionate Life: A Christian Perspective*, ed. M. Schut (Denver: Living the Good News/Moorhouse Group, 1999) 110.

the earth. We are both bounded and free. Acknowledging and entering into a deep appreciation of those interconnections can be a door into awe and gratitude for the mystery of life. It can be a way to cultivate space for the Sacred.

Another profound source of testimony to the fullness of life that comes from careful attention to our limits is the stories told by people facing death or serious illness. These accounts come in several varieties.[20] There are those that speak of triumph over illness, and those that detail the trauma, pain, and suffering of illness. There are also those that sing of all that is learned of life as its end is faced. Life's freedom, joys, and ultimate meaning can come into focus. This is not to suggest any value in voluntarily choosing a path of suffering. That is masochism. Nor is there any value in refraining from the relief of suffering whenever possible. But it is to suggest that there is immeasurable value in attending to the natural limits we all encounter in life.

Although the cultivation of voluntary simplicity is usually negotiated in the details of our daily choices, there are significant implications for our collective lives and for the health of creation. Our current economic life is structured to require growth, and much good is promised from that growth. Who benefits from the growth, which is sometimes also called development, very much depends on the structures of power and the distribution of entitlements.[21] In the name of those goods, limits to economic growth are removed regardless of the cost to creation or costs in human suffering. The cultivation of voluntary simplicity provides a window into the inner dynamic of "our public belief in growth" and its addictive culture of consumption.[22] It also opens a door to a whole host of alternative practices that exist in unpublicized corners of communities throughout the world. Even simple acts, perhaps especially simple acts, can have profound effects.

---

[20] Arthur Frank, *The Wounded Storyteller: Body, Illness and Ethics* (Chicago: University of Chicago Press, 1995), is an insightful guide to this literature.

[21] See John Cobb, "Liberation Theology and the Global Economy," *Liberating the Future: God, Mammon and Theology,* ed. J. Rieger (Minneapolis: Augsburg Fortress, 1998); also H. E. Daly and John B. Cobb, *For the Common Good: Redirecting the Economy Toward Community, the Environment and a Sustainable Future* (Boston: Beacon Press, 1989).

[22] T. C. Weiskel, "Some Notes From Belshaz'zar's Feast," *Simpler Living, Compassionate Life: A Christian Perspective,* ed. M. Schut (Denver: Living the Good News/ Moorhouse Group, 1999).

STATION 2 LITANY:
IN THE BEGINNING . . . FOOD

Voices 1: For your glory shining through the world around us;
for galaxies, stars, the sun, moon, and our planet earth;
for all its forces of renewal and evolution;
All: **for the mysteries of creation, we thank You.**

Voices 2: For the extravagant diversity of life,
for skin and scales, feathers and fur, leaves and needles;
for the intricate interplay of all our differences,
All: **for the sheer abundance of creation, we thank You.**

Voices 1: You have bound us together into a dynamic whole—
interconnected, interdependent;
Voices 2: flows of energy and matter, air and water, life and death;
a resilient web of life greening and growing;
All: **for the ever-unfolding elegance of creation, we thank You.**

Voices 1: We pray that we might enter into your joy and delight,
your love of this creation.
All: **Touch us with your Spirit.**

Voices 2: We pray for your wisdom to know the way of the banquet.
All: **Feed us with your Word.**

Voices 1: In the enduring lure of the new;
in all the seductions of our time;
Voices 2: in the hardness and hurt of encounters with our limits,
in the gaps when you seem absent;
All: **give us discernment to choose your way,
that we might use our freedom for the good of all.**

Voices 1: Guide the consuming desires of our hearts;
shape our wants and needs,
All: **that we might reach, take, and share your word as food
for the world.**

Voices 2: At the foot of the tree of all our choices,
open our hands, minds, and souls to you;

All: that in the spaciousness of our lives
we might welcome you home.
For we are yours, we belong to you.

All: **Creator God, Giver of all good gifts,**
Source of all life, Path of abundant life, Breath of life itself,
We give you praise and honor and glory forever.

Visual focus: A full bowl of fruit with a piece off to one side.

Station 3

HEAR "THE CRIES OF MY PEOPLE"

Would that all the LORD's people were prophets,
and that the LORD would put his spirit on them!

—Numbers 11:29

The garden's simplicity, harmony, abundance, and intimacy with the Holy may be our first home, but they are certainly no longer the defining characteristics of our world. Even in our origin stories, the original humans are plunged into a world of fractured relationships, missed connections, and decisions gone very wrong. Brothers kill each other, evil flourishes, wholesale destruction almost envelops the earth. We enter a very ambiguous world. It is not always easy to distinguish between the invitation to wisdom's banquet and folly's banquet. The word of God and the word of the tempter can sound very similar. The stories of our relationship with the Holy, from the garden on, have been accounts of moving two steps closer and then one step away. At times the dance may even have seemed like two steps closer and three steps away, with each misstep compounding our suffering. Yet the dance floor is vast and God's presence is constant. The dance continues.

Prophets, then and now, are those who hear the heartbeat of God and feel in their bones the missteps of our dance. Prophets are those who cry to God, to the leaders, and to the people, the pain of a dance gone wrong. Abraham Heschel writes that "the fundamental experience of the prophet is a sympathy with the divine pathos. . . . The prophet hears God's voice and feels [God's] heart."[1] Lest that sound too romantic, Sandra Schneiders adds a note of realism: "To feel the pathos of God is not a warm and comfortable religious experience; it is an experience of the howling wilderness driving one to protest."[2] Prophets are voices of the desert, of the exile from the garden. Prophets, then and now, speak the agony of the moment: the earth's, ours, and God's, and call us to hear, to see, to acknowledge the truth at the heart of our universe.

THE VOICES OF THE TRADITION

The simplicity of Jesus' parable of the rich man and his feasts focuses the question of the prophet's voice. The initial situation is stark.

> There was a rich man who was dressed in purple and fine linen and who feasted sumptuously every day. And at his gate lay a poor man, named Lazarus, covered with sores, who longed to satisfy his hunger with what fell from the rich man's table; even the dogs would come and lick his sores (Luke 16:19-21).

In contemporary parlance we know this as the "income gap," although the Scripture's "great chasm" (v. 26) might be more accurate. This picture of great hardship in the midst of great prosperity is enacted in almost every corner of the globe today. Television, the Internet, celebrity magazines at grocery store check-out stations bring the disparities of rich and poor into our homes, indeed right to "our gates." Bane and Coffin refer to this reality as a "paradox," but is it really a paradox?[3] Is it not our daily reenactment of the contradictions and fracture lines in our world, that our faith down through the ages has labeled sin?

---

[1] Abraham Heschel, *The Prophets* (New York: HarperCollins, 1962; Perennial Classics edition, 2001) 31.

[2] Sandra M. Schneiders, *Finding the Treasure: Locating Catholic Religious Life in a New Ecclesial and Cultural Context* (New York: Paulist Press, 2000) 141.

[3] Mary Jo Bane and Brent Coffin, "Introduction," *Who Will Provide? The Changing Role of Religion in American Social Welfare*, ed. Mary Jo Bane, Brent Coffin, Ronald Thiemann (Boulder, Colo.: Westview Press, 2000) 2.

The second act of the parable is set in the time/space after death that is continuous with our lives in this time and space.

> The poor man died and was carried away by the angels to be with Abraham. The rich man also died and was buried. In Hades, where he was being tormented, he looked up and saw Abraham far away with Lazarus by his side. He called out, "Father Abraham, have mercy on me" (Luke 16:22-24a).

The situations of the rich man and Lazarus have been reversed. Jesus was very fond of such reversals in the order of things. Lazarus is in the heart of the Holy and the rich man is in torment. The rich man begs for mercy first for himself and then for his five brothers. He entreats Abraham to send Lazarus to bear the word of life to his brothers, so they might repent and change in time to avoid his torment. He prays, not that they be filled with understanding, compassion, remorse, and sadness, but that they actually be transformed. Abraham's response is simple: "They have Moses and the prophets; they should listen to them" (Luke 16:29).

Parables always have at their heart a question, a puzzle, a surprise, or a riddle. The question in this parable is surely not the message. It is all too familiar to us. What is the question of this parable? With all our sophistication, can we see and hear any better now than then? If not, why not? What is the word of life for our time and place? Who bears it? Are we listening? Can we hear and do we move to the beat of the heart of God?

Moses is one of the great prophets in our tradition. Joseph, son of Jacob and Rachel, had prepared the way in Egypt, so that his people could escape and survive a devastating famine in the land. Moses was the son who led his people home from Egypt. In between there came a time when the Egyptians "set taskmasters over them to oppress them with forced labor . . . and made their lives bitter with hard service . . . [and] were ruthless in all the tasks that they imposed" (Exod 1:11, 14).

Moses, who had escaped the imperial edict to kill all the male children at birth through the good work of his midwives, Puah and Shiphrah, and the quick wits of his sister, Miriam, was raised with all the privileges of Pharaoh's home as an adopted grandson. Yet, when confronted with the realities of "the forced labor of his people" as an Egyptian beat a Hebrew, he chose to stand with his kin and against the empire. He killed the Egyptian and then fled all the privilege of his adopted home to become an "alien residing in a foreign land" (Exod 2:11-15, 22). That was the first step in Moses' transformation.

God then meets Moses, now a shepherd, in the burning bush. In that encounter Moses becomes God's agent of deliverance for his people from their captivity. God says to Moses: "I have observed the misery of my people who are in Egypt; I have heard their cry on account of their taskmasters. Indeed, I know their sufferings, and I have come down to deliver them" (Exod 3:7, 8).

And Moses becomes a reluctant prophet of liberation. He, like many[4] after him, ask: "Who am I that I should go. . . . Suppose they do not believe me or listen to me. . . . I am slow of speech, slow of tongue. . . . O my Lord, please send someone else" (Exod 3:11; 4:1, 10b, 13). But he goes, defies Pharaoh, and indeed leads his people out of Egypt.

Liberation was not accomplished with the crossing of the Red Sea and the destruction of Egyptian power. Physically free, the people were still psychically captive to the empire they had left. They want to sell their freedom for bread:

> The whole congregation of the Israelites complained against Moses and Aaron in the wilderness. . . . "If only we had died by the hand of the LORD in the land of Egypt, when we sat by the fleshpots and ate our fill of bread; for you have brought us out into this wilderness to kill this whole assembly with hunger" (Exod 16:2, 3).

It took forty years in the wilderness school of desires for the hearts of the people to become attuned to God's. It took more than a generation to learn to walk to the beat of God's heart.[5] The seductions of the empire are deeply embedded in the psyche. Liberation is the journey of a lifetime or more, and prophecy is long, hard, repetitive work.

Over the centuries God's people appropriated the ways of the cultures around them. They adopted a monarchy and, with the monarchy, a state religion, and a system of privilege. The system became corrupt.[6] Pharaoh and the empire were not out there, a foreign power,

---

[4] See Isa 6:5; Jer 1:6; Zechariah, father of John the Baptist in Luke 1:18; and even Jesus in John 2:4.

[5] This chapter of the Exodus story is revisited in Station 9.

[6] Just as Samuel had warned them: 1 Sam 8:1-22.

but were within, indeed were one's own. And again God sent prophets to the people.

The prophets cry out in judgment.[7] Ezekiel shouts his protest to the leaders and all those with responsibility for the care of others: "Ah, you shepherds of Israel who have been feeding yourselves! Should not shepherds feed the sheep? You eat the fat, you clothe yourselves with the wool, you slaughter the fatlings; but you do not feed the sheep" (Ezek 34:2b, 3).

He spells out the metaphor of feeding to avoid any literal or minimalistic interpretation: "You have not strengthened the weak, you have not healed the sick, you have not bound up the injured, you have not brought back the strayed, you have not sought the lost, but with force and harshness you have ruled them" (Ezek 34:4).

The fruits of injustice: power misused, responsibility obfuscated, relationship denied, are born: "My sheep . . . wandered over all the mountains . . .; my sheep were scattered over all the face of the earth. . . . My sheep have become prey, . . . food for all the wild animals" (Ezek 34:6, 8b).

The people, God's beloved, have become lost, alienated, and alone. The bonds of community are shattered. They are now prey for all the predators: not only enemy states, but also the deceptions of the serpent, that "wiliest of all the wild animals" (Gen 3:1). Ezekiel, claiming the authority of God, speaks judgment: "Thus says the Lord GOD, I am against the shepherds" (Ezek 34:10a).

With all the drama of a courtroom prosecutor, Isaiah speaks to the suffering of his time/place:

> The LORD rises to argue his case;
>> he stands to judge the peoples.
> The LORD enters into judgment
>> with the elders and princes of his people:
> It is you who have devoured the vineyard;
>> the spoil of the poor is in your houses.
> What do you mean by crushing my people,
>> by grinding the face of the poor? (Isa 3:13-15).

Jeremiah in his time cries out warning and "woe" to a person who builds property with unjust means, with "dishonest gain": "who makes

---

[7] This cry of the prophets is revisited in Stations 10 and 13.

his neighbors work for nothing, / and does not give them their wages. . . . / [Who practice] oppression and violence" (Jer 22:13-17). And Amos adds his voice and names again the signs of injustice:

> Hear this, you that trample on the needy,
>   and bring to ruin the poor of the land,
> saying, "When will the new moon be over
>   so that we may sell grain;
> and the sabbath,
>   so that we may offer wheat for sale?
> We will make the ephah [the measure] small and the shekel [the price]
>   great,
>   and practice deceit with false balances,
> buying the poor for silver
>   and the needy for a pair of sandals,
>   and selling the sweepings of the wheat" (8:4-6).

Amos then goes on to predict dire repercussions and times of great tragedy and suffering:

> I will turn your feasts into mourning,
>   and all your songs into lamentation;
> I will bring sackcloth on all loins,
>   and baldness on every head;
> I will make it like the mourning for an only son,
>   and the end of it like a bitter day.
> The time is surely coming, says the Lord GOD,
>   when I will send a famine on the land;
> not a famine of bread, or a thirst for water,
>   but of hearing the words of the LORD.
> They shall wander from sea to sea,
>   and from north to east;
> they shall run to and fro, seeking the word of the LORD,
>   but they shall not find it (8:10-12).

A people who have lost the way, like Ezekiel's sheep, seek and seek, but have no ears to hear the beat of God's heart. Amos predicts a time of starvation, when the people are once again lost in the wilderness starving for the Word of Life.

This cry of the prophets has resonated down through the centuries whenever and wherever the people and the land suffer. The injustices and the suffering they describe are familiar. The hurt is as real today as then. The language of judgment is uncomfortable, but judgment is not the only voice of prophecy.[8] Many can find a meeting place and shared language in lament.

Lamentations, "a small psalter of communal laments,"[9] was written in the people's second great time of captivity, the Babylonian exile. It is a time of loss, confusion, and disorientation.

> By the rivers of Babylon—
> > there we sat down and there we wept
> > when we remembered Zion.
> On the willows there
> > we hung up our harps (Ps 137:1-2).

Lament is the language of this time:

> How the gold has grown dim,
> > how the pure gold is changed!
> The sacred stones lie scattered
> > at the head of every street.
> The precious children of Zion,
> > worth their weight in fine gold—
> how they are reckoned as earthen pots,
> > the work of a potter's hands![10]
> Even the jackals offer the breast
> > and nurse their young,
> but my people have become cruel,
> > like the ostriches in the wilderness.
> The tongue of the infant sticks
> > to the roof of its mouth for thirst;
> the children beg for food,
> > but no one gives them anything (Lam 4:1-4).

In such times, it is not only the leaders who devour the vineyard. When any order or ethic has been sucked into the turmoil and terror of complete chaos, the nightmare of all times is spoken:

---

[8] The language of judgment is discussed in Station 10.

[9] Bruce M. Metzger and Roland E. Murphy, eds., *The New Oxford Annotated Bible: New Revised Standard Version* (New York: Oxford University Press, 1991) 1047.

[10] See also Jer 18:1-12.

The hands of compassionate women
    have boiled their own children;
they became their food
    in the destruction of my people (Lam 4:10).[11]

Oh, the precious children! The suffering of the innocents, the devastation of neglect and abandonment, the gift of new life, of the future, is warped, crushed, and discarded, consumed by their own. It unleashes lament.

A voice is heard in Ramah,
    lamentation and bitter weeping.
Rachel is weeping for her children;
    she refuses to be comforted for her children,
    because they are no more (Jer 31:15; see also Matt 2:18).

Parents, aunts, uncles, grandparents, sisters, brothers, people everywhere weep for the children consumed by deprivation, destitution, disease, and malnutrition.

Yet moving into the pain of our world with an open heart in lament can crack a soul. The flame of compassion can burn to the ash of psychic numbness, the paralysis of despair, or the resignation of hopelessness. The light goes out and darkness is all there is:

Your terrors annihilated me.
They flood around me all day long,
    close in on me all at once.
You have deprived me of friends and companions
    and all that I know is the dark (Ps 88:17, 18).[12]

In this place God is absent, dead, taken down from the cross and laid in a tomb, like any mortal, any human construction.

Fools say in their hearts, "There is no God."
    They are corrupt, they do abominable deeds;
    there is no one who does good.

---

[11] See also 2 Kgs 6:24-33, and the horrors of the curses proclaimed by Moses in Deuteronomy 28, especially verses 53-57.

[12] Translation: *The New Jerusalem Bible* (New York, N.Y.: Doubleday, 1990).

The LORD looks down from heaven on humankind
>   to see if there are any who are wise,
>   who seek after God.
They have all gone astray, they are all alike perverse;
>   there is no one who does good,
>   no, not one.
Have they no knowledge, all the evildoers
>   who eat up my people as they eat bread,
>   and do not call upon the LORD? (Ps 14:1-4; parallel Ps 53:1-4).

For some the Creator is consumed and spit out with utter disregard. For others God is not cursed, but this place of suffering is a stripped-down God-forsaken place, full of tears, terror, abandonment.

My God, my God, why have you forsaken me?
>   Why are you so far from helping me, from the words of my groaning?
O my God, I cry by day, but you do not answer;
>   and by night, but find no rest (Ps 22:1-2).

The psalms of lament cry out over and over: "How long, O Lord, how long?"[13] In this place, God is not denied, but is far away.

Why have you forgotten us completely?
>   Why have you forsaken us these many days?
Restore us to yourself . . .
unless you have utterly rejected us,
>   and are angry with us beyond measure (Lam 5:20, 21a, 22).

God seems not to hear the cries of God's people.

God's voice is never heard in Lamentations, although there is an amazing declaration of hope at its heart. Hope is spoken to various degrees in the great laments of our Scriptures, but in this place of suffering it comes only as grace's pure gift of faith: "[For] faith is the assurance of things hoped for, the conviction of things not seen" (Heb 11:1). "It comes from elsewhere, unbidden, illusive, uncontrollable, and surprising, given in the pit, the place of no hope."[14]

---

[13] See Psalms 6; 13; 35; 74; 79; 80; 82; 89; 90; 94.

[14] Lam 3:21-33; Kathleen O'Connor, *Lamentations and the Tears of the World* (Maryknoll, N.Y.: Orbis Books, 2002) 57. See also Station 8.

In the face of great suffering, the alternative to lament is the natural impulse to silence. When Job's three friends went to him to "console and comfort him" they found that

> they did not recognize him, and they raised their voices and wept aloud; they tore their robes and threw dust in the air upon their heads. They sat with him on the ground seven days and seven nights, and no one spoke a word to him, for they saw that his suffering was very great (Job 2:12-13).

Language disintegrates in the face of suffering.

At the same time there is also the cry for a witness, for people, and for God to see, to attend, to hear.[15] The cry for a witness, for accompaniment in suffering, that is most deeply etched into the souls of Christians, is Christ's request for prayer in the garden of Gethsemane. "Remain, . . . stay awake and pray" (Matt 26:36-46; Mark 14:32-42; Luke 22:40-46).

Yet the disciples sleep through the Lord's agony, and awake only to see the betrayal of Jesus to the soldiers of the empire and its accomplices. To see, to watch, to hear, to be present to suffering, to God's pathos, and to speak that suffering remains a challenge of faith even, and perhaps especially, today.

SPIRITUAL CHALLENGE: WITNESS

The spiritual challenge in our information age is what to see, what to pay attention to, what to witness of all the suffering of people and the earth. Given the sheer volume, complexity and diversity of information that is available, we have real choices about what to know and also, by implication, what not to know. Could we ever say, as many decent Germans said of the death camps after World War II: "We didn't know"? As demanding and even counterintuitive as it might seem, our faith claims that the path of abundant life requires attending to God's pathos, the ache of God's heart as God hears the groaning of creation

---

[15] Lamentations cries out again and again for witnesses: 1:9, 11, 12, 18, 20; 2:20; 3:36, 50, 59-63; 4:16; 5:1.

and the cries of God's people. As people of faith we are called to the task of prophecy.

Yet we seem to be living in a time like Isaiah's when we:

> say to the seers, "Do not see";
> and to the prophets, "Do not prophesy to us what is right;
> speak to us smooth things,
> prophesy illusions,
> leave the way, turn aside from the path,
> let us hear no more about the Holy One of Israel" (Isa 30:10-11).

Many are suggesting that we live in this same culture of denial. We are wrapped in a worldwide web of information available virtually with the click of a computer key, yet it is as if God has poured out upon us a spirit of deep sleep, closed our eyes, and covered our minds (Isa 29:10).[16] All at the same time, we know and don't know, see and don't see, or at least see only what we want to.

W. H. Auden in his poem "Musee des Beaux Arts" writes:

> About suffering they were never wrong,
> the Old Masters: how well they understood
> its human position; how it takes place,
> while someone else is eating or opening a
> window or just walking dully along.[17]

---

[16] Indeed, God's mission statement to Isaiah was:

> "Go and say to this people:
>   'Keep listening, but do not comprehend;
>   keep looking, but do not understand.'
> Make the mind of this people dull,
>   and stop their ears,
>   and shut their eyes,
> so that they may not look with their eyes,
>   and listen with their ears,
> and comprehend with their minds,
>   and turn and be healed" (Isa 6:9-10).

This passage is used in Matt 13:14-15; see also Isa 5:20; 29:8-13; 42:18-23; Jer 5:21; Ezek 12:2; Mark 8:18; John 12:40; and 2 Tim 4:3, 4.

[17] See Stanley Cohen, *States of Denial: Knowing about Atrocities and Suffering* (Malden, Mass.: Blackwell, 2001) in its entirety, but particularly his discussion of Auden's quote on page 295. See also Bruce Morris "About Suffering: Voice, Genre, and Moral Community," *Social Suffering*, ed. Arthur Kleinman, Veena Das and Margaret Lock (Berkeley: University of California Press, 1997).

It is true that in the midst of great suffering, life goes on. In part, the separation of suffering from people's ongoing lives *is* "the human position." Yet it is only partly in the nature of things.

Our ability to continue our lives' smooth movement undisturbed by suffering is accomplished by conscious and unconscious choices to avert the eye, to walk by, to close the windows of our hearts, minds, and souls. We retreat into an inner defended space of peace either psychically or more literally as gated communities or armed compounds.[18] Denial, this "deep sleep," has many faces: cognitive, emotional, moral, behavioral. "Blocking out knowledge, moral obliviousness, and 'concern' without action" are each aspects of denial.[19] In contemporary life, denial enters virtually every aspect of our lives, from our intimate relationships, to life in organizations and bureaucracies, to our whole culture. It also has a spiritual dimension. Christ's invitation to watch with him in the garden is still his invitation to us today. Our spiritual challenge is to attend to God's world with all the love and wisdom of Christ, or more simply "to hear with our ears and see with our eyes."

The rationalizations and justifications for the degrees of denial in which we live are infinite. Certainly, there is a limit to how fully we can understand the suffering of another. There is an "inherent pressure within affliction to isolation and silence."[20] And it hurts to attend deeply to suffering. It is true that an addiction or fascination with witnessing suffering can dissolve a soul.[21] Some degree of denial is probably essential—but the degree of denial matters.

In our culture, we, as bystanders or observers of the world's suffering, "have greater variety and intensity of demands in an average media day than the Good Samaritan would have seen in a lifetime."[22] The demands are immense. There are not just the demands of the information itself, but also the moral demands accompanied by appeals to action. Many root our current level of denial in the phenomena of

---

[18] Here I am really only talking about the bystander component of denial and bracketing off considerations of the denial of victims and of perpetrators.

[19] Cohen, *States of Denial*, 74.

[20] Morris, "About Suffering."

[21] See Arthur Kleinman and Joan Kleinman's discussion of Kevin Carter and his famous famine photograph in "The Appeal of Experience; The Dismay of Images: Cultural Appropriations of Suffering in Our Times," *Social Suffering*, ed. Arthur Kleinman, Veena Das, and Margaret Lock (Berkeley: University of California Press, 1997).

[22] Cohen, *States of Denial*, 163.

desensitization, psychic numbing, shortening of our attention span, compassion fatigue, and despair. Yet Cohen argues that "the sheer repetition of images of suffering, their easy accessibility, or even their intrusiveness need not cause a state of exhaustion. There is, after all, no such thing as love fatigue."[23] He suggests that "the instinct to want to do something" in response to suffering is "a universal human response."[24] That desire to do something may not be triggered by every photo, article, video clip, appeal, or chance encounter with suffering in the street, but it is triggered at least sometimes, by some events. Faith suggests that the natural inclination of the human spirit to respond to suffering is rooted in our connection to the Source of infinite love. Love is not scarce. In fact, it is infinitely renewable. It is our connection to its source that can get stretched and thin at times, although it can never be severed. Participation in communities of compassion that nurture and sustain our connection to the Holy are, therefore, critical for us to remain responsive to the suffering around us.

"The problem with multiple images of distant suffering," Cohen argues, "is not their multiplicity but their psychological and moral distance. Repetition just increases the sense of their remoteness from our lives."[25] In our North American culture of comfort, the challenge may actually be to decrease the remoteness of our contact with suffering—our own, others', and the earth's. It is one of the gifts of the food pantries, meal programs, and such activities. They do not solve the problem,[26] but they can reduce the distance, the abstractness, the dehumanization and objectification of the issues and suffering in our communities. Not only is our responsiveness to suffering fed in such encounters, but it is in that place of connection with the tangible needs of another that we meet God.[27] It is there our love can be renewed and strengthened rather than drained. Certainly to nurture a relationship with God and not attend to suffering misses the beat of God's heart and runs the risk of creating a Hollywood God, something of our own wishes.

Against a larger screen, Cohen hypothesizes about the roots of denial in our culture. He suggests that it "has little to do with fatigue or

[23] Ibid., 194.

[24] Ibid., 195.

[25] Ibid., 194.

[26] The sense of being overwhelmed by the scale of the problems is the topic of Station 8.

[27] See Station 5.

the sheer repetition of images." Rather, the message being received is: "get real, wise up and toughen up; the lesson is that nothing, nothing after all, can be done about problems like these or people like this."[28] This message is to the advantage of those who benefit from the way things currently are. But faith names this sense of "no alternative" as a lie. There may be a "great chasm" between the rich and poor, the suffering and the comfortable, but the empire's way is not the only way. The choice is not between life as slaves of the empire or death by starvation in the wilderness. God hears the cries of God's people and beloved creation and indeed "comes to deliver them" (Exod 3:8).

Spiritual Practice: Lament

There is a Chinese proverb: "To know and not to act is not to know."[29] The great gift of an aphorism is to clarify and focus an issue, but in its simplicity it can obscure the true complexity of the moment. The impulse to act in the face of suffering, "to want to do something," is sacred. It is a gift to be treasured and treated with respect. We must act to relieve suffering in order to be fully human. Yet too often we act before we know. We jump to what to do or say, before we have truly heard or seen. Sometimes we act to avoid knowing—knowing ourselves, knowing the other (victim, perpetrator, and webs of relationships), knowing suffering, hearing the fullness of God's heart beat. It is also true that we learn in our acting, that we cannot know apart from engagement. Yet the pause before action or taken in the midst of action, the space we take to truly attend, hear, see, and know the suffering, carries the possibility of transformation.

Suffering touches us all at one time or another. Although it is probably not useful to compare suffering, for Arthur Frank there is a critical difference between the suffering that has its cry heard, seen, and known and the suffering that is left in its own uselessness, in its own silence.[30] In the hearing of suffering, the potential for meaning is born. The transformative potential or the growth of something more than

[28] Cohen, *States of Denial*, 195.
[29] Ibid., 23; quoting Wang Yang-Ming.
[30] Arthur Frank, *The Wounded Storyteller: Body, Illness, and Ethics* (Chicago: University of Chicago Press, 1995) 167, 179.

the suffering itself emerges as the hearing shapes the stories of both the sufferer and the witness. This is in no way to support inaction. It is rather to underline the importance of being present to all the truth of the moment. It is to encourage a practice of attending to the whole person with a mind-in-the-heart kind of listening that is based on empathy. This is not pity that distorts our hearing by turning a suffering person into an object of our sympathy or a statistic in our program. Practicing empathy nurtures the heart space from which we reach out in solidarity with those who suffer.

To be present to suffering, either our own or others', involves learning the language of lament. "Lamentations is ancient poetry of truth-telling, an act of survival that testifies to the human requirement to speak the unspeakable, to find speech in traumatized numbness and to assert boldly . . . the sheer fact of pain."[31] It is the cry, sometimes scream, sometimes raw statement or gesture of suffering. It is sometimes filled with anger, with self-pity, with irrational hurts, crazy accusations, and incomprehensible connections. Lament is often uncomfortable for its hearers. It often pushes the boundaries of polite conversation. But the emotion expressed, the articulateness of the speech, and correctness of the theology are all less important than the simple act of speaking itself. In speaking, there is an opening to something more than suffering. There is an opening to the other, to relationship, to the Holy. In that opening that the speaking and hearing of our suffering creates, there is the possibility of the restoration of wholeness.

Any lament, any testimony of suffering, is necessarily incomplete. "The more that is told, the more we are made conscious of remaining on the edge of silence."[32] It is true that lament begs interpretation. Certainly, lies and confusion as well as truth can come out of the cauldron of suffering. All the tools of understanding can be brought to bear—from psychology, to sociology, to the health sciences, to art and hermeneutics. Yet, "any analysis is always left gazing at what remains in excess of the analyzable. What is testified to remains the really real, and in the end what counts are duties toward it."[33] Those duties are the action born of knowing—knowing with the heart, mind, and spirit.

[31] O'Connor, *Lamentations*, 5.
[32] Frank, *The Wounded Storyteller*, 138.
[33] Ibid., 138ff.

The depth knowing of suffering is part of the nourishment of wisdom's banquet. It is what allows us to tell our part of the truth. It is what frees us to hear the beat of God's heart and respond without weariness:

> Have you not known? Have you not heard?
> The LORD is the everlasting God,
>   the Creator of the ends of the earth.
> He does not faint or grow weary;
>   his understanding is unsearchable.
> He gives power to the faint,
>   and strengthens the powerless.
> Even youths will faint and be weary,
>   and the young will fall exhausted;
> but those who wait for the LORD shall renew their strength,
>   they shall mount up with wings like eagles,
> they shall run and not be weary,
>   they shall walk and not faint (Isa 40:28-31).

STATION 3 LITANY:
HEAR "THE CRIES OF MY PEOPLE"

Voices 1: For the witness of scientists, journalists, and artists,
          For all their statistics, words, and images;
Voices 2: For their careful unflinching gaze
          Into the suffering of people and of our planet, both near
            and far,
    All: **We give You thanks, O God.**

Voices 1: For the prophets in the wilderness places of our time,
          For their courageous call to hear the beat of your heart;
Voices 2: For those who howl the laments of our day, and
          For the patience, compassion and wisdom of those who
            listen,
    All: **We thank You.**

Voices 1: But, Jesus, I am exhausted by my sadness:
          Our earth is cracking,
          the silence of the spring is growing,
          the web of life is tearing.
    All: **Wake us from our sleep; save us.**

Voices 2: But, Jesus, I am afraid,
          Of all that lies in the silences, the shadows,
          The closets, attics, basements of our lives,
          Of all that is not said, or half said, boxed up and almost
            forgotten;
    All: **Melt our fear with your love; save us.**

Voices 1: But, Jesus, it hurts—all the severed connections:
          Our elders put away, dignity erased;
          Our children dying, futures voided;
          Families lost, homes destroyed, trust betrayed;
    All: **Heal the ragged edges of our love; save us.**

Voices 2: We gather up all the words that cover the silences of our
            suffering:
          Anguish . . . despair . . . sorrow . . . terror . . .
          Abandonment . . . deprivation . . . violence . . . loss . . .

All: **We offer them, and all that has no name, to You,**
       Hear the cries of your people; restore us, O God.

Voices 1:   For You are the rock that gathers up the tears of our world;
            You are the knowing that will not crack;
Voices 2:   You are the fire that stirs us to act,
            the impulse of an open heart, a hand outstretched;
All: **We praise and honor your name forever.**

Visual Focus: An empty bowl with stones around it.

Station 4

"I AM THE BREAD OF LIFE"

O taste and see that the LORD is good;
happy are those who take refuge in him.
—Psalm 34:8 [1]

Standing present to the misery of people and of the earth itself is a stark, stripped-down, raw place to be. The larger philosophical questions of life and death, of the relationship of the material and spiritual dimensions of life, of the ultimate meaning and worth of things, and all the hungers and thirsts of the human journey, are thrown into sharp relief in this place of open attention to the suffering of our world. This is a decisive place, a hinge place. Choices matter in this place. This creates the edge, the fierceness, the sense of urgency in those who speak from this place, the prophets in our midst.

In the world of empires, where the well-being of the few is predicated on the deprivation of the many and where the few can distance themselves from the suffering of the many, "the prophetic alternative is a bad joke either to be squelched by force or ignored in satiation."[2] Many try to turn away from the prophet's voice. Many have no option. "But we [people of faith] are a haunted people because we believe the bad joke is rooted in the character of God, in God's very self, a God

---

[1] See also: "How sweet are your words to my taste, / sweeter than honey to my mouth!" (Ps 119:103); and "God provides food for all living creatures, / for God's faithful love endures for ever" (Ps 136:25; New Jerusalem Bible).

[2] Walter Brueggemann, *The Prophetic Imagination* (Philadelphia: Fortress Press, 1978) 42.

43

who is not the reflection of Pharaoh or of Solomon," or for that matter any elite of the empire of the day.[3] In the place of suffering, deprivation, and lamentation, who is God? Where is the God of love in this place? The journey of the banquet leads into the hard-edged light of this place, rather than into the diffused gentle light of the palace.

VOICES OF THE TRADITION

For Christians, Christ is the prophet, but more than prophet. Christ is our icon of the Holy, our window into the heart and wisdom of the universe, our answer to the questions: Who is God? and Where is God in this place of suffering, deprivation, and lament? Christ not only stands and speaks in the place where the cries of the poor and the suffering meet the ear of God as a prophet does; Christ transforms that place. And, right at the heart of this mystery, just as in the garden, is food—two kinds of food.

Isaiah's invitation, resonating with Wisdom's invitation to her banquet,[4] is also Christ's invitation.

> Ho, everyone who thirsts,
>   come to the waters;
> and you that have no money,
>   come, buy and eat!
> Come, buy wine and milk
>   without money and without price.
> Why do you spend your money for that which is not bread,
>   and your labor for that which does not satisfy?
> Listen carefully to me, and eat what is good,
>   and delight yourselves in rich food (Isa 55:1-2).

Into the place of hungering and thirsting, that all too real place of famine and dehydration where there is not enough hard-earned money to buy food and drink to sustain life, comes the invitation to good, rich food, food to delight and satisfy. How are we to respond? The host says only: come, buy (but without money, without price), and listen carefully.

[3] Ibid.
[4] Prov 9:3-6; see also Station 2.

Jesus, after feeding the five thousand,[5] encourages those who came looking for him: "Do not work for the food that perishes [the loaves they had eaten the day before], but for the food that endures for eternal life, which the Son of Man will give you" (John 6:27).

Here again are the two foods: the perishable (the material) and the eternal (the spiritual).[6] In response to the people's request: "'Sir, give us this bread always.' Jesus said to them, 'I am the bread of life. Whoever comes to me will never be hungry, and whoever believes in me will never be thirsty'" (John 6:34-35).

Christ is both the one who feeds the five thousand with the food that perishes but sustains life *and* the bread that gives enduring life to the world. In Christ, both kinds of food are unified. The place of deprivation is reshaped. On this redefinition, the journey of the banquet hinges. The verbs of this invitation are again only "come" and "believe."

Christ is our glimpse in the present of the fullness of the banquet to come. It is not by accident that Luke places the infant Jesus in a manger, the feed container for all the creatures of that sixth day of creation. Nor is it by chance that at the center of Mary's great song of thanksgiving to the God she knew so intimately we find:

> [God] has brought down the powerful from their thrones,
> and lifted up the lowly;
> he has filled the hungry with good things,
> and sent the rich away empty (Luke 1:52-53).[7]

"Good things" are, have been, and always will be God's desire for the hungry.

Jesus' invitation is the starting point for the journey that re-knits our fractured relationships with each other, the Holy and the earth, into the unity of the garden. Jesus is the hinge point of the journey of the banquet. He is the turning point at which

[5] John 6:1-14; see also Station 9.

[6] John 4:1-15 tells a parallel account about water. There is the water that the Samaritan woman must come everyday to fetch and there is the water that becomes "a spring of water gushing up to eternal life."

[7] Joseph Grassi, *Broken Bread and Broken Bodies: The Lord's Supper and World Hunger* (Maryknoll, N.Y.: Orbis Books, 1985) 55ff.

> Those who go out weeping,
>> bearing the seed for sowing,
> shall come home with shouts of joy,
>> carrying their sheaves (Ps 126:6).

The two kinds of foods are two kinds of eating. They are two very different banquets. "The contrast between the eating of the fruit of the forbidden tree by Adam and Eve, and the banquet of wisdom which is Jesus' Last Supper with his disciples . . . is the contrast between a meal—and a 'knowledge'—which divides and a meal which unites."[8] But how does this happen? What is this turning point, this hinge, that Jesus is? What is the food, the nourishment of this "meal which unites"?

A starting point for these questions is Mark's account of this "banquet of wisdom which is Jesus' Last Supper with his disciples." The supper starts in the city: "So the disciples set out and went to the city, and found everything as he had told them" (Mark 14:16; parallels: Matt 26:17ff.; Luke 22:7ff.). And it ends in a garden deep in the shadows of the cross to come. It grows in the rich symbolic soil of the Passover. For the Passover is the feast of liberation that marks the journey of the people out from under the oppression of the empire.

Yet the tentacles of the empire—betrayal, abandonment, anger, and fear—surround even this banquet of wisdom which foreshadows all the meals of the church to come. The seeds of evil are there even in Jesus' intimate circle:

> When they had taken their places and were eating, Jesus said, "Truly I tell you, one of you will betray me, one who is eating with me." They began to be distressed and to say to him one after another, "Surely, not I?" He said to them, "It is one of the twelve, one who is dipping bread into the bowl with me" (Mark 14:18-20).

Jesus and his disciples eat together, sing a hymn, and then go to the Mount of Olives, the place described as a garden in John 18:1. "And Jesus said to them:

---

[8] Bruno Barnhart, *The Good Wine: Reading John from the Center* (New York: Paulist Press, 1993) 137.

You will all become deserters; for it is written,
> "I will strike the shepherd,
>> and the sheep will be scattered."

Peter said to him, "Even though all become deserters, I will not." And all of them said the same (Mark 14:27, 29, 31b).

The banquet, then and now, is celebrated in the midst of the empire. It is sandwiched between the realities of sin: our fractured relationships with each other, God, and creation. This is the story of life in the midst of death, not in spite of death. This banquet of wisdom is about the redemption and re-creation of the integrity of all of life. It is not an escape from life. It is not fantasy. It is a table prepared "in the presence of my enemies" (Ps 23:5).

And so:

> While they were eating, [Jesus] took a loaf of bread, and after blessing it he broke it, gave it to them, and said, "Take; this is my body." Then he took a cup, and after giving thanks he gave it to them, and all of them drank from it. He said to them, "This is my blood of the covenant, which is poured out for many. Truly I tell you, I will never again drink of the fruit of the vine until that day when I drink it new in the kingdom of God."
>
> When they had sung the hymn, they went out to the Mount of Olives (Mark 14:22-26).

That initial action echoes that first taking and giving of food: "She took of its fruit and ate; and she also gave some to her husband, who was with her, and he ate. Then the eyes of both were opened, and they knew that they were naked" (Gen 3:6b-7a). Yet Jesus' action, this sharing of food at the Last Supper, radically reverses the effect of that first taking and sharing. In the fruit of this tree, our flimsy fig leaves are transformed into the clothes Paul describes: "[We] have clothed ourselves with the new self, which is being renewed in knowledge according to the image of its creator" (Col 3:10). For as Paul writes: "As many of you as were baptized into Christ have clothed yourselves with Christ" (Gal 3:27). In this clothing, indeed "we will not be found naked" (2 Cor 5:3).

What is the fruit of this tree? In what ways does Jesus' taking, breaking, and sharing of bread reverse that first taking and sharing in the garden? First, in Jesus' banquet, we are invited to take and eat the very flesh and blood of "the one who came from heaven" (John 6:33, 38, 41, 42, 50, 51, 58), the Holy One of God (John 6:69). The intent of "the one who came from heaven" is "to raise it up on the last day" (John 6:37, 39, 44, 54). It is to reweave heaven and earth. Could there be a more radical enactment of the reintegration of heaven and earth, the spiritual and physical, than the actual eating and drinking of God's very self?

At the base of the tree in the original garden, God was objectified into a topic of conversation and dubious intentions. At Jesus' table, this distant externalized God offers to enter into our very embodied selves and we are invited to become what we eat. The bread and wine of Jesus' table is our path into the heart of the Holy and the Holy into our very bellies.[9] It is food to nourish body and soul. What was enacted in that Last Supper and is enacted every time we celebrate the Eucharist is God reconciling the world to God's self in unconditional self-giving.

> The creative Word, from which the earth came, is one with the earth and its life, and this creation begins to shine again from within. . . . The Word has become "nature," and now nature herself speaks wordlessly, with color and sound, as trees do speak with liquid syllables of light.[10]

It is in the bread that is fully God's self and also of this earth, a product of our time and labor offered to God, that the path of reconciliation that makes whole the pattern of creation is opened up for all to see. And it is in our amen, our yes, our eating and drinking of that bread and that wine, that we become part of that reconciliation process. "All this is from God, who reconciled us to himself through Christ, and has given us the ministry of reconciliation" (2 Cor 5:18).

Second, the shape of this reconciliation is cruciform. It is bread broken and torn apart. It is grapes crushed and wine poured out. This reconciliation does not deny, sublimate, reject, or circumnavigate the

---

[9] Or more poetically: "God cannot be seen externally, with human eyes; *he*—the absolute center who is in God—*has opened the way* into that place for us. . . . Jesus walks through the world as through a garden, awakening within each creature its own fullness by his light. . . . Jesus invites us to come into this place, this center." Barnhart, *The Good Wine*, 54, 55; emphasis in the original.

[10] Ibid., 80.

suffering of history. The movement is not away from suffering, but right into the heart of it in love. It is not negotiated in an otherworldly domain. In the garden, Jesus aligns his will with the One he knew as his beloved parent. Then, with his eyes open, he walks in absolute freedom into the center of the empire's power, into all that tears the world apart. Christ walks directly into the heart of history and absorbs into himself all the destructive forces of evil with no return. Where is God in our suffering world? God stands fully present without reserve in the heart of suffering. God in Christ enters the place of God's absence, the place of darkness, negation, and nothingness. And there, "where God's absence was most loudly expressed, God's presence was most profoundly revealed."[11] In the breaking and pouring out that is Christ's death, the temple veil is torn in two to reveal the heart of the Holy, the desire of God to be one with us and at one with creation. The power of this movement, its initiative and transformative energy, is boundless, costly love, poured out from the heart of the Divine. This is the food of the banquet, the bread of life.

God knows the evil of this world not from a distance, but from the depths of it. God in Christ bears its marks in his hands and feet and God takes those wounds into God's very heart. In absorbing the power of the empire without return, Christ shows us the path that transforms violence and death into life. This path is not about winners and losers. It is not about who gets bread and who is left without. It is about transforming evil so it is possible for all to be fed and for all to have a place at the table. The goal is transformation, not rejection, condemnation, or damnation (John 3:17). In the cross God stands irrevocably allied with all those rejected, cast out, and forsaken by those interested in status, security, and coercive power. All our categorizations of people as evil or good, worthy or not, deserving or undeserving, acceptable or beyond the pale are forever suspect. For Christ freely chose to live and die on the wrong side of all our dichotomies—in a smoldering garbage mound outside the walls of the holy city between two criminals: one murmuring of power and one murmuring of faith (Luke 23:39-43).

In this place of violence, evil, and death, God is present and present as pure love. Indeed,

---

[11] Henri Nouwen, *Reaching Out: The Three Movements of the Spiritual Life* (Garden City, N.Y.: Doubleday, 1975) 91.

God loves beyond our dreams, extravagantly, without limit. Whatever we might imagine God's love for us to be, it is far deeper, steadier, gentler. It cannot be manipulated or bargained with. It cannot be earned or lost. . . . It fills the whole creation with light. It shines with a kind of joy in the heavens, and it illuminates each blade of grass, each tiny bug, opening our eyes to see them. It is the air we breathe, the ground we walk on, the food we eat.[12]

This is the Word of God spoken in real time and space, with blood, sweat, and tears. This is the bread of life broken for all to be the bread that, in faith, satisfies all hunger. This is the food of wisdom's banquet. In this our relationships with God, each other, and creation are knit together into a whole. This is God's covenant with us in Christ. It is this Word that draws us into song even in the shadow of the cross. It is a Word to be trusted, even with our lives.

> For as the rain and the snow come down from heaven,
>   and do not return there until they have watered the earth,
> making it bring forth and sprout,
>   giving seed to the sower and bread to the eater,
> so shall my word be that goes out from my mouth;
>   it shall not return to me empty,
> but it shall accomplish that which I purpose,
>   and succeed in the thing for which I sent it (Isa 55:10-11).

The journey of the banquet is the flowering of this Word in our midst.

SPIRITUAL CHALLENGE:[13] FAITH

What gives this reconciling word its transformative power in our lives? What gives us the eyes to see its truth and to participate in its flowering? Only our yes, our amen, are required. The invitation to the banquet reads simply: come and believe. The invitation is pure gift and grace is the vehicle of our response. Before we earn it, deserve it, or

---

[12] Roberta Bondi, *To Love as God Loves: Conversations with the Early Church* (Philadelphia: Fortress Press, 1987) 101.

[13] The spiritual challenges of the banquet are many. For focus, we start with "faith" and many of the others are addressed in the stations to come.

achieve it, God offers this grace: for free, for all, forever.[14] No one is excluded from the banquet except those who themselves choose exclusion. All that is required is our yes.

But as the disciples said to Jesus: "This teaching is difficult; who can accept it?" (John 6:60). Indeed the large crowds that open this food-centered account in John dwindle at the end to only the twelve (John 6:2, 70). "Even to them [Jesus'] message of sharing, of non-violence, of ultimate generosity and self-gift, of trust in love rather than power, seems a hard saying and we see them repeatedly looking for some sort of magic to give more force to God's covenant with them."[15] Paul encountered the same challenge. For seen with one set of eyes, the food Jesus offers is indeed crazy, offensive, or at least counterintuitive.

> For Jews demand signs and Greeks desire wisdom, but we proclaim Christ crucified, a stumbling block to Jews and foolishness to Gentiles, but to those who are the called, both Jews and Greeks, Christ the power of God and the wisdom of God. For God's foolishness is wiser than human wisdom, and God's weakness is stronger than human strength (1 Cor 1:22-25).

The religious among us want conviction, an assurance of the rightness of this claim; and the worldly wise, the scientists and philosophers of the age, want something that makes sense, a power that is predictable, a useful tool. The cross satisfies neither.

The invitation to the banquet is rather an invitation to faith: come and believe. It is an invitation to say yes to the One who died outside the bounds of all that seems useful or acceptable. In that death, in the bread broken and wine poured out, God utters a statement of unconditional love, of unqualified commitment to God's beloved creation. In faith, God is even now reconciling creation, in all its fullness, to God's self. But, it is only in the surrender of our desire for power, certainty, and control to this God that we can see it. With the eyes of faith,

- we see the power of life that even the empire cannot silence;[16]

---

[14] See Mary Jo Leddy, *Radical Gratitude* (Maryknoll, N.Y.: Orbis Books, 2002) 65.

[15] Monika Hellwig, *The Eucharist and the Hunger of the World*, 2d ed. (Franklin, Wis.: Sheed and Ward, 1999) 63.

[16] Eph 1:17-19.

- we see the material world shining with the light of the transcendent, as gift not as possession or resource;

- we see people—all people, as children of God, bearers of the image of God; and

- we see history as God's, not ours; as something we contribute to and participate in certainly, but as a narrative ultimately shaped by God in love.

Life for all comes only in the surrender of the desire to know for sure in a predictable, manageable, humanly controllable way. The other path diminishes life and only the few can participate in its gifts. Yet how much of the energy of our culture, our technology, our politics and economics is about our control?

The first step of the journey of the banquet, the redemption of creation, is belief: come and believe. "[The gospel] is the power of God for salvation to everyone who has faith. . . . For in it the righteousness of God is revealed through faith for faith" (Rom 1:16-17). Yet faith is about more than "believing beliefs [or] assenting to doctrines. Actually, the response Paul sought included both consent to the truth of his statements about God's act in Christ, and personal entrustment of the self to the God who had done this and to Christ."[17] What is this trust that lies at the root of "entrustment"?

> To trust is to commit oneself. To trust a person is to rely on that person and to allow oneself to be shaped by that person on a deep level, for the object of trust shapes the truster. To trust a message is to rely on it, to act on it, to be shaped by it. . . . When Paul called for trust he was calling for reconfiguration of the self.[18]

The invitation of the banquet is an invitation to enter into an unfolding relationship of trust with the Holy.

In this relationship with God in Christ not only are we clothed with Christ, but our very selves are reshaped. The "I" that is the subject of all the verbs of my life [I do, I think, I create, I plan, I decide, I eat, I serve, etc.] is reconfigured by another subject: the Holy. In the space

---

[17] Leander E. Keck, *Paul and His Letters*, 2d ed. (Philadelphia: Fortress Press, 1988) 52.

[18] Ibid.

that grace creates, with the permission of trust, we open ourselves to another "I"; not an "it," an object of attention, devotion, or even a truth. We open to another subject whom we allow to shape us. That open space between two subjects is the creative arena of the Spirit. It is the place where the breath of God generates life beyond our asking or imagining. Our part is "to love God with all our heart, all our soul, all our mind, all our strength." It is to bring all of ourselves into our relationship with God: to come and believe. It is to be as fully committed as the widow who gave her "two small copper coins [which was] . . . all she had to live on" (Luke 21:1-4). She gave not out of her excess or her discretionary time, talent, or energy. She gave with no reserve, an unconditional yes, in complete trust.

The challenge is not to foreclose the openness of our engagement with the Holy. The temptation is to turn faith into a noun rather than a verb and turn God into an "it" rather than a "you." The danger is to turn a living relationship with God into a holiness project or a good and worthy cause or something that we do to align ourselves correctly, properly, fully with God, as if that had not already been accomplished by God in Christ. Our simple "yes—amen" in response to God, repeated over a lifetime, in an infinite number of circumstances, is the core of the life of faith.

Gathering at Christ's table, our life *is* shaped by the food and etiquette of that table. But it is at the table that we learn the table etiquette.[19] Faith creates morality. It is not the other way around. The invitation to the table is unconditional. That is the freedom we feast on in Christ. Yet, it is a freedom based on consent to an open-ended engagement with another Subject. It is not a freedom that we can control. It is not earned, owned, or managed. "Take, eat" is the offer, regardless of who is present. It is offered to the betrayer. It is offered to the justly judged criminals at Jesus' side. It is eaten in the midst of the empire. It is given as pure gift. And it is by grace that we hear ourselves say "yes" to the host of the banquet (Eph 2:8).

The cross does not "solve" the problem of suffering or of hunger. It reframes it. We see with different eyes and understand with a different heart. We see from a place of connection with God. The banquet

---

[19] Keck, following Paul, makes this point by saying the indicative [you are in Christ/you are at Christ's table] generates the imperative [live in Christ/follow that table etiquette]; ibid., 86.

is already served with a place at the table set for everyone, always. Food that satisfies every hunger is offered at this table in abundance. Isaiah's invitation, "Come, buy wine and milk without money and without price," is Jesus' invitation: come and believe. Our yes, our amen, is the step of faith. With grace we take our place at the table. With grace we consent to the shaping of our lives by the food of the banquet table: the Word of God that leavens the whole loaf of history.

SPIRITUAL PRACTICE: PRAYER

Prayer is intentional time spent at the banquet table. In prayer we bring all of ourselves: all our thinking, feeling, being, talking, listening, doing, loving, singing, crying, into the presence of God. It is not that we are ever or anywhere not in the presence of God (Psalm 139; Rom 8:38, 39). It is rather that we choose to turn away from that presence. Prayer is an intentional choosing to be with God. The advice of the ages is to "pray without ceasing" (1 Thess 5:17; Luke 18:1). It is in prayer that we are shaped by the table: its food, its etiquette, its conversation.

At the heart of a life of prayer, there is what appears initially to be a paradox. "Praying without ceasing" requires real effort and discipline, yet it is the pure gift of grace that makes prayer possible. Sarah Coakley describes prayer as "a peculiarly active form of passivity in which the divine pressure upon us meets not blockage but clarification."[20] The energy of our hearts, hands, and minds, all the demands of work, home, and community life, and the commitments made with the best of intentions create a whirling centrifugal force that sends us outward in all sorts of directions. The discipline of prayer is attention to the centripetal force that, like a magnet, draws us to the very center of our lives wherever we find ourselves. Time spent in prayer is time spent at the heart of the universe. At the center, through the Spirit, we are connected to the whole web of life, and the healing of that web begins. We clean our glasses so we see again the transcendent shining in the ordi-

---

[20] Sarah Coakley, "Deepening Practices: Perspectives from Ascetical and Mystical Theology," *Practicing Theology: Beliefs and Practices in Christian Life*, ed. Miroslav Volf and Dorothy C. Bass (Grand Rapids, Mich.: Eerdmans, 2002) 83.

nariness of our lives. Through grace, at the center, we encounter a quietness, a love, a welcome that satisfies every hunger and thirst. We love and work then from a place of fullness, not emptiness. At the center, through the Spirit, we can hear the direction in which God is pulling us. All the centrifugal energy of our lives, our actions, commitments, and intuitions, is shaped and focused by our time at the center.

The disciples, seeing Jesus at prayer, ask what seekers through all the ages ask: "Teach us to pray" (Luke 11:1). The request itself is prayer. Jesus responds with what has come to be known as the Lord's Prayer (Luke 11:2-4; Matt 6:9-13). The Lord's Prayer is like a seed that, buried in the right soil, grows and yields thirty, sixty, a hundredfold.[21] From the yield of that seed comes our food and seed for further plantings. Through the ages, a variety of prayer forms have grown in response to that request: "teach us to pray." They are as diverse and plentiful as the plants in any botanist's field guide.[22] In response to the prayer "teach us to pray," the seed is always offered and the Spirit nurtures its growth,[23] for even when "we do not know how to pray as we ought, . . . that very Spirit intercedes with sighs too deep for words" (Rom 8:26). The critical turn in the journey of the banquet is that initial prayer of the heart: "teach us to pray."

In Matthew's account, Jesus' teaching about prayer also includes a caution that prayer is not about public ritual filled with "empty phrases . . . [and] many words." It is about time spent in the presence of God (Matt 6:5-8). This is not to say that prayer with others is unimportant. In fact, Jesus assures us later in Matthew's gospel: "If two of you agree on earth about anything you ask, it will be done for you by my Father in heaven. For where two or three are gathered in my name, I am there among them" (Matt 18:19-20). But Jesus does direct our attention past the ritual and words of any one prayer-form to the heart of the matter: time spent consciously in the presence of God, listening to God.

---

[21] Matt 13:1-9; Mark 4:1-9; Luke 8:4-8.

[22] Just as Roberta Bondi writes about the desert dwellers of the early church (the fourth and fifth centuries), "there is intentionally a huge variety in their prayer, for they insist at every turn that God reveals God's self to each person according to that person's needs." *To Love as God Loves*, 85.

[23] There is a whole host of resources for developing a prayer life that include books, spiritual directors, prayer groups, and simply time spent in prayer.

For prayer is so much more than words. Today in our exciting, stimulating, and relentlessly noisy culture, many are finding that the language of silence is fertile soil for prayer. When Elijah retreated from the opposition and danger of his ministry to the mountain, God invited Elijah into God's presence.

> Now there was a great wind, so strong that it was splitting mountains and breaking rocks in pieces before the LORD, but the LORD was not in the wind; and after the wind an earthquake, but the LORD was not in the earthquake; and after the earthquake a fire, but the LORD was not in the fire; and after the fire a sound of sheer silence. When Elijah heard it, he wrapped his face in his mantle and went out and stood at the entrance of the cave. Then there came a voice to him that said, "What are you doing here, Elijah?" (1 Kgs 19:11b-13).

Elijah met God in that "sheer silence" and is sent out from that place. It is not that our words are irrelevant. In fact, in speaking our own words, thoughts, and feelings in the presence of God, we can find those words transformed. We see them in a new light. Yet, sometimes in our prayers we are so busy talking to God and asking God to hear us, that there is hardly any room for us to hear God. Just as in the garden God called, "Where are you?" to the original humans, God is still calling, "Where are you?" and we cannot hear because we have hidden ourselves in all the noise of our lives (Gen 3:8, 9). Real time spent in the silence at the center of our beings: heart, mind, and body resting in God, before, beneath, beyond all the verbs of our lives, is time spent at the banquet table. It is nourishment for the journey. Our souls are satisfied there as with a rich feast (Ps 63:5), and we in turn can become food for the world. We too are sent out.

STATION 4 LITANY:
"I AM THE BREAD OF LIFE"

Voices 1: We bring our emptiness to You:
Empty bellies, empty hearts, empty hands;

Voices 2: In your presence we are filled,
Satisfied with good things;

All: **For the rich, dark bread of your love,**
We thank You, O God.

Voices 1: In those hard, scorched holes of absence:
No one, no thing, no love, no God,

Voices 2: You are there, touching the edges of the void,
Speaking love in the sheer silences of our lives;

All: **Our thanks, O Word of Life.**

Voices 1: For all who hunger, let there be a place at the table;

Voices 2: For all crushed by the empire, let the banquet be served;

All: **Gather us, feed us, form us, around your table, O God.**

One: Grow our faith:

Voices 1: Like crocuses under the late snows of spring;
Like cacti in the desert.

One: Open our ears to hear and our eyes to see:

Voices 2: The light that graces the ordinariness of our days with
subtle joy;
The heartbeat that tunes the noise of our day into music.

One: Teach us to pray:

Voices 1: To rest in your presence;
To be nourished by your Word.

One: Clothe us in your love:

Voices 2: That we might welcome all people to your table,
And become ourselves food for the world:

All: **Bread broken, wine poured out.**

[pause]

<table>
<tr><td align="right">**One:**</td><td>Host of the Banquet,</td></tr>
<tr><td align="right">**Voices 1:**</td><td>You stretch wide your arms to embrace the whole world,</td></tr>
<tr><td align="right">**All:**</td><td>**We enter your embrace; You are our love, our beloved.**</td></tr>
</table>

One:	You are the sap that feeds us,
Voices 2:	Greening each leaf on the tree that unites heaven and earth;
All:	**We bless and honor your name forever.**

Visual Focus: Bread broken open.

Station 5

TABLE ETIQUETTE 1
LOVE—"I WAS HUNGRY AND
YOU GAVE ME BREAD"

*You yourselves are our letter, . . . to be known and read by all; and
you show that you are a letter of Christ, . . . written not with ink
but with the Spirit of the living God, not on tablets of stone but on
tablets of human hearts.*

—2 Corinthians 3:2-3

Food is at the heart of human culture. It is a part of all of our lives. We
each eat every day, and hopefully more than once a day. It is part of
our material life as day six creatures, yet it also opens to the Sacred.
Even in such a simple act as breaking and sharing bread, the transcendent dimension can shine in the midst of our ordinary human experience. The ways we eat—the food we eat when, with whom, with
what, the etiquette of eating, the tables we gather around—reveal
much about our material, social, and spiritual culture. Cultural and
nutritional anthropologists study these food ways. They read them as a
book about who we are. Our food ways reflect our relationships: with
the earth, with each other, and with God. Our food ways are integral
to the flourishing of life on our planet—to life abundant for all.

When our faith tradition speaks of the food of the banquet as
boundless, costly love, poured without restraint from the heart of the
Holy, there are real implications for our food ways: our ways of relating to each other, God, and the earth. There is an etiquette or ethos at

the banquet table of God. Every day we participate in the etiquette of the banquet, or not. Even among Jesus' disciples at the Last Supper, "a dispute arose" about this etiquette (Luke 22:24). Every day in very concrete ways the possibility of the banquet is renewed or disregarded. This station and the two following explore this etiquette, its roots, and its broader implications.

VOICES OF THE TRADITION

Jesus' Last Supper with his disciples is recounted quite differently in John than in the other gospels. The dinner is set with the same backdrop: the Passover festival of the liberation of the people. It is also held in the shadow of the betrayal of Christ and the cross. Yet in John the focus is directly on table relationships, on the etiquette of the banquet.

> Now before the festival of the Passover, Jesus knew that his hour had come to depart from this world and go to the Father. Having loved his own who were in the world, he loved them to the end. The devil had already put it into the heart of Judas son of Simon Iscariot to betray him. And during supper Jesus, knowing that the Father had given all things into his hands, and that he had come from God and was going to God, got up from the table, took off his outer robe, and tied a towel around himself. Then he poured water into a basin and began to wash the disciples' feet and to wipe them with the towel that was tied around him (John 13:1-5).

In spite of, or perhaps because of, the cosmic context of his whole life, "knowing that the Father had given all things into his hands, and that he had come from God and was going to God," Jesus chooses the menial role of servant. This is his defining gesture of love, the lens through which to interpret his whole ministry.

Paul summarizes the radical nature of Jesus' action:

> Though [Christ] was in the form of God,
>   [he] did not regard equality with God
>   as something to be exploited,
> but emptied himself,
>   taking the form of a slave,
>   being born in human likeness.

And being found in human form,
  he humbled himself
  and became obedient to the point of death—
  even death on a cross.
Therefore God also highly exalted him
  and gave him the name
  that is above every name (Phil 2:6-9).

In the name of love, Christ reverses all the categories of power. He brings a different lens to our understanding of fullness and emptiness. The implications are inescapable . . . or are they?

Have the implications of Jesus' gesture ever been inescapable? From the criminal dying at his side to his closest disciples and friends, there has always been a struggle to see the world from Jesus' perspective.[1] In Luke's account of the Last Supper, power is exactly what the disciples argued about.

> A dispute also arose among them as to which one of them was to be regarded as the greatest. But [Jesus] said to them, "The kings of the Gentiles lord it over them; and those in authority over them are called benefactors. But not so with you; rather the greatest among you must become like the youngest, and the leader like one who serves. For who is greater, the one who is at the table or the one who serves? Is it not the one at the table? But I am among you as one who serves (Luke 22:24-27).

Jesus knows that in the empire the "one at the table" is the greatest. So he, in the shadow of the cross, "took off his outer robe and tied a towel around himself," and on his knees with a wash bowl, concretely, with no possible ambiguity, reverses that order. He washes the feet of his disciples.

Paul spells out the implications of this act: "Do nothing from selfish ambition or conceit, but in humility regard others as better than yourselves. Let each of you look not to your own interests, but to the interests of others. Let the same mind be in you that was in Christ Jesus" (Phil 2:3-5).

---

[1] Even at the beginnings of the church the expectations were for the widow to "wash the saints' feet," not the other way around (1 Tim 5:10).

This is a hard teaching. It contradicts the whole way we have been taught to see the world. And so Peter, and actually most of us since then, naturally object:

> [Jesus] came to Simon Peter, who said to him, "Lord, are you going to wash my feet?" Jesus answered, "You do not know now what I am doing, but later you will understand." Peter said to him, "You will never wash my feet." Jesus answered, "Unless I wash you, you have no share with me" (John 13:6-8).

It is the only way to walk with Christ. It is non-negotiable. It lies at the very heart of the ethos of the banquet.

In the enthusiasm of his yes, Peter misses the point. It is not about cleanliness. "'Lord, not my feet only but also my hands and my head!' Jesus said to him, 'One who has bathed does not need to wash, except for the feet, but is entirely clean'" (John 13:9-10). Jesus keeps the focus on the matter at hand. The issue is power; not the negation of power, but its redefinition.

> After he had washed their feet, had put on his robe, and had returned to the table, he said to them, "Do you know what I have done to you? You call me Teacher and Lord—and you are right, for that is what I am. So if I, your Lord and Teacher, have washed your feet, you also ought to wash one another's feet. For I have set you an example, that you also should do as I have done to you. Very truly, I tell you, servants are not greater than their master, nor are messengers greater than the one who sent them. If you know these things, you are blessed if you do them (John 13:12-17).

In the midst of real differences in power, relationships can be patterned in all sorts of ways. Power can be used to "lord it" over another, or can be used to serve the interests of another. The etiquette of the banquet is clear on this point: "Let the same mind be in you that was in Christ Jesus" (Phil 2:5).

However, the sequence of the event is also important. Peter's feet are washed. We experience Christ's unconditional love. We receive the food of the table: that "boundless, costly love, poured out without restraint from the heart of the Holy."[2] It is that food that can open,

---

[2] Station 4.

with the power of the Spirit, the inner eye of our knowing. Then, "if we know these things," the blessing comes "if we do these things." The movement of redemption begins with our knowing, our experience, of the love of God. Our eating of the fruit of this tree is then transformed into our doing, our acting. When the receiving turns into the giving, the wisdom of the banquet is welded to the compassion of the banquet. "If you know these things, you are blessed if you do them" (John 13:17).

This is the nature of blessing.

> A blessing is a creative act; it brings something new into existence. . . . But a blessing is always expected to make the one who receives it, the source of blessing for others; it is not expected to come to rest in its recipient and to end there. . . . One is not blessed at the expense of others, but for the benefit of others.[3]

This transformation from blessing received into blessing given is the crucial alchemy in the heart of believers. It is what changed as the followers of Jesus became apostles of Christ. It is not an optional step in the journey of faith, but lies right at the very center of it. Hellwig's words are quite decisive on this point.

> It is not possible to cross over in the sacrifice of the death of Jesus into the life of God, and to leave behind the poor and the oppressed of the world. To accept the bread of the Eucharist is to accept to be bread and sustenance for the poor of the world.[4]

To receive the sacrament is to become, ourselves, the sacrament— bread for the world, wine poured out for all. We are the food of the banquet.

The alchemy that transforms receiving the sacrament into being the sacrament is the blessing that links: "If you know these things, you are blessed if you do them" (John 13:17). It is what welds together the banquet of wisdom or communion with the Divine that yields understanding, and the banquet of compassion in which we love as God

---

[3] Monika Hellwig, *The Eucharist and the Hunger of the World,* 2d ed. (Franklin, Wis.: Sheed & Ward, 1999) 38, 42.

[4] Ibid., 72.

loves God's creation.[5] It is the same alchemy that unites the two great commandments into one.

> One of the scribes came near and heard them disputing with one another, and seeing that he answered them well, he asked [Jesus], "Which commandment is the first of all?" Jesus answered, "The first is, 'Hear, O Israel: the Lord our God, the Lord is one; you shall love the Lord your God with all your heart, and with all your soul, and with all your mind, and with all your strength.' The second is this, 'You shall love your neighbor as yourself.' There is no other commandment greater than these" (Mark 12:28-31).

The confusion in the singular and plural forms of speech in that last verse: "there is [singular] no other commandment [singular] greater then these [plural]" is perhaps no confusion, but rather, as Sandra Schneiders notes, insightful theology.

> Jesus' whole life consisted in identifying love of God and love of neighbor. . . . Christian love is not simply the observance of the two great commandments, but the integration of the two in a Jesus-like identification that focuses on the neighbor in need. Loving the neighbor is more than an expression or result of loving God; it is loving God.[6]

In Luke, the discussion of the great commandment is extended with a parable. "A lawyer stood up to test Jesus. 'Teacher,' he said, 'what must I do to inherit eternal life?'" (Luke 10:25). In his typical fashion, Jesus responds to his question with a question: "What is written in the law?" The lawyer responds with the great commandment. The Good Samaritan parable that Jesus offers in response to his tester's second question, "Who is my neighbor?" is a reflection on the singularity of the great commandment. It paints a sharp contrast between the absence of care offered the robbery victim left for dead on the side of the road by two specialists in this law (the priest and Levite) and the extravagance of care offered by the one considered a religious apostate (the Samaritan; Luke 10:29-37). Paul makes the same point, but his

---

[5] This linkage is repeated at a deeper level in the movement from Station 11 to Stations 12 and 13.

[6] Sandra Schneiders, *Finding the Treasure: Locating Catholic Religious Life in a New Ecclesial and Cultural Context* (Mahwah, N.J.: Paulist Press, 2000) 314; emphasis in the original.

contrast to the love ethic is our familiar "dog-eat-dog" world: "The whole law is summed up in a single commandment, 'You shall love your neighbor as yourself.' If, however, you bite and devour one another, take care that you are not consumed by one another" (Gal 5:14-15).[7]

Whether the alternative to "love of neighbor" is walking by on the other side of the road or Paul's more actively destructive picture, the point is Jesus' imperative: "Go and do likewise" (Luke 10:37b). The lawyer who stood up to test Jesus knew the right answer. But for Jesus, the emphasis is on living the answer: "If you know these things, you are blessed if you do them" (John 13:17).

This is the wisdom of the ones who choose to build houses on solid foundations:

> Everyone then who hears these words of mine and acts on them will be like a wise man who built his house on rock. The rain fell, the floods came, and the winds blew and beat on that house, but it did not fall, because it had been founded on rock. And everyone who hears these words of mine and does not act on them will be like a foolish man who built his house on sand. The rain fell, and the floods came, and the winds blew and beat against that house, and it fell—and great was its fall! (Matt 7:24-27; parallel: Luke 6:46-49).

Faith is linked to action. Love of God and love of neighbor are two sides of the same coin. The banquet of wisdom is inextricably intertwined with the banquet of compassion.

James is insistent on this integration of our God-talk with our God-walk.[8]

> What good is it, my brothers and sisters, if you say you have faith but do not have works? Can faith save you? If a brother or sister is naked and lacks daily food, and one of you says to them, "Go in peace; keep warm and eat your fill," and yet you do not supply their bodily needs, what is the good of that? So faith by itself, if it has no works, is dead.
>
> But someone will say, "You have faith and I have works." Show me your faith apart from your works, and I by my works will show you my faith (Jas 2:14-18).

---

[7] See also Rom 13:8-10.

[8] See Frederick Herzog, *God-Walk: Liberation Shaping Dogmatics* (Maryknoll, N.Y.: Orbis Books, 1988).

And this integration is reiterated in the first letter of John: "How does God's love abide in anyone who has the world's goods and sees a brother or sister in need and yet refuses help? Little children, let us love, not in word or speech, but in truth and action" (1 John 3:17-18). It is there that the reason for the univocal voice of our tradition on this point is put most simply:[9] "Beloved, let us love one another, because love is from God; everyone who loves is born of God and knows God. Whoever does not love does not know God, for God is love. . . . Those who abide in love abide in God and God in them" (1 John 4:7-8, 16b). The etiquette of the table is inherent in the nature of the Holy. By "really loving our neighbor, we as it were fall or penetrate into the ultimate realities of created reality; and even if we do not explicitly say so, are really mysteriously concerned in this love with the God of our eternal, supernatural salvation."[10] The two great commandments cohere.

One of the early church monks, Dorotheus of Gaza, offers a wonderful analogy for this coherence.

> Suppose we were to take a compass and insert the point and draw the outline of a circle. The center point is the same distance from any point on the circumference. . . . Let us suppose that this circle is the world and that God himself is the center: the straight lines drawn from the circumference to the center are the lives of human beings. . . . Let us assume for the sake of the analogy that to move toward God, then human beings move from the circumference along the various radii of the circle to the center. But at the same time, the closer they are to God, the closer they become to one another; and the closer they are to one another, the closer they become to God.[11]

The inverse is also true: "as we move away from God we move away from other people, and as we move away from people, we also move away from God."[12]

---

[9] Leander Keck makes a cogent case that this stance in no way contradicts Paul's insistence that faith is the only basis for right relationship with God; see *Paul and His Letters*, 2d ed. (Philadelphia: Fortress Press, 1988) 85–90.

[10] Karl Rahner, *Every Day Faith*, trans. W. J. O'Hara (New York: Herder and Herder, 1968) 108.

[11] Roberta Bondi, *To Love as God Loves: Conversations with the Early Church* (Philadelphia: Fortress Press, 1987) 25.

[12] Ibid.

In this light, it is possible to understand the fierceness of John the Baptist's call for repentance:

> You brood of vipers! Who warned you to flee from the wrath to come? Bear fruits worthy of repentance. Do not begin to say to yourselves, "We have Abraham as our ancestor"; for I tell you, God is able from these stones to raise up children to Abraham. Even now the ax is lying at the root of the trees; every tree therefore that does not bear good fruit is cut down and thrown into the fire (Luke 3:7b-9).

In contrast his call to action seems quite modest. "The crowds asked him, 'What then should we do?' In reply he said to them, 'Whoever has two coats must share with anyone who has none; and whoever has food must do likewise'" (Luke 3:10-11).

When "knowing these things" is welded together with "doing these things," it is possible to appreciate that the intensity and urgency of the Baptist's call to repentance is actually not disproportionate to the simplicity and decency of his call to action. Love of neighbor and especially those in need profoundly affects and reflects our relationship with the Holy.

Similarly, the intensity of the last parable in Matthew's Gospel, the parable of the sheep and goats, can be more fully appreciated as the implications of the unity of the great commandment are plumbed (Matt 25:31-46). The drama of the judgment scene before "the Son of Man . . . on the throne of his glory" surrounded by "all the angels . . . and all the nations" is not simply a rhetorical flourish added for color. It reveals what is at stake in love of neighbor. It reveals the possibility present in mundane, concrete acts of compassion: giving food to the hungry, drink to the thirsty, welcome to the stranger, clothing to the naked, care to the sick, and presence to the prisoners. And so the king in the parable says:

> Truly I tell you, just as you did it to one of the least of these who are members of my family, you did it to me. . . . Truly I tell you, just as you did not do it to one of the least of these, you did not do it to me (Matt 25:40, 45).

In the simplest gestures of love, the Holy is present.

In fact in such gestures the whole mystery of the incarnation is reproduced:

> If we love this other—if we do not as it were culpably impede the dy-
> namism of this love and fundamentally turn it back towards ourselves,
> then there occurs precisely the divine descent into the flesh of human-
> ity, so that God is in the place where we are and gazes at us in a human
> being. . . . Where the other human being confronts me, there Christ
> really is, asking me whether I will love him, the incarnate Word of God,
> and if I say Yes, Christ replies that he is in the least of his [kin].[13]

The mystery of the incarnation is not just a historical reality, years ago
in Palestine, or merely a theological concept. It is true and ongoing
today. God is always the God who becomes human.

In the simple act of feeding the hungry, we do not just do a good
thing or follow a moral imperative to care for our neighbor; we are actually invited to encounter the living Christ, the mystery of the universe from before time to after the end of time. "I was hungry and you
gave me food." This was certainly the experience of the Samaritan
woman. In a tired, hot, and thirsty Jewish man sitting by a well with
no bucket, she met "the Messiah, . . . Savior of the world, . . . [the
one who gives the water that] will become in them a spring of water
gushing up to eternal life" (John 4:25, 42, 14). Yet is it our experience?
Do we meet the living Christ in "the least of the members of Christ's
family"? Is the experience of "the least of the members of Christ's
family" that they have been addressed by us as the Christ? It is true
that "if we know these things, we are blessed if we do them" (John
13:17).

SPIRITUAL CHALLENGE: LOVE

Love is the core verb and noun in our faith: love of God, of each other,
of God's beloved creation, to love as God loves. Paul's commentary on
love ends with: "And now faith, hope, and love abide, these three; and
the greatest of these is love. Pursue love and strive for the spiritual gifts,
and especially that you may prophesy" (1 Cor 13:13– 14:1). Our spiritual challenge today is to "pursue love" in concrete and life-generating
ways that are sturdy enough to withstand the pressures of our culture
in contrary directions. Yet, as Roberta Bondi notes: "[Love] is not some-

---

[13] Rahner, *Every Day Faith*, 114–5.

thing we can grit our teeth and do; nor is it a possession that, once we have it, makes us good or acceptable. Delight in love is the gift of God, God loving in us."[14]

"Love" is one of those big, multifaceted words that is used in all sorts of ways in our culture. Disregarding popular culture's reduction of love to a transitory emotional event like "falling in love" or "being in love," most people catch a glimpse of a sturdier, deeper understanding of love through experiences of love as child, parent, partner, friend; as lover and beloved. Yet those experiences, even at their best, are always only partial. The love our faith speaks to, the love of God, is a love that comes from a bottomless aquifer. It is love inseparably intermingled with infinite wisdom. It is love that embraces enemies and can absorb evil without return. It is, therefore, not simply a matter of affection, temperament, or emotion. It is rather a deep disposition of the heart: "a commitment that shapes our ways of seeing, understanding, and acting."[15] It is a commitment to the well-being of others in which we cultivate "the same mind . . . that was in Christ Jesus" (Phil 2:5). We come to this disposition, this habit, or shaping of our hearts and minds "as a result of God's grace and our own choices and commitments lived out over a very long period of time. . . . It is a way of seeing habitually and responding to the real, separate, individual needs of each of the people we encounter in our lives every day."[16] It is not something we achieve or possess. Love is something that is cultivated. We are constantly growing into it as we gather around the table and the full ethos of the banquet unfolds and deepens in our lives.

In a study of the ways Christianity is lived out among members of mainstream churches, Nancy Ammerman characterizes the most common approach as "Golden Rule Christianity."[17] This way of understanding and living out one's faith

> emphasizes relationships and caring. The good person invests heavily in care for family (especially children) and friends, tries to provide friendly help in the community, and seeks ways to make the larger world a better

[14] Bondi, *To Love as God Loves*, 22.

[15] Ibid., 30.

[16] Ibid., 33–5.

[17] Nancy T. Ammerman, "Golden Rule Christianity," *Lived Religion in America: Toward a History of Practice*, ed. David D. Hall (Princeton, N.J.: Princeton University Press, 1997).

place. . . . God is located in moments of transcendence and in the everyday virtues of doing good.[18]

There is much to commend in this way of living out the gospel. The emphasis on the everyday practice of love of neighbor and the attention to relationships in family, community, and world are central to the etiquette of the banquet table. This is the Christianity many of us were taught as children. It is the way many outside of the faith also characterize Christianity. Yet there are two ways in which the simple decency of this approach can be subverted.

The first challenge is the power dynamics in relationships and particularly in relationships of care.[19] When Jesus washed the feet of his disciples, he was the one with the most power who was offering a gift to his friends. It was not a service provided out of obligation, fear, or coercion by a person of little or no standing. It was also not offered by one who needed to be needed. It was not offered because the disciples deserved to have their feet washed. It was pure gift offered to show a path of liberation, not servitude, self-negation, or indebtedness.[20] The fundamental inequality between Jesus and his disciples was not dissolved,[21] but it was set aside to attend to their interests. Martin Buber describes this kind of attention to another as attention to a "you" or a "thou," as opposed to an "it."[22] The other is neither an object (even of my love), nor a means to serve another end. The other is not a statistic, a type, an experience, let alone a potential member. The other is distinctly herself or himself, and, for a moment, all that there is in my attention. I attend to the other and his or her interests. That open attention, for however brief and/or unconscious a moment that it lasts, creates the space for grace, for blessing. Not only is the dignity and freedom of the other maximized in such a moment; not only are our ears opened to hear the voice of the other; but that moment of open

---

[18] Ibid., 211.

[19] Richard Rohr has noted that power without attention to love tends toward domination and love without attention to power tends toward sentimentality. *Jesus' Plan for a New World: The Sermon on the Mount* (Cincinnati: St. Anthony Messenger Press, 1996) 41.

[20] See Sandra Schneiders, *Written That You May Believe: Encountering Jesus in the Fourth Gospel* (New York: Crossroad, 1999) 167–74.

[21] See John 13:13.

[22] Martin Buber, *I and Thou*, trans. Walter Kaufmann (New York: Charles Scribner's Sons, 1970).

attention makes possible the subtle but critical shift from *serving* Christ in our neighbor to *meeting* Christ in our neighbor. Can such a moment happen in the midst of differences in power? Yes. Martin Buber describes this interaction with trees and cats as well as people. Can such a moment happen when differences in power are enacted in dominating, dehumanizing, or paternalistic ways? No. We cannot get to that place without laying aside "our outer robes," without surrendering our power to control the other.

Many faith communities are involved in providing care in one form or another to their neighbors. Tex Sample reflects on his conversations with mainstream church people working with hard living people:

> In my interviews I would on occasion become too preoccupied with the *how* questions: *How* does one find effective programs? . . . One day I was straightened out: "It's the wrong question, Tex. You can't do this with gimmicks. . . . You can't build relationships on style, you build them on involvement and being." . . .The key ingredient is not the *function* or *form* of the ministry, but the *quality* of the relationships.[23]

It is in the quality of the relationships that the authenticity of our loving, our "Golden Rule Christianity," is judged. For "care as a practice involves more than simply good intentions. It requires a deep and thoughtful knowledge of the situation and of all the actors' situations, needs and competencies."[24] It also requires judgments about needs, many of which can conflict, and it requires honesty, reflection, and respect for the emotional dynamics of both the care giver and receiver. Taking relationships seriously, particularly in situations of inequality, is challenging work. It is our capacity to hear the voice of the other with open unguarded attention and learn from it that allows us to find our path through these challenges. And it is the promise of faith that it is in the midst of just these challenges that we encounter the living Christ in our day.

The second challenge to the simple decency of Golden Rule Christianity comes from the structure of our society. Dorothee Soelle tells an old Jewish story about heaven and hell that illustrates the wisdom

---

[23] Tex Sample, *Hard Living People and Mainstream Christians* (Nashville: Abingdon Press, 1993) 95–6; emphasis in the original.

[24] Joan C. Tronto, *Moral Boundaries: A Political Argument for an Ethic of Care* (New York: Routledge, 1993) 136–7.

of Paul's admonition: "Let each of you look not to your own interests, but to the interests of others" (Phil 2:4).

> Rabbi Mendel wanted to know what heaven and hell looked like, and the prophet Elijah took him to show him. Elijah led him into a large room where a big fire was burning and where there was a large table with a huge pot of spoons that were longer than their arms, and because the people could not eat with these spoons, they sat around the table and starved. Rabbi Mendel found this room and what he saw there so terrible that he quickly ran outside. . . . Then Elijah took Rabbi Mendel to heaven and into another room where a big fire was burning and where there was a large table with a big pot of steaming soup on it. And around this table sat people with the same spoons, but they did not have to starve because they were feeding each other.[25]

Who would not want to be in heaven? The advantages of cooperation and mutual aid over competitive individualism are clear. Yet the foundation of our culture is competitive individualism. Love in our culture may be a virtue in the intimacy of the home and among close friends, but it seems increasingly irrelevant anywhere else. Soelle characterizes the critique: "excessive demands, unrealistic thinking, and sentimentality are the hallmarks of those apostles of love who want to heal the world's ills with more neighborly love from one person to another."[26] In contrast, our faith asserts that "true humanity is realized only when people live with one another in such a way that they do not live against one another or simply next to one another but *for* one another."[27]

The options in the face of such a pervasive, deeply rooted, systemic challenge are:

• to embrace the ethos of our dog-eat-dog, survival-of-the-fittest culture and consign the ethos of the banquet to history; or

• to compartmentalize the two table etiquettes, love of neighbor and competitive individualism, into different spheres of activity: the private sphere of family, friends, and faith, and the public sphere of politics and economics, respectively; or

[25] Dorothee Soelle, *The Strength of the Weak: Toward a Christian Feminist Identity*, trans. Robert and Rita Kimber (Philadelphia: Westminster Press, 1984) 159–60.

[26] Ibid., 38. See also Station 8.

[27] Miroslav Volf, *Work in the Spirit: Toward a Theology of Work* (New York: Oxford University Press, 1991) 191.

- to commit to the ethos of the banquet and with all the gifts God gives walk into whatever situations present themselves and to the degree possible attend to and seek the well-being of the other.

In the midst of our current economic and political realities, the option to compartmentalize is becoming increasingly impossible. Yet, even within the very real constraints of our twenty-first-century culture, a life of faith is possible. For the Spirit creates all sorts of opportunities to participate in the banquet if we can but notice and move in that direction. Paul's prayer to the church in Philippi is still appropriate today, for the table etiquette of the banquet has always been counter-cultural: "This is my prayer, that your love may overflow more and more with knowledge and full insight to help you to determine what is best" (Phil 1:9-10a).

SPIRITUAL PRACTICE:
ACTS OF COMPASSION

How do we cultivate a disposition that consistently orients toward the other whether we find ourselves in corporate boardrooms or soup kitchens? How do we learn to attend to the world as God's beloved creation, to see each other as bearers of God's image? There is a folk saying that the devil is in the details, and so is salvation. Whether we are poor and challenged or rich and powerful, it is in the daily concrete interactions of our lives that we practice love and weaken the hold of all that distracts us from that practice. Indeed, all sorts of things can distract us from a practice of compassion. There are the great "isms": racism, classism, sexism, and paternalism. But there are also all sorts of preoccupations of the heart that can distract us. There are insatiable hungers or thirsts for food, drinks, stuff, status, admiration, sex, or money. An awkwardness or hesitancy in giving and receiving gifts can inhibit us. Depression, sadness, nostalgic regret; anxieties and fears, as well as anger, resentment, animosity; boredom; envy, judgmental and/or self-righteous attitudes—the list could go on—all can distract or inhibit our compassion. These are all very common, quite human, parts of our experience. They have been known through the ages, although called by different names.[28] The issue is not that they exist in our lives. The issue is rather their power over us or the hold they have on our attention. In contrast to these all too real phenomena, acts of compassion are what nourish our practice of love. Practical gestures of care and real material assistance (in time, money, and talents) are critical for the health of our souls. It is in these moments in the very midst of our lives, at table with the stranger, the hungry, the prisoner, the sick, that we meet the Holy.

Acts of compassion can be grand, noticeable acts of heroism and self-sacrifice, or they can be quite mundane, simple gestures of care. It is ironic that the sheep in Matthew's great judgment parable ask: "Lord, when was it that we saw you?" (Matt 25:37-39). They did not even remember when they had met Christ! Just as it is not a particular food choice or any one meal that defines a diet, but the habitual pattern and diversity of choices that leads to health and vitality, so it is not one compassionate act, but rather a steady diet of them that matters. Again, the issue is not so much the quantity of gestures, but rather a dependable disposition of the heart and mind. It is not about earning God's favor, for we are already assured of God's love. It is rather a matter of sharing that grace in which we already live.

Many trivialize the importance of acts of compassion and argue against placing love at the center of the table etiquette of the banquet on the assumption that "if one takes care seriously then justice will be displaced. This argument presumes that care is particular, justice universal; that care draws out of compassion, justice out of rationality."[29] Certainly, it is a very complex, interlocking set of structures—political, economic, bureaucratic, and cultural—that create the situations of vast inequality, violence, and deprivation around the globe, in our own cities, and sometimes homes. It is important to be clear-eyed and informed on the far-reaching structural bases for the pain and suffering in our world to "determine what is best" in any given situation (Phil 1:10a). Yet that determination must be deeply rooted in a compassionate knowing.[30] Miroslav Volf asserts that as much as we need to

---

[28] See Bondi's discussion of the early Church's understanding of "the passions"; *To Love as God Loves*, ch. 4.

[29] Tronto, *Moral Boundaries*, 166.

[30] See Karen Lebacqz, "Bridging the Gap: Pain and Compassion," *The Future of Prophetic Christianity: Essays in Honor of Robert McAfee Brown*, ed. Denise Lardner Carmody and John Tully Carmody (Maryknoll, N.Y.: Orbis Books, 1993).

recognize that acts of compassion are insufficient to create the kind of structural change our planet needs, we also have to insist that structural change on its own is inadequate and compassion is needed.[31] It is not enough to simply be right or to have the right analysis. For this can too easily slip into ideology or an "idolatry of a particular political program. . . . [This] emerges from a hope cut loose from its moorings in community with people of many backgrounds when love for people and respect for the wisdom of people is lost in working for the masses instead of working with people."[32] Our actions must come from a place of understanding that fully includes the other in order to move toward fullness of life for all. A table etiquette of love is concretely what it means to live for others, rather than against or simply beside others. It is love as a disposition of the heart and a commitment of the mind that prompts the move to inclusion. It is acts of compassion that keep that heart space from which we reach out in solidarity with those who suffer open, limber, green, and growing.[33]

[31] Volf, *Work in the Spirit*, 191.

[32] Sharon Welch, *A Feminist Ethic of Risk*, rev. ed. (Minneapolis: Fortress Press, 2000) 166. The blood shed in the twentieth century in the name of various ideologies working for the masses stands as a caution against this path.

[33] In contrast to some who "think of care in an apolitical context by tying it to a narrow psychological concern, or argue that it is a kind of practice that is corrupted by broader social and political concerns," Jane Tronto argues that "care as a practice can inform the practices of democratic citizenship." *Moral Boundaries*, 167ff.

STATION 5 LITANY:
TABLE ETIQUETTE: LOVE

Voices 1:   For the gift of your presence shining in the face of a
                    neighbor,
             For the moments when your Spirit turns another toward us;
Voices 2:   For all the times when grace enters the space between us,
             And we become blessings to each other,
       All: **We thank you, O God.**

Voices 1:   For all who challenge our compassion—
             From worthy charities, to street people, to our next-door
                    neighbor;
Voices 2:   For all who focus and deepen our compassion,
             To make our best intentions fruitful;
       All: **We are thankful and ask You to bless their work.**

Voices 1:   We take off our outer garments,
Voices 2:   We stand before you vulnerable, naked;
       All: **In your infinite wisdom and compassion**
             Dissolve all that stands in the way of our loving.

       One: In situations of conflict,
       All: **open our hearts and minds without prejudice to the**
                    other;
       One: In situations of inequality,
       All: **let us see and respect the full humanity of the other;**
       One: In situations of suffering,
       All: **fill our hearts with courage and our hands with healing;**
       One: In situations of practical need,
       All: **let us serve the other with dignity and generosity;**
       One: In situations of stress and ambiguity,
       All: **still our minds to hear the heart of the other;**
       One: In situations of joy, achievement, and goodness,
       All: **let us wholeheartedly affirm and celebrate.**

All: **Let our daily acts of compassion and love**
be cracks in the walls that surround us,
places that sustain life, and
openings to the fullness of the Banquet.

[pause]

Voices 1: O Center of the circle of life,
You draw us to Yourself and to each other like a magnet.
Voices 2: Your love is contagious;
We delight in your touch, we delight to be your touch.
All: **We praise You with all that we are;**
Glory to You, O Love Incarnate!

Visual focus: A bowl of water and towel.

Station 6

TABLE ETIQUETTE 2
HOSPITALITY—"INVITE EVERYONE
YOU FIND TO THE BANQUET"

*Do not neglect to show hospitality to strangers, for by doing that
some have entertained angels without knowing it.*

—Hebrews 13:2

Nothing is more natural than for people to break bread together. Sharing food at table is one of the universal ways that relationships are created. Patterns of table fellowship can be studied to identify social groups: families, friendship networks, communities, and whole cultures. The word for the social patterns created by eating together is "commensality," which the dictionary defines as "fellowship at table; the act or practice of eating at the same table.[1] The tables we gather around are infinitely varied. There are family dinner tables, worksite canteens, buffet tables at community suppers, fancy restaurant tables, the simple rock or log of a picnic site, school cafeterias, soup kitchen tables, and church altars. The patterns of food sharing and the ethos of the group that gathers around each of these tables, its commensality, are different. What, then, is the commensality of the banquet table? What is the table etiquette of God's hospitality?

[1] *Webster's Revised Unabridged Dictionary,* © 1996, 1998 MICRA, Inc.

VOICES FROM THE TRADITION

Jesus' table fellowship, the company he kept, his enjoyment of food, and his attention to the customary "rules" of the table are not tangential to his ministry. Rather, they define his ministry and us as his followers.

In the typical pattern of table fellowship, one invites relatives, friends, and neighbors usually with similar social standing. Jesus reverses that pattern: "When you give a luncheon or a dinner, do not invite your friends or your brothers or your relatives or rich neighbors, in case they may invite you in return, and you would be repaid" (Luke 14:12). The table for Jesus is not about building up a cohesive web of mutual obligation among relatives or near neighbors. Rather, in the spirit of the banquet table, Jesus suggests: "But when you give a banquet, invite the poor, the crippled, the lame, and the blind" (Luke 14:13). In this attention to the vulnerable and excluded, Jesus is drawing on clear and honored roots in his Jewish tradition.

> For the LORD your God is God of gods and Lord of lords, the great God, mighty and awesome, who is not partial and takes no bribe, who executes justice for the orphan and the widow, and who loves the strangers, providing them food and clothing. You shall also love the stranger, for you were strangers in the land of Egypt (Deut 10:17-19).

Attention to the needs of the widow, orphan, and stranger or resident alien is part of faithful covenant practice.[2] Those who have no benefactors do have a place and a claim on the community. They have some entitlements.

Jesus honors and radicalizes this tradition. In Jesus' parable of the wedding banquet, the king's invited guests are like the seed sown among the thorns: "The cares of the world, and the lure of wealth, and the desire for other things come in and choke the word, and it yields nothing" (Mark 4:19). They decline the invitation to the banquet. "They would not come." The king then says to his slaves: "'Go therefore into the main streets, and invite everyone you find to the wedding banquet.' Those slaves went out into the streets and gathered all whom

---

[2] See Exod 22:21-27; Deut 14:28-29; 16:13-15; 24:14-22; 27:18, 19, and the equivalent tradition among the prophets: Isaiah 1; Jeremiah 7, Ezekiel 22; Zechariah 7; Malachi 3.

they found, both good and bad; so the wedding hall was filled with guests" (Matt 22:9-10; parallel Luke 14:16-24). What does it mean to invite everyone and anyone to the banquet, "both good and bad"?[3] What is the meaning or implication of such an open, inclusive, non-discriminating invitation to table?

As Dominic Crossan points out: "A feast for society's outcasts could easily be understood . . . as a benefaction." It could be understood within a tradition of benevolence as a charitable act of taking care of those in need. Yet, the "everyone" is provocative. It means anyone, and that "anyone negates the very social function of table, namely, to establish a social ranking by what one eats, how one eats, and with whom one eats. . . . One could, in such a situation have classes, sexes, ranks and grades all mixed up together."[4] The banquet is clearly about more than benevolence. "The good and bad," the righteous and unrighteous, rich and poor are all together at the banquet table. The ethos of Jesus' table fellowship is rooted in a vision that is about something more than maintaining a coherent, compatible, even charitable community.

The shape of Jesus' ministry and the nature of this wedding banquet are tightly intertwined. Jesus' actual table companions were very diverse. They included "the good and the bad" together.

> And as he sat at dinner in Levi's house, many tax collectors and sinners were also sitting with Jesus and his disciples—or there were many who followed him. When the scribes of the Pharisees saw that he was eating with sinners and tax collectors, they said to his disciples, "Why does he eat with tax collectors and sinners?" When Jesus heard this, he said to them, "Those who are well have no need of a physician, but those who are sick; I have come to call not the righteous but sinners" (Mark 2:15-17; parallels: Matt 9:10-13; Luke 5:29-32).

Jesus does not do away with categorizations of people, but he radically changes their meaning. The "sinners" are not shunned or excluded. Rather, they are his table companions, the focus of his love.

---

[3] Luke underlines this question by extending this part of the story into a two-stage process: first, the host of the great dinner says: "bring in the poor, the crippled, the blind, and the lame"; then, because there is still room, the host continues: "Go out into the roads and lanes, and compel people to come in" (Luke 14:21, 23).

[4] John Dominic Crossan, *The Historical Jesus: The Life of a Mediterranean Jewish Peasant* (San Francisco: HarperSanFrancisco, 1992) 262.

Not only does Jesus keep dubious company at his table, but he clearly enjoys the table:

> To what then will I compare the people of this generation, and what are they like? They are like children sitting in the marketplace and calling to one another,
>
> > "We played the flute for you, and you did not dance;
> > we wailed, and you did not weep."
>
> For John the Baptist has come eating no bread and drinking no wine, and you say, "He has a demon"; the Son of Man has come eating and drinking, and you say, "Look, a glutton and a drunkard, a friend of tax collectors and sinners!" Nevertheless, wisdom is vindicated by all her children (Luke 7:31-35; parallel Matt 11:16-18).

Jesus' reputation, his identity, was defined by his unusual table etiquette: "'Look, a glutton and a drunkard, a friend of tax collectors and sinners!" Although he knew hunger,[5] fasting was not part of his pattern of life:

> Now John's disciples and the Pharisees were fasting; and people came and said to him, "Why do John's disciples and the disciples of the Pharisees fast, but your disciples do not fast?" Jesus said to them, "The wedding guests cannot fast while the bridegroom is with them, can they? As long as they have the bridegroom with them, they cannot fast. The days will come when the bridegroom is taken away from them, and then they will fast on that day" (Mark 2:18-20; parallels Matt 9:14-15; Luke 5:33-35).

The tenor of Jesus' table was joy and fullness to overflowing.[6] There is no evidence of a body-denying or purifying ethos. There is no evidence of the creation of an exclusive table group. Rather, there seems to be a delight in the gifts of creation and an embrace of all the different people in his midst.

All cultures have "rules" or generally recognized acceptable patterns of behavior at table and understandings about what counts as accept-

---

[5] Beyond the forty days of fasting which preceded Jesus' temptations, both Matthew (21:18) and Mark (11:12) testify to Jesus' experience of hunger: "he was hungry."

[6] Stations 10 and 12 extend this theme.

able food.[7] These shared expectations often serve the function of defining who can share a table and who is excluded, who is part of the group and who is not. Jewish culture in Jesus' day was no exception. But Jesus did not follow the customary "rules" of his time. "Together, [Jesus'] open commensality and free healing symbolized the shattering of social boundaries and affirmed unbrokered access to God [a sharing of material and spiritual resources], both revolutionary actions in a world constituted by boundaries and brokerage."[8] Marcus Borg interprets Jesus' approach as holiness rooted in the "politics of compassion." Jesus emphasized inclusion, the renewal of relationships, and access of all to the fullness of God's love. In contrast, the Pharisees, another reform movement within the Jewish community of Jesus' day, pursued holiness as careful adherence to traditional principles and practices of the faith. In contrast to Jesus' emphasis on inclusion, the Pharisee's approach required members to separate themselves from the culture into a distinct group defined by their intentional pursuit of holiness. Their practices created clear boundaries and a unique identity for the group. It also created distinctions among members as different life circumstances permitted such separation and the full pursuit of all the prescribed practices. Many of the debates about Jesus' table fellowship are about the contrast between the principles and social visions of these two reform movements.

One example is the debate about the accepted pattern of hand washing, which Mark notes as one aspect of a larger set of food "rules":

> Now when the Pharisees and some of the scribes who had come from Jerusalem gathered around him, they noticed that some of his disciples were eating with defiled hands, that is, without washing them. (For the Pharisees, and all the Jews, do not eat unless they thoroughly wash their hands, thus observing the tradition of the elders; and they do not eat

---

[7] Food anthropologists have studied these food and table "rules" extensively. See Mary Douglas, *Leviticus as Literature* (New York: Oxford University Press, 1999) for an example of the application of that discipline to Leviticus with its "law pertaining to land animal and bird and every living creature that moves through the waters and every creature that swarms upon the earth, to make a distinction between the unclean and the clean, and between the living creature that may be eaten and the living creature that may not be eaten" (Lev 11:46-47).

[8] Marcus J. Borg, *Conflict, Holiness and Politics in the Teachings of Jesus*, 2d ed. (Harrisburg, Pa.: Trinity Press International, 1998) 5.

anything from the market unless they wash it; and there are also many other traditions that they observe, the washing of cups, pots, and bronze kettles.) So the Pharisees and the scribes asked him, "Why do your disciples not live according to the tradition of the elders, but eat with defiled hands?" (Mark 7:1-5; parallel Matt 15:1, 2).

Jesus first addresses the Pharisees, but then turns to the crowd, and generalizes the issue:

Then he called the crowd again and said to them, "Listen to me, all of you, and understand: there is nothing outside a person that by going in can defile, but the things that come out are what defile."

When he had left the crowd and entered the house, his disciples asked him about the parable. He said to them, "Then do you also fail to understand? Do you not see that whatever goes into a person from outside cannot defile, since it enters, not the heart but the stomach, and goes out into the sewer?" (Thus he declared all foods clean.) And he said, "It is what comes out of a person that defiles. For it is from within, from the human heart, that evil intentions come: fornication, theft, murder, adultery, avarice, wickedness, deceit, licentiousness, envy, slander, pride, folly. All these evil things come from within, and they defile a person" (Mark 7:14-23; parallel Matt 15:10-20).

At this level of first principles, the radical core of Jesus' practice emerges. It is not that Jesus' path is without "rules" or a sense of righteousness or holiness. For Jesus, protection against what harms or defiles, and, therefore more generally, the pursuit of holiness, is *not* an issue of boundaries, of what is in and out, an issue of the stomach. It is not about separation from the world. Rather, it is a matter of the conversion of the heart. Jesus' focus on compassion as the root of holiness places the accent of his table etiquette on the invitation to the banquet, on inclusion, on building relationships. By altering the understanding of table rules, Jesus changes the boundaries of community. There is a place at the table for everyone.

The openness of Jesus' table was not only a challenge for the religious authorities of his day and for his disciples. Even Jesus struggled with the boundaries of the table. Any table "rule" can become a boundary and a defining feature of a bounded community. In both Mark and Matthew, there is the account of Jesus' conversation with the Syrophoenician woman:

> From there [Jesus] set out and went away to the region of Tyre. He entered a house and did not want anyone to know he was there. Yet he could not escape notice, but a woman whose little daughter had an unclean spirit immediately heard about him, and she came and bowed down at his feet. Now the woman was a Gentile, of Syrophoenician origin. She begged him to cast the demon out of her daughter. He said to her, "Let the children be fed first, for it is not fair to take the children's food and throw it to the dogs." But she answered him, "Sir, even the dogs under the table eat the children's crumbs." Then he said to her, "For saying that, you may go—the demon has left your daughter." So she went home, found the child lying on the bed, and the demon gone (Mark 7:24-30; parallel Matt 15:21-28).

Jesus is able to listen to the woman's argument, extend his heart, and change his mind. The gifts of Jesus' ministry[9] and grace of his table are not limited by traditional group boundaries. In fact, there are no barriers to Jesus' table except self-imposed ones.[10]

Just as the implications of the etiquette of love developed into a politics of compassion during Jesus' ministry, so there was much contention about the implications of this etiquette of hospitality for community life in the early Church. The church in Corinth offers several examples of this struggle. One was about food rules: What foods could be eaten? In particular, should food from pagan temples be eaten? Differentiation among acceptable foods is often associated with differentiation among eating situations and therefore the people who are a part of those events. In addressing these food rules, Paul stresses the openness and freedom of the gospel: "All things are lawful," but he adds, "not all things are beneficial . . . not all things build up" (1 Cor 10:23). Our freedom is to be tempered by care for others. There is no preset simple rule for the discernment of the path of freedom conditioned by the table etiquette of love, but Paul offers the guideline: "Whether you eat or drink, or whatever you do, do everything for the glory of God" (1 Cor 10:31).

---

[9] Several of Jesus' healing miracles have food or table references: Matt 8:11 and parallel; Mark 1:30-31; Mark 5:43; John 12:1-2; as of course do several of his resurrection appearances: Luke 24:30, 34, 41, 42; John 21.

[10] Judas leaves the table of the Last Supper; the brother of the prodigal son cannot be persuaded to join the banquet (Station 11); and the rich man cannot follow (Station 8).

How open was the table to be? Peter struggled with this question early in the life of the Church. The vision he was given that allowed Jewish Christians and Gentile Christians to sit at table without "distinction" was about the food rules of the purity code in Leviticus. It is told twice as if for emphasis.

> Now the apostles and the believers who were in Judea heard that the Gentiles had also accepted the word of God. So when Peter went up to Jerusalem, the circumcised believers criticized him, saying, "Why did you go to uncircumcised men and eat with them?" Then Peter began to explain it to them, step by step, saying, "I was in the city of Joppa praying, and in a trance I saw a vision. There was something like a large sheet coming down from heaven, being lowered by its four corners; and it came close to me. As I looked at it closely I saw four-footed animals, beasts of prey, reptiles, and birds of the air. I also heard a voice saying to me, 'Get up, Peter; kill and eat.' But I replied, 'By no means, Lord; for nothing profane or unclean has ever entered my mouth.' But a second time the voice answered from heaven, 'What God has made clean, you must not call profane.' This happened three times; then everything was pulled up again to heaven. At that very moment three men, sent to me from Caesarea, arrived at the house where we were. The Spirit told me to go with them and not to make a distinction between them and us" (Acts 11:1-12; Acts 10:1-36).

Christ's way is not about distinctions or separation among foods or people, but love of God and neighbor. It is about open hospitality and an etiquette of inclusion.

But even that is not saying enough. Not only does the inclusivity of the open table work to diminish distinctions of access to the table, it is also invoked to address enmity. Quoting Proverbs 25:21 and 22, Paul writes: "'If your enemies are hungry, feed them; if they are thirsty, give them something to drink; for by doing this you will heap burning coals on their heads.' Do not be overcome by evil, but overcome evil with good" (Rom 12:20-21).

This is the very antithesis of the too common practice of withholding food to induce or coerce a change of heart among antagonists. In the radical inclusivity of Jesus' ethic of love there is no place for the use of food as a weapon (Matt 5:43-48). In times of great insecurity, oppression, and change when there is much to fear, not just strangers but even those antagonistic to us have a place at the table.[11] Compassion rules.

Not only are there to be no distinctions in invitation to the banquet, there are to be no distinctions at the table. Not only is there a place for everyone at the table, those places are not to be arranged by status.

> When [Jesus] noticed how the guests chose the places of honor, he told them a parable. "When you are invited by someone to a wedding banquet, do not sit down at the place of honor, in case someone more distinguished than you has been invited by your host; and the host who invited both of you may come and say to you, 'Give this person your place,' and then in disgrace you would start to take the lowest place. But when you are invited, go and sit down at the lowest place, so that when your host comes, he may say to you, 'Friend, move up higher'; then you will be honored in the presence of all who sit at the table with you. For all who exalt themselves will be humbled, and those who humble themselves will be exalted" (Luke 14:7-11).

Just as with Jesus washing the feet of his disciples, so here too Jesus' table etiquette subverts status differentiation. However, it does not come naturally. It is a pattern of relating that has to be learned.

The lesson had to be learned and relearned in the early Church. We hear James correcting all the ways that even today we make distinctions among ourselves by the places that are assigned:

> For if a person with gold rings and in fine clothes comes into your assembly, and if a poor person in dirty clothes also comes in, and if you take notice of the one wearing the fine clothes and say, "Have a seat here, please," while to the one who is poor you say, "Stand there," or, "Sit at my feet," have you not made distinctions among yourselves, and

---

[11] The Old Testament offers a story of just such a feast. In the chaos of the closing days of his reign, Saul consults a medium, even though he had expressly forbidden "mediums and wizards from the land." Yet the woman, seeing Saul's distress and imminent destruction, has compassion and serves Saul and his servants a feast that he might have strength to go on his way (1 Samuel 29). Ironically, counter-examples come from David's children (2 Samuel 13). "Under the pretense of requesting a meal, Amnon raped Tamar; under the pretense of offering Amnon a meal, Absalom murders his brother. Throughout, this allusion to a meal is evocative, for a meal should conjure up a covenant ceremony, a symbolic gesture of cohesion, instead of a bloodbath." Regina M. Schwartz, *The Curse of Cain: The Violent Legacy of Monotheism* (Chicago: University of Chicago Press, 1997) 100.

become judges with evil thoughts? Listen, my beloved brothers and sisters. Has not God chosen the poor in the world to be rich in faith and to be heirs of the kingdom that he has promised to those who love him? But you have dishonored the poor (Jas 2:2-6a).

Similarly, but with more irony, Paul writes to "admonish" the church in Corinth for similar pretensions (1 Cor 4:8-13). Even the disciples were offered lesson after lesson. In the midst of their discussion about who was the greatest among them, Jesus draws a child into their midst. "Taking [the child] in his arms, he said to them, 'Whoever welcomes one such child in my name welcomes me, and whoever welcomes me welcomes not me but the one who sent me'" (Mark 9:36b-37; Luke 9:46-48; Matt 18:1-5). Our hospitality to the least is our hospitality to the Holy. It seems that every generation in the Church must learn the subversive table etiquette of the banquet.

Paul encapsulates the heart of the radical, open commensality of Jesus' table:

> For in Christ Jesus you are all children of God through faith. As many of you as were baptized into Christ have clothed yourselves with Christ. There is no longer Jew or Greek, there is no longer slave or free, there is no longer male and female; for all of you are one in Christ Jesus. And if you belong to Christ, then you are Abraham's offspring, heirs according to the promise (Gal 3:26-29).

No distinctions are made at Christ's table: no "us" and "them," up and down, in and out, greater or lesser distinctions, neither by faith, race, class, age, or gender. It is not that differences are erased or become meaningless. It is the meaning that we make of them that matters. For example, Jesus never negated his Jewishness. Rather, it was in his faithfulness to his ancestry that he could bring the invitation to the fullness of the banquet to those who had been excluded from those promises.

In the midst of the quarrelsome, divisive church in Corinth, we can hear Paul's advice for negotiating difference without distinction:

> For just as the body is one and has many members, and all the members of the body, though many, are one body, so it is with Christ. For in the one Spirit we were all baptized into one body—Jews or Greeks, slaves or free—and we were all made to drink of one Spirit (1 Cor 12:12-13).

There is one table, one body in Christ. Paul's insistence on "oneness," on inclusion regardless of our differences, is not at the expense of difference or the uniqueness of the "varieties of gifts . . . services . . . activities" the Spirit has given the members (1 Cor 12:4-6). It is rather to build up the integrity of the whole *with* our differences, not *in spite of* them. This is the oneness of Pentecost, not the totalitarian oneness of Babel. Our diversity serves the whole: "To each is given the manifestation of the Spirit for the common good" (1 Cor 12:7). In this sense of the common good there is such a web of interdependent relationship, that we know that "if one member suffers, all suffer together with it; if one member is honored, all rejoice together with it" (1 Cor 12:26). This is the image of the oneness that Jesus weaves, then and now, in his radical open table commensality.

But how quickly oneness, even a oneness that honors difference, can become an over-against-another oneness. How easily we can begin to argue about the correctness or rightness or appropriateness of one etiquette versus another. And how intense those arguments can become when it is faith that divides us. But, Christ's table is different from other tables around which people gather, for Jesus' ministry, death, and resurrection cast a permanent suspicion over all passionately drawn and defended boundaries.[12] Jesus took his faith outside the city walls, into the company of tax collectors and sinners, thieves and criminals, into the company of the forsaken, even into the silence of the dead, to invite all—everyone and anyone—to the marriage supper of the Lamb (Rev 19:9).

❋

SPIRITUAL CHALLENGE: SOLIDARITY

Dorothee Soelle recounts an old Jewish story which captures the promise of this table etiquette:

> An old rabbi once asked his students how one could recognize the time when night ends and day begins. "Is it when, from a great distance, you can tell a dog from a sheep?" one student asked. "No," said the rabbi. "Is

---

[12] See Gil Bailie's outline of the revolutionary implications of this suspicion in *Violence Unveiled: Humanity at the Crossroads* (New York: Crossroad, 1995).

it when, from a great distance, you can tell a date palm from a fig tree?" another student asked. "No," said the rabbi. "Then when is it?" the students asked. "It is when you look into the face of any human creature and see your brother or your sister there. Until then, night is still with us."[13]

Night ends and day begins as our eyes refocus on what connects us rather than on what divides us. This is the spiritual challenge of solidarity.

Solidarity is all about seeing the world from the vantage point of our interconnectedness with each other and with all of creation. With the eyes of solidarity we see through our particular interests to our common interests. We see not just conflicting or competing interests, but also shared interests and all that binds us together. "Solidarity [also] moves away from the false notion of disinterest, or doing for others in an altruistic fashion. Instead it is grounded in 'common responsibilities and interests.'"[14] Solidarity is not, however, about self-sacrifice or loss of self. Rather, it is about "an enlargement of the self to include community with others. To work with others is not to lose oneself, but first and foremost it is to find a larger self."[15] We find we belong to the web of life, to the earth. We are not alone, but are related with others all around the globe. "The dichotomy between love of self and love of others is a dangerous one created by alienation and sustained by structures of alienation."[16]

In the work of solidarity we begin to understand that we all eat at the same table and that all the tables that we gather around in our daily lives are connected. For people of faith these connections are rooted in the Holy. It is God's table around which we gather, whether it is a food table, a board table, a desk, or an altar. It is the love of God for all of God's creation that binds us together. That is the shared food

[13] Dorothee Soelle, *The Strength of the Weak: Toward a Christian Feminist Identity* (Philadelphia: Westminster Press, 1984) 41.

[14] Ada Maria Isasi-Diaz, "Solidarity: Love of Neighbor in the 1980s," *Feminist Theological Ethics: A Reader*, ed. Lois K. Daly (Louisville, Ky.: Westminster John Knox Press, 1994) 78–9.

[15] Sharon D. Welch, *A Feminist Ethic of Risk*, rev. ed. (Minneapolis: Fortress Press, 2000) 162. She goes on to note that "when we begin from a self created by love for nature and for other people, choosing not to resist injustice would be the ultimate loss of self" (165).

[16] Ibid., 163.

of the table. As Douglas Meeks writes: "Those who live from the table of God's household are no longer simply advocates of those who struggle to live without what is necessary for life; [we] have become brothers and sisters."[17] It is not simply that we care. We are actually kin. We are bound in a deeper relation than that created by ideology, affection, utility, our own engineering, or the happenstance of birth or life circumstance. Solidarity is about more than shared beliefs, feelings, or strategic interests. It is about the radical hospitality of the banquet, the extravagantly inclusive invitation to the table and the relationships born at the table. This is the faith foundation of solidarity.

Today, however, the realities of globalization heighten the challenge of a Christ-shaped understanding of solidarity. We live with more people in the world, with more of us living closely together in urban environments and with denser, more immediate economic and communication ties than ever before in history. Our current history is filled with dramatic movements toward full community: progressive democratization of structures of government, diversification of populations, increasing acceptance and international enforcement of human rights, and tremendous improvements in access to health, education, food, and water in most parts of the world.[18] At the same time, it is also filled with horrific examples of community torn apart: ethnic cleansing, segregation, genocide, and species extinctions as well as the more mundane, almost invisible forms of the erosion of solidarity: the rise of gated communities, private schools, tougher immigration and social welfare policies, and the degradation and loss of environmental integrity. The prevalence and persistence of hunger in our world is a sign of the scale of the challenge we face. Clearly, with plenty of food for everyone in the world, the people still without food have been excluded in various ways from the common table.[19] It is only from a place of solidarity, of kinship, and of a deep appreciation of our interconnectedness that we can constructively engage all that tears apart the community of life.

[17] M. Douglas Meeks, *God the Economist: The Doctrine of God and Political Economy* (Minneapolis: Fortress Press, 1989) 92.

[18] See the annual reports of the United Nations Human Development Unit for extensive data and analysis on these trends.

[19] See the annual reports of Bread for the World, Washington, D.C., for ongoing documentation and analysis of this challenge.

There are two fundamental ways that solidarity is challenged: (1) by breaking the bonds that connect us and claiming independence rather than interdependence; and (2) by erasing the separateness or distinctiveness of each entity by domination or more insidiously through assimilation.[20]

In the first case we distance ourselves from others. The distanced "other" becomes a threat, an enemy, a nonentity, an abandoned or disregarded one. We reject or exclude the "other." In the second case, we erase the differences between us. We see the "other" as an inferior who must somehow be made like us or be in a relationship to us that is defined by us. We absorb the other and refuse to see or respect his or her particularities. In both cases, the "other" remains a stranger to us. Yet, it is this stranger whom Christ invites to the banquet table and welcomes as is.

Who is this "other" who is welcomed at the table? Anyone who is different from us can be our "other." Given all the ways we can be different from each other, anyone can be an "other." There are the "others" within our community and "others" outside our community. If we define community as our nation, "others" become immigrants, refugees, allies, or opponents of "our" way of life, "our" policies, "our" understandings of what is good and right. If we define community as our faith community, "others" become those with different beliefs or practices, those of a different congregation, denomination, or religious tradition. If we define community as those who share a common experience of either suffering or privilege, "others" become those who do not, and perhaps cannot, understand us. These divides can easily come to define our sense of ourselves and our identities individually and as a group. "I" am, or "we" are, not "them."

Differences among people become sharply defined in an insecure world where fear is real and often justified, where resources are scarce and where a sense of belonging is uncommon. In our world of identity and special interest politics of both the left and the right, the boundaries of who "I" am distinct from who "you" are can be passionately drawn with epithets for anyone who trespasses the boundaries: sexist, racist, heterosexist, classist, ageist, communist, fascist, heretic, etc. In this environment, bridges and places of connection, trust, or openness

---

[20] Miroslav Volf, *Exclusion and Embrace: A Theological Exploration of Identity, Otherness and Reconciliation* (Nashville: Abingdon, 1996) 67.

between people become harder to find and negotiate. As Monica Hellwig has noted:

> We have all learned to trust rather in armaments and fortifications, in accumulation of goods and power over others, than to trust in others. Then, as now, people were convinced they were more likely to survive by excluding than by including others, by dominating rather than by befriending them. . . . This was true not only of the Roman conqueror but also of the oppressed people in their relations with one another.[21]

The challenge for Christians, as for the Pharisees and well-to-do, is that Jesus ate with "them." He befriended the tax-collectors and sinners of his day. The hospitality of the table is more than a metaphor. In very concrete ways our table practices enact a different basis for human community. They are places of connection where the love that casts out fear can grow (1 John 4:18a).

There is, however, another category of "otherness" which is central to the full life of the table. Over centuries, we have learned to define ourselves as over against and separate from the rest of creation. We have emphasized our distinctiveness from rather than our relationship to nature. This alienation from creation allows us to destroy the very air, water, soil, and other life forms upon which we depend for life. It leaves us restless, homeless, without a sense of belonging, divorced from our relations. What would it mean to consider ourselves part of the whole community of life? What would the full inclusion of creation mean to the table etiquette of the banquet?

Sallie McFague has outlined a whole theology based on an ecological paradigm. In such a theology, "the God whose glory is each creature fully alive revels in differences, not in sameness. The God that fits with the ecological paradigm is the God for whom oneness is only achieved through the infinitely complex interrelationships and interdependencies of billions of different constituents, beings, and events."[22] A deep understanding of ecology is a better starting place for appreciating the possibilities and structure of a fully inclusive table etiquette than one based on mechanistic principles. It is a critical complement

---

[21] Monika Hellwig, *The Eucharist and the Hunger of the World*, 2d ed. (Franklin, Wis.: Sheed & Ward, 1999) 61.

[22] Sallie McFague, *Life Abundant: Rethinking Theology and Economy for a Planet in Peril* (Minneapolis: Fortress Press, 2001) 150.

to the solely human paradigms elaborated in philosophy, history, political or the human sciences. By stretching solidarity to include creation, a whole new intellectual basis for understanding complex interrelationships becomes available to us and a door to a different theology is opened.

Jesus not only redraws and makes us forever suspicious of the boundaries we draw between ourselves and others, but he shows over and over a clear preference for the "hard-living" of his day, the vulnerable, those who suffer, the oppressed and excluded. Why is this so, and does this preference undermine the inclusiveness of his table? Christ's table etiquette is about the way past all humanly created and defended barriers to the banquet that God intends for all. Jesus knows the banquet as a reality, he lives out of it, and invites all he meets to join him. The vulnerable, the "hard-living," the oppressed, marginalized, and excluded hear the invitation and understand it more easily than those who have something to lose, than those who are captive by their own vision of "the good and just," or who are preoccupied with their own affairs. Christ's preference for the "other" is not because "the poor, the crippled, the blind and the lame" are better, inherently more virtuous, or less likely to become oppressors given the opportunity. It is because they respond to the invitation. From their experiences and vantage point, they can grasp the essence of the banquet and appreciate it as good news.[23]

There is no need to fear Christ's preference for the poor. There is no need to protect one's place at this table, or for anyone, rich or poor, to fear exclusion. The etiquette of Christ's table, as irrational as it seems, is that even if 99 percent of the sheep are present, the 1 percent are sought after. The house is turned upside down for the single missing coin (Luke 15:1-10; Matt 18:12-13). The "all," "anyone," "everyone" in the invitation to Christ's table is serious. The challenge of solidarity is to make this real for real people in real time and space.

---

[23] This is the topic of Stations 9 and 10. "The preferential option is based on the fact that the point of view of the oppressed, pierced by suffering and attracted by hope, allows them, in their struggles, to conceive another reality. Because the poor suffer the weight of alienation, they can conceive a different project of hope and provide dynamism to a new way of organizing human life for all." J. M. Bonino as quoted by Isasi-Diaz in *Feminist Theological Ethics*, 80.

SPIRITUAL PRACTICE: INCLUSION

As we learn to see with the eyes of solidarity, we learn to practice genuine inclusive commensality, to welcome the stranger to table, to build communities where all may flourish.

People of faith cannot claim a privileged position in the work of inclusion. Whether from Jesus' interactions with the religious authorities of his day or from the bloody history of the Christian Church, there is clearly something in the religious perspective that requires scrupulous attention to our practices of inclusion/exclusion. Our definitions of goodness, truth, and what is right can all too easily be used to justify exclusion. This is the dynamic that lies at the heart of the debate between Jesus and the Pharisees. In fact, it was "'the good and just' [who] could not understand Jesus because their spirit was 'imprisoned in their good conscience' and [who] crucified him because they construed as evil his rejection of their notions of good."[24] Duly cautious, then, about the seductiveness of practices of exclusion to the faithful, and concomitantly alert to the danger of a radical practice of inclusion, our faith calls us to the etiquette of an open table.

To deepen our practice of inclusion we must understand the practices of exclusion. First, exclusion must be distinguished from differentiation. Inclusion without differentiation is a recipe for formless, norm-less chaos that is opposed to life in its fullness and is a nightmare for anyone interested in a just order. It was out of just such chaos that creation was formed through the differentiation of light and darkness, day and night, the earth and the seas (Genesis 1). Creation is an intricate network of interdependent relationships among vast numbers of different, distinct entities: living and nonliving, human and non-human. The integrity of the community of life depends upon interactions of distinct, separate entities that are bound together in relationship. The fullness of community is with our differences, not in spite of them. The goal of inclusion is not necessarily consensus or a cohesive, well-integrated, unified whole. In fact, "the intention of solidarity is potentially more inclusive and more transformative than is the goal of consensus," for it is about connection with room for divergence.

---

[24] Volf, *Exclusion and Embrace*, 61.

In trying to dismantle structures of exclusion, however, it is all too easy to simply mimic them. It is all too common to replace one "in" group with another "in" group or simply draw the boundaries differently but still defend them energetically. It is all too easy to claim that we are part of a welcoming, inclusive community. The true test of such a claim are the stories of the excluded. What do those outside the community say of our hospitality? Are they even present for us to hear their voices? Do we have the ears and heart to hear what they do say? Finally, what do they say with their words, presence, and body language about their experiences of exclusion and inclusion? They are our teachers in this matter.

Miroslav Volf's "drama of embrace"[25] describes critical ingredients of the practice of inclusion. An embrace starts with the opening up of my arms to another. I create space in myself to welcome another. I acknowledge my interest and stand vulnerable before another. I am prepared for a moment to move beyond myself. This is an open invitation offered with respect of the other's integrity and freedom to decide whether to reciprocate or not. There is no force, manipulation, or hidden intent. The response of the other is free. There is a pregnant moment of waiting, of uncertainty, of risk. The hug of welcome takes "two pairs of arms." We connect in the middle ground between separation and merger. We acknowledge our relation and our difference. In that connection, my "identity is both preserved and transformed." I am more than I was. And then our arms open again. There is no "disappearance of the 'I' into the 'we.'" We are both connected and free and the dance of difference and relation, connection and distance, love and freedom continues.

This drama of embrace and its close cousin, genuine dialogue or conversation oriented to mutual understanding, can occur whether reading a book, talking on the phone, or sitting at table with a friend or stranger. In all sorts of big and small ways we are given opportunities to welcome the "other." These unfolding, indeterminate threads of connection create the space for the mutual development of the community of life. The open table is built by creating real space for the other, respecting the freedom of the other, being vulnerable, and risking connection and transformation while maintaining distinctness and difference. This is the creative space of the Spirit "who by the power

---

[25] Ibid., 40–7.

at work within us is able to accomplish abundantly far more than all we can ask or imagine" (Eph 3:20). In time even the deep divisions of animosity and oppression can be healed. Understanding can flourish in the midst of all the diversity of languages and life forms at the table. Night ends and day begins in the fine-grained, everyday work of solidarity.

Station 6 Litany:
Table Etiquette: Hospitality

Voices 1: For the splendor and infinite variety of life on this planet,

Voices 2: For the rainbow beauty of our brothers and sisters around the globe,

All: For the invitation to share your table, we give You thanks.

One: For the civil engineers of the soul,

Voices 1: who build bridges to span the extraordinary divides amongst us,

Voices 2: who design tables to accommodate the whole community of life,

All: We thank You.

One: For the poets of community,

Voices 1: Who give us language to speak with our kin,

Voices 2: Who speak the yearnings of our hearts for connection,

All: We thank You.

One: For the ecologists of the web of life,

Voices 1: Who give us eyes to see our place and love it,

Voices 2: Who map the intricate interdependencies that link us together,

All: We thank You.

One: O Pentecost Spirit,
Who knows no bounds of language or color, of capacity or suffering,

Voices 1: Give us courage to dismantle the barriers that separate us;
And grace to create real space for the other;

Voices 2: Give us courage to welcome the stranger in our midst;
And grace to value the "all," "everyone," and "anyone" of your embrace;

Voices 1: Give us courage to risk the unknowns of genuine relation-ship;
And grace to stay fluid in the dance of connection and distance;

Voices 2: Give us courage to trust that harm does not come from
the outside;

And grace to hear the table stories of all our brothers and
sisters;

All: **Stir our spirits to reach out in welcome, curiosity, and
embrace; and**

**Explore the constantly unfolding possibilities of
community.**

Voices 1: Your hospitality is as expansive as the prairie sky,

The joy of your table is as at a wedding feast,

Voices 2: We sing the magnificence of your table,

The warmth of your welcome,

All: **All Glory, Praise, Delight, and Honor**

Is Yours, Host of the Banquet.

Visual Focus: Chairs at a round table.

Station 7

TABLE ETIQUETTE 3
ECONOMICS—"WHERE YOUR TREASURE IS, THERE YOUR HEART WILL BE ALSO"

The earth is the LORD's and all that is in it,
the world, and those who live in it.

—Psalm 24:1

Food is more than good to eat and a delight to the eyes [Gen 3:6a]. Food is also a commodity of value bought and sold, given and received, in market and gift economies all over the world. The banquet etiquette of love and hospitality is transacted in these economies. The ethos of the table has everything to do with our patterns of giving and receiving, buying and selling. Said another way: "love without economics is empty rhetoric."[1] Love of God and neighbor is our faith's language of relationship. Economics is increasingly our culture's language of relationship. If we are not to speak out of both sides of our mouth, we must become bilingual. How does the "revolution in the structure of human relationship"[2] that Jesus initiated, that was symbolized by his washing of the disciples' feet and his table fellowship, get translated into our patterns of exchange? How in our world of buying and selling, where

[1] Sallie McFague, *Life Abundant: Rethinking Theology and Economy for a Planet in Peril* (Minneapolis: Fortress Press, 2001) 128.

[2] Bruno Barnhart, *The Good Wine: Reading John from the Center* (New York: Paulist Press, 1993) 141; and Station 5.

103

market logic seems to reign supreme, are we to understand Christ's economy—an economy of life? Do we spiritualize it and keep the gospel economy in one compartment and the economy of the market, of wealth and property, in another compartment? Or do we struggle with the economic dimension of this profound revolution in the structure of human relationships that is the etiquette of the table? For, "there is no meaning in love for a hungry person which leaves that person hungry."[3]

This Station introduces the economic face of this struggle; Station 9 takes up the themes of scarcity, abundance, and a gift economy; and Station 10 reflects on justice as the journey moves into ever broader dimensions of the life of the banquet.

VOICES OF THE TRADITION

The table etiquette of the banquet has always been a real stretch for Jesus' followers. Several of Jesus' parables affront the logic of a market-based economy. Then as now, they challenge our common sense and what is accepted as fair. That is, of course, in the nature of parables. Parables exist as invitations into the "revolution in the structure of human relationships" that is at the heart of gospel economics. They do not give answers. They do yield thought-provoking questions. To entertain the richness of the parables' logic, we must be open to the interplay of two ways of thinking operating at the same time: the common-sense logic of the everyday, and the uncommon-sense or wisdom of the banquet table. In mathematics, a numeral written in base ten means something different than that same numeral written in base five. So God's economy works with the same realities—property, work, wealth, food, gain, debt—as our market economy, but it works on a quite different base.

The first of four challenging parables is Luke's account of "the parable of the talents."

> [Jesus] went on to tell a parable, because he was near Jerusalem, and because they supposed that the kingdom of God was to appear immediately. So he said, "A nobleman went to a distant country to get royal power for himself and then return. He summoned ten of his slaves, and

---

[3] Monika Hellwig, *The Eucharist and the Hunger of the World*, 2d ed. (Franklin, Wis.: Sheed & Ward, 1999) 46.

gave them ten pounds, and said to them, 'Do business with these until I come back.' But the citizens of his country hated him and sent a delegation after him, saying, 'We do not want this man to rule over us.' When he returned, having received royal power, he ordered these slaves, to whom he had given the money, to be summoned so that he might find out what they had gained by trading. The first came forward and said, 'Lord, your pound has made ten more pounds.' He said to him, 'Well done, good slave! Because you have been trustworthy in a very small thing, take charge of ten cities.' Then the second came, saying, 'Lord, your pound has made five pounds.' He said to him, 'And you, rule over five cities.' Then the other came, saying, 'Lord, here is your pound. I wrapped it up in a piece of cloth, for I was afraid of you, because you are a harsh man; you take what you did not deposit, and reap what you did not sow.' He said to him, 'I will judge you by your own words, you wicked slave! You knew, did you, that I was a harsh man, taking what I did not deposit and reaping what I did not sow? Why then did you not put my money into the bank? Then when I returned, I could have collected it with interest.' He said to the bystanders, 'Take the pound from him and give it to the one who has ten pounds.' (And they said to him, 'Lord, he has ten pounds!') 'I tell you, to all those who have, more will be given; but from those who have nothing, even what they have will be taken away. But as for these enemies of mine who did not want me to be king over them—bring them here and slaughter them in my presence.'"

After he had said this, he went on ahead, going up to Jerusalem (Luke 19:11-27; parallel: Matt 25:14-30).

To anyone who is at home in our market society, the internal logic of this story sounds familiar, even comforting: sound investment to produce growth in capital; no risk, no gain; winner take all. So why does this parable include such a violent ending and such a picture of absolute deprivation for the least, for "those who have nothing"? Such sentiments sound strangely out of place in the Gospels. It is our natural inclination to assume the king and the king's economy are endorsed by God and to imagine they might even be a metaphor for God and God's economy. But, why then do the citizens of the king hate him so? In spite of the familiarity of the internal logic of the parable, there is something deeply troubling about it. Who would not invest the king's money in a bank and benefit from a good interest-bearing account? Because interest rates play such a central role in our economy, many contemporary readers might not find this as jarring as Jesus' audience who knew that interest was forbidden in Jewish law.[4] With whom do the righteous stand in this parable? Why do our hearts want to believe that Jesus stands with those who made such sound investments even though the opening and closing verses[5] make it clear that Jesus is on his way to Jerusalem and the cross?

The second parable about the vineyard workers creates a picture of a very different economy:

> For the kingdom of heaven is like a landowner who went out early in the morning to hire laborers for his vineyard. After agreeing with the laborers for the usual daily wage, he sent them into his vineyard. When he went out about nine o'clock, he saw others standing idle in the marketplace; and he said to them, "You also go into the vineyard, and I will pay you whatever is right." So they went. When he went out again about noon and about three o'clock, he did the same. And about five o'clock he went out and found others standing around; and he said to them, "Why are you standing here idle all day?" They said to him, "Because no one has hired us." He said to them, "You also go into the vineyard." When evening came, the owner of the vineyard said to his manager, "Call the laborers and give them their pay, beginning with the last and then going to the first." When those hired about five o'clock came, each of them received the usual daily wage. Now when the first came, they thought they would receive more; but each of them also received the usual daily wage. And when they received it, they grumbled against the landowner, saying, "These last worked only one hour, and you have made them equal to us who have borne the burden of the day and the scorching heat." But he replied to one of them, "Friend, I am doing you no wrong; did you not agree with me for the usual daily wage? Take what belongs to you and go; I choose to give to this last the same as I give to you. Am I not allowed to do what I choose with what belongs to me? Or are you envious because I am generous?" (Matt 20:1-15).

Each person gets paid "the usual daily wage." There is no undercutting of the wage scale in the vineyard. But clearly in the vineyard owner's

---

[4] The law is clear that interest is forbidden between the people of Israel: Exod 22:25; Lev 25:36-37; Deut 23:19-20; Neh 5:6-12; Psalm 15; Ezek 18:5-9; 22:12, 13; Luke 6:34.

[5] Matthew draws attention to this same question by placing this parable immediately before the parable about the judgment of the sheep and goats ("I was hungry and you gave me food"), which is right before the account of Jesus' Last Supper with his disciples.

full employment world, equal pay for equal work is not the operative principle for wage calculations. The winners in this economy are clearly "the last." It is not an economy of "just deserts"—or is it? Envy and the predisposition to compare our position with another's have such a claim on our minds and hearts that it is almost impossible to delight in the extravagant generosity of the landowner. All these reflections sidestep the question: What *does* "belong" to the landowner?

The third parable about the rich farmer starts with that property ownership question: "What does belong to me?"

> Someone in the crowd said to him, "Teacher, tell my brother to divide the family inheritance with me." But [Jesus] said to him, "Friend, who set me to be a judge or arbitrator over you?" And he said to them, "Take care! Be on your guard against all kinds of greed; for one's life does not consist in the abundance of possessions." Then he told them a parable: "The land of a rich man produced abundantly. And he thought to himself, 'What should I do, for I have no place to store my crops?' Then he said, 'I will do this: I will pull down my barns and build larger ones, and there I will store all my grain and my goods. And I will say to my soul, 'Soul, you have ample goods laid up for many years; relax, eat, drink, be merry.' But God said to him, 'You fool! This very night your life is being demanded of you. And the things you have prepared, whose will they be?' " (Luke 12:13-20).

The rich farmer's story is such a straightforward account of success and bad luck that it is easy to skip over this parable in its apparent simplicity. But like all good parables, we are left dangling with a provocative unanswered question. Exactly why is this farmer a fool? He does what farmers have always done. As in many parables, the concluding question bites the tail of the opening question. The person with a property inheritance question is left with a question of property inheritance: "And the things you have prepared, whose will they be?" It remains an open-ended, unanswered question. To whom *do* they belong?[6] Is the abundance of the farmer related to the abundance that Jesus promises: "I came that they may have life, and have it abundantly" (John 10:10). What is the nature of that abundance and how is it inherited?

---

[6] The parable of the wicked tenants (Matt 21:33-41; Mark 12:1-9; Luke 20:9-16) continues the challenge that this parable presents to our common assumptions about property ownership.

The fourth parable continues to explore the question of ownership, but with a different twist.

> Then Jesus said to the disciples, "There was a rich man who had a manager, and charges were brought to him that this man was squandering his property. So he summoned him and said to him, 'What is this that I hear about you? Give me an accounting of your management, because you cannot be my manager any longer.' Then the manager said to himself, 'What will I do, now that my master is taking the position away from me? I am not strong enough to dig, and I am ashamed to beg. I have decided what to do so that, when I am dismissed as manager, people may welcome me into their homes.' So, summoning his master's debtors one by one, he asked the first, 'How much do you owe my master?' He answered, 'A hundred jugs of olive oil.' He said to him, 'Take your bill, sit down quickly, and make it fifty.' Then he asked another, 'And how much do you owe?' He replied, 'A hundred containers of wheat.' He said to him, 'Take your bill and make it eighty.' And his master commended the dishonest manager because he had acted shrewdly; for the children of this age are more shrewd in dealing with their own generation than are the children of light" (Luke 16:1-8).

The manager is admittedly dishonest and profligate in spending his master's money. So what are we to make of the master's commendation of the steward's shrewdness? Certainly the steward's generous debt relief program would build (or rebuild) relationships in his community. The rich man's loss is the debtors' gain. For one who was so often welcomed into people's homes, it is hard to imagine that Jesus would not appreciate the steward's natural inclination to ensure his place in the community. And so there is the summary comment: "And I tell you, make friends for yourselves by means of dishonest wealth so that when it is gone, they may welcome you into the eternal homes" (Luke 16:9). Yet the Scriptures are realistic about the impact of such an approach: "The Pharisees, who were lovers of money, heard all this, and they ridiculed him" (Luke 16:14).

A parable like this would certainly jar "lovers of money" in any day. Yet, this parable not only provokes, it also raises the deeper question of what uses we make of wealth. What *does* make wealth honest or dishonest? What are good uses of wealth? What are the bases for our judgments about how money is acquired and used?

These parables challenge us to think about the fundamental economic assumptions of our life together. They invite us to imagine a different base for our economic relationships. Jesus and his followers lived in the midst of a vast, demanding international economic system, full of inequities, with a vastly disproportionate set of winners and losers whose discontent was kept in check with all the force of the Roman Empire. But rather than suggest a practical set of economic policy proposals, Jesus' parables invite his hearers to look at that system and explore its foundations. What does shape our imaginations and our hearts' desires economically? The bread of the banquet table not only feeds our bodies and souls, but also nourishes a very different understanding of economic priorities. The economic relationships of the banquet table have a very different ethos than that of the empire.

This dimension of Jesus' table fellowship was and continues to be challenging. Yet, there was no hedging of that challenge. Our scriptural tradition is unequivocal. "For Jesus . . . the way in which a person used money and possessions was an issue that demanded a clear choice between God and idolatry."[7] "No one can serve two masters; for a slave will either hate the one and love the other, or be devoted to the one and despise the other. You cannot serve God and wealth" (Matt 6:24; parallel Luke 16:13).

Do we trust God or money? Our primary allegiance is decisive. This does not exclude participation in market economies. It does mean, however, a choice about the fundamental purposes for whatever wealth we have. Jesus does not reject money. But he does challenge our deepest commitments.

> Then they sent to him some Pharisees and some Herodians to trap him in what he said. And they came and said to him, "Teacher, we know that you are sincere, and show deference to no one; for you do not regard people with partiality, but teach the way of God in accordance with truth. Is it lawful to pay taxes to the emperor, or not? Should we pay them, or should we not?" But knowing their hypocrisy, he said to them, "Why are you putting me to the test? Bring me a denarius [a coin] and let me see it." And they brought one. Then he said to them, "Whose

---

[7] Joseph A. Grassi, *Broken Bread and Broken Bodies: The Lord's Supper and World Hunger* (Maryknoll, N.Y.: Orbis Books, 1985) 29.

head is this, and whose title?" They answered, "The emperor's." Jesus
said to them, "Give to the emperor the things that are the emperor's,
and to God the things that are God's." And they were utterly amazed at
him (Mark 12:13-17; parallels Matt 22:15-22; Luke 20:20-26).

If anything, taxes were more burdensome then than now. An anti-tax
position was popular in Jesus' day as well. But Jesus does not accept a
simple "should we pay taxes or not?" For him, the central question is
one of allegiance. What is the empire's and what is God's? What does
belong to God?

Jesus was very clear about the seductive power of money and the
allure of all that money can buy.

> Do not store up for yourselves treasures on earth, where moth and rust
> consume and where thieves break in and steal; but store up for your-
> selves treasures in heaven, where neither moth nor rust consumes and
> where thieves do not break in and steal. For where your treasure is,
> there your heart will be also (Matt 6:19-21; parallel Luke 12:33-34).

Our treasure defines our worldview. It claims our heart, we become
attached to it, and it can displace or, at least, distract us from our love
of God and neighbor. As Douglas Meeks notes: "The way we relate to
our possessions embodies our response to God and neighbor. The biblical traditions make plain that all possessing has a proclivity toward
idolatry. . . . Idolatry is being possessed by a possession."[8] We think
our possessions buy us freedom, but often, quite subtly, we find ourselves captive to that very treasure.

And so our tradition requires decision. Commitment is unavoidable.
Fence sitting is not an option.

> The kingdom of heaven is like treasure hidden in a field, which someone
> found and hid; then in his joy he goes and sells all that he has and buys
> that field.
>   Again, the kingdom of heaven is like a merchant in search of fine
> pearls; on finding one pearl of great value, he went and sold all that he
> had and bought it (Matt 13:44-46).[9]

[8] M. Douglas Meeks, *God the Economist: The Doctrine of God and Political Economy*
(Minneapolis: Fortress Press, 1989) 117.
[9] Whenever there is this kind of "either/or" line drawn in the sand, a judgment is
implied. Judgment is the accent of the third mini-parable in this sequence from

It is true that there is a radical cost to discipleship. It does indeed require our lives:

> [Jesus] called the crowd with his disciples, and said to them, "If any want to become my followers, let them deny themselves and take up their cross and follow me. For those who want to save their life will lose it, and those who lose their life for my sake, and for the sake of the gospel, will save it. For what will it profit them to gain the whole world and forfeit their life? Indeed, what can they give in return for their life? (Mark 8:34-37).

The journey of the banquet starts, as it did for the first disciples, with a reorientation of our basic livelihoods. Jesus calls, and "immediately [the disciples] leave" nets, boats, family . . . and follow (Matt 4:20, 22; Mark 1:18, 20; Luke 5:11, 28).

For Christians who are comfortably satiated with full stomachs, it is all too easy to miss the fullness of life that is offered in the gospel.

> And to the angel of the church in Laodicea write: . . . I know your works; you are neither cold nor hot. I wish that you were either cold or hot. So, because you are lukewarm, and neither cold nor hot, I am about to spit you out of my mouth. For you say, "I am rich, I have prospered, and I need nothing." You do not realize that you are wretched, pitiable, poor, blind, and naked. Therefore I counsel you to buy from me gold refined by fire so that you may be rich; and white robes to clothe you and to keep the shame of your nakedness from being seen; and salve to anoint your eyes so that you may see. Listen! I am standing at the door, knocking; if you hear my voice and open the door, I will come in to you and eat with you, and you with me (Rev 3:14a, 15-18, 20).

The imagination of the Christians of Laodicea has been dulled by their prosperity. Their sense of themselves relative to all that is possible is diminished. They have settled for the abundance of the rich farmer, and have no sense of the abundance of the banquet. Sharing the feast

---

Matthew 13. "Again, the kingdom of heaven is like a net that was thrown into the sea and caught fish of every kind; when it was full, they drew it ashore, sat down, and put the good into baskets but threw out the bad. So it will be at the end of the age. The angels will come out and separate the evil from the righteous and throw them into the furnace of fire, where there will be weeping and gnashing of teeth" (Matt 13:47-50). The judgment aspect of this either/or logic is discussed in Stations 10 and 13.

of the Holy One—"if you hear my voice and open the door, I will come in to you and eat with you, and you with me"—comes when we "hear . . . and open the door." But to get there from here, we must "buy" in. And that requires the commitment of all of who we are.

SPIRITUAL CHALLENGE: PROPERTY

Luke Johnson calls "the connection between being a Christian and the way we own and use things, one of the knottiest questions imaginable."[10] Indeed it seems always to have been so. From the people who made a golden calf to worship from the jewelry that they had brought from Egypt (Exod 32:1-6), to Naboth who staked his life on a different understanding of property than that of King Ahab (1 Kgs 21:1-25), to Judas, the keeper of the common purse, who betrayed Jesus for money (John 13:29; Luke 22:5), our ways of relating to property have challenged our relationships with God and neighbor. Indeed, like Judas, people today still betray the Holy in our midst for money and all that money can buy; like Ahab, we still destroy our neighbor and community relationships; and like the people in the wilderness, we still ascribe ultimate power to the creations of human hands.

The caution from First Timothy is very much to the point: "For the love of money is a root of all kinds of evil, and in their eagerness to be rich some have wandered away from the faith and pierced themselves with many pains" (1 Tim 6:10). It is not just we ourselves who are distracted from a life of faith and "pierced with many pains," but creation, community, and others, near and far from us, are affected by our choices about property, money, and possessions.

Yet property, money, possessions are not to be rejected. At its core, our tradition is not ascetic. Earlier in First Timothy, in contradiction to a group advocating various renunciations to do with food and marriage, there is the affirmation that echoes through all the Scriptures: "Everything created by God is good, and nothing is to be rejected, provided it is received with thanksgiving; for it is sanctified by God's word and by prayer" (1 Tim 4:4-5). There is no renunciation of property per se in our tradition. What is contentious is property relations: what kind

---

[10] Luke T. Johnson, *Sharing Possessions: Mandate and Symbol of Faith* (Philadelphia: Fortress Press, 1981) 1.

of relations are created, what values govern those relations, what uses we make of "our" property, and who has legitimate claims on "our" property?

Jubilee practices[11] are an early witness to a time when economic relations were structured for the good of the whole community. The jubilee year builds on the Sabbath practice of a regular time of rest and re-creation for humans, animals, and the land itself so that all might experience wholeness and glorify the Creator. Jubilee was a time not just for rest but also for the restoration of community relationships that had been distorted through the accumulation of wealth and power by the few. So in the fiftieth year [after seven Sabbath years], property was to be returned to its original owners, debts were to be forgiven, slaves freed. Not only the land, but community relationships themselves were to be renewed. "The intention of the biblical jubilee was to break periodically the inevitable historical dynamic of acquisitiveness and domination, leading to exclusion, and to restore the opportunities for life in community to all."[12] There is no sense that this time of restitution was ever fully or regularly implemented, but it continued to shape the imagination of the people. The association of Jesus' ministry with the proclamation of "the year of the Lord's favor" links Jesus' invitation to the banquet to this Jubilee time of renewal and restitution of community (Luke 4:19; Isa 61:2).

A second example of a time when economic relations were structured for the good of the whole community comes from the earliest days of Pentecost. Out of an intimate experience with Jesus and the Spirit, the early Church structured its economy on a communal property base:

> All who believed were together and had all things in common; they would sell their possessions and goods and distribute the proceeds to all, as any had need. Day by day, as they spent much time together in the temple, they broke bread at home and ate their food with glad and generous hearts, praising God and having the goodwill of all the people. And day by day the Lord added to their number those who were being saved (Acts 2:44-47).

[11] See Leviticus 25 and its related Sabbath-year practices: Exod 23:10; Deut 15:1-18.

[12] Konrad Reiser, "Utopia and Responsibility," *The Jubilee Challenge: Utopia or Possibility, Jewish and Christian Insights*, ed. Hans Ucko (Geneva: World Council of Churches Publications, 1997) 22.

This is an image of a loving, growing, joyful, banquet-centered community in which everyone's needs are met through the redistribution of their shared possessions. In the same way that the Spirit at Pentecost had created mutual understanding among people who shared no common language, so the Spirit created community filled "with glad and generous hearts, praising God and having the goodwill of all people." This is a vision of many utopian communities down through the centuries. Contemporary religious communities of monks and nuns are a living part of this tradition. To different degrees, the co-operative movement and aspects of community banking also incorporate parts of this vision. It is a vision of a banquet-centered balance between freedom from poverty and its grinding struggle for the basics of life and the freedom that comes from poverty and the relinquishment of all acquisitiveness.[13]

Yet our Scriptures are not simplistic. This picture of the early Jerusalem church is repeated almost immediately but with subtle differences.

> Now the whole group of those who believed were of one heart and soul, and no one claimed private ownership of any possessions, but everything they owned was held in common. With great power the apostles gave their testimony to the resurrection of the Lord Jesus, and great grace was upon them all. There was not a needy person among them, for as many as owned lands or houses sold them and brought the proceeds of what was sold. They laid it at the apostles' feet, and it was distributed to each as any had need (Acts 4:32-35).

Again there is a picture of property held in common by a faith-centered community with the redistribution of resources to ensure the well-being of all in the community. But warning shadows have emerged. In contrast to the emphasis on diversity in the Pentecost experience, there is now mention of a uniformity of beliefs within the group, a "oneness" of heart and soul that is linked to common ownership of property. Indeed property relations often define who is included and excluded in community. In addition to the "great grace" of the community, there is now an emphasis on "the apostles" and a new image of hierarchical power relationships: the proceeds from property

---

[13] See Aloysius Pieris, *An Asian Theology of Liberation* (Maryknoll, N.Y.: Orbis Books, 1988) 80.

sales were placed "at the feet" of those who testified "with great power." If the image of placing money at those same feet that Jesus had so recently washed is not jarring enough, the story of Ananias and his wife, Sapphira, immediately follows this text. They withhold a portion of the proceeds from the sale of their property. When confronted they each drop instantly to their death, with Sapphira falling at Peter's feet (Acts 5:1-11). The harmony of the garden and Pentecost is gone. There is no reference to the banquet, to table fellowship, prayer, praise, or gladness in this text. For property relations to bring life and abundance for all, they must be banquet-centered. There must be a place for the Ananiases and Sapphiras in our midst.

To love God and our neighbor with all of who we are includes our property. Our faith asserts that the whole earth is God's. We are always, only tenants or stewards. All that we have is a gift from God.[14] In faith then, God has an ultimate claim on our property. Ironically, "the mode of God's possessing is giving, not the hoarding by which human beings claim dominion."[15] The extravagant generosity of the landowner of the vineyard most closely resembles God's economic style. In the vineyard, all are included, even the least. The last employed are entitled to "the usual daily wage." What is God's claim on our property? Do the least have a claim on "our" property?

The challenge is that our current economy more closely resembles that of the hated king than that of the vineyard. Our economy with its "winner take all" logic has allowed the income disparities between the winners and losers to widen seemingly inexorably.[16] In fact, despite some of its rhetoric, the marginalized, voiceless, and creation in general have little or no place in our economic communities.[17] The least have no claim on even the basics for life. The last in line have diminishing entitlements to the goodness of creation. But, abundant life for all requires that all have at least some entitlements. As Monika Hellwig

[14] See Lev 25:23; Exod 19:4; Deut 26:10; Ps 50:8.

[15] Meeks, *God the Economist,* 114.

[16] Income disparity (and related measures) and the rates of its change do differ markedly between countries. Those differences give an idea of the effect that public policy can have. Increasing disparity among people is the result of choices we make. See the annual Human Development Reports issued by the United Nations Development Programme.

[17] For a succinct summary and critique of that rhetoric, see John B. Cobb, "Liberation Theology and the Global Economy," *Liberating the Future: God, Mammon and Theology,* ed. Joerg Rieger (Minneapolis: Augsburg Fortress, 1998) 27–42.

has noted: "The gospel does not say anywhere that there must be no inequality, only that there must be no one in need."[18] Amartya Sen has provided a detailed account of four twentieth-century famines in which the structures of human community so diminished people's entitlements to the food that was available that they starved to death. He and colleagues have also outlined, with the same detail, the kind of public policies that have been and can be used to alleviate the entitlement failures that lead to deprivation and starvation.[19] It is not for a lack of food, knowledge, or ways and means that people are unfed or underfed in our communities, countries, and around the globe. It is a lack of will, of our hearts' commitment to act together. It is our choices about property, rooted in our sense of community, that determine the patterns of buying and selling, giving and receiving, and these in turn determine whether there is fullness of life for all or just the few.[20] It is not impossible. Indeed, for a time when we were very present to the Spirit, "there was not a needy person among them."

The "goodwill for all people" that is basic to the banquet ethos seems as far away as that original Pentecost moment. A sense of a common good or of a common interest among people and between people and creation seems to have all but evaporated from our economic relationships. In this context "love of neighbor" takes on a sentimental or nostalgic ring. Even the dishonest manager understood the value of a "welcome" among people and spent resources shrewdly to build up relationships. How much more could the "children of light" be doing?

SPIRITUAL PRACTICE: ALMS, TITHES, AND TAXES

How do we acknowledge God's claim on all of our lives? How can we acquire and use our wealth and possessions sacramentally: as tangible,

[18] Hellwig, *The Eucharist*, 49.

[19] Amartya Sen, *Poverty and Famines: An Essay on Entitlement and Deprivation* (Oxford: Clarendon, 1981) 154–6. See also Jean Dreze and Amartya Sen, *Hunger and Public Action* (Oxford: Clarendon Press, 1989); and Amartya Sen, "Property and Hunger," *Economics and Philosophy* 4 (1988) 57–68.

[20] United Nations Development Programme, Human Development Report 1998 (New York: Oxford University Press, 1998).

outward manifestations of the inward grace that permeates our lives and creation as a whole? Can we reimagine the web of relationships of which we are a part, so that our financial transactions build up the health of the community as a whole?[21] Can we imagine ways to direct our economic lives for "the goodwill of all people"?

Beyond the jubilee and Sabbath-year practices and the experience of the early Jerusalem church, our Scriptures discuss three other practices in which wealth was redistributed. All are still relevant today. One is almsgiving.

> If there is among you anyone in need . . . do not be hard-hearted or tight-fisted toward your needy neighbor. You should rather open your hand, willingly lending enough to meet the need, whatever it may be. Give liberally and be ungrudging when you do so, for on this account the LORD your God will bless you in all your work and in all that you undertake. Since there will never cease to be some in need on the earth, I therefore command you, "Open your hand to the poor and needy neighbor in your land" (Deut 15:7-8, 10-11). [Or] Give to everyone who begs from you, and do not refuse anyone who wants to borrow from you (Matt 5:42; see also Luke 12:33).

Almsgiving is a concrete, everyday practice not only of compassion, but also of detachment from our natural acquisitive impulses. As a spiritual discipline, it benefits the giver as well as receiver.

Closely related to almsgiving is the collection or "the voluntary gift" or tithe that Paul organized to help the church in Jerusalem which is described in detail in 2 Corinthians 8 and 9. Paul mentions two issues that continue to run through the heart of any redistribution of resources.

> In this matter I am giving my advice: it is appropriate for you who began last year not only to do something but even to desire to do something— now finish doing it, so that your eagerness may be matched by completing it according to your means. For if the eagerness is there, the gift is acceptable according to what one has—not according to what one does not have. I do not mean that there should be relief for others and pressure on you, but it is a question of a fair balance between your present abundance and their need, so that their abundance may be for your need, in order that there may be a fair balance (2 Cor 8:10-14).

---

[21] Interestingly, "wealth" and "well" have the same root in our language.

In contrast to Jesus' unbounded "give to anyone who begs from you," Paul speaks pragmatically to the question of "fair balance" among people. The question of what constitutes a "fair balance" between one's abundance and another's need, and who adjudicates that balance, is always at the heart of the justice concerns of any community. But Paul's prior question of our "desire [or eagerness] to do something" is also a crucial question today. Nurturing a generous, openhanded "desire to do something" is an integral part of the journey of the banquet.

Medieval Jewish scholar Maimonides described eight styles of giving, or ways our benevolence or "desire to do something" can be shaped. He arranged "eight degrees of charity" hierarchically.[22] The lowest style of assistance is to give grudgingly, reluctantly, or with regret: "morosely." Then there is the one "who gives less than is filling but gives with a gracious mien." Then there is giving what one should, but only after being asked. The fourth approach is to give "before the poor person asks." One step higher is a gift in which "the poor person knows from whom he [sic] is taking, but the giver knows not to whom he is giving." Then there is the situation where "the giver knows to whom he gives, but the poor person knows not from whom he receives." Better yet is the situation when the gift is anonymous to both giver and recipient. Finally, the ideal gift is one that helps another to become self-supporting, by means of a gift, a loan, business partnership, or employment. "With reference to such aid, it is said, 'You shall strengthen him, be he a stranger or a settler, he shall live with you' (Lev 25:35), which means strengthen him in such manner that his falling into want is prevented." This is the wisdom of the twelfth century. It is as pertinent today as then.

Jesus in his day clarifies the heart of the matter. He was invited to dinner and his host raised concerns about his table practices. Jesus responds:

> Now you Pharisees clean the outside of the cup and of the dish, but inside you are full of greed and wickedness. You fools! Did not the one who made the outside make the inside also? So give for alms those things that are within; and see, everything will be clean for you. But woe

---

[22] Moses ben Maimon (1135–1204), "Book Seven: Seeds," *A Maimonides Reader*, ed. Isadore Twersky (New York: Behrman House, 1972) 136, 137.

to you Pharisees! For you tithe mint and rue and herbs of all kinds, and neglect justice and the love of God; it is these you ought to have practiced, without neglecting the others (Luke 11:39-42; parallel Matt 23:23).

Almsgiving and tithing are set in those inner, fundamental banquet concerns of justice and love. It is the food of the banquet that nurtures the "desire to do something" of which Paul speaks, and that will continue to lead us to that "fair balance" between one's abundance and another's need and teach us to give in ways that nurture the whole.

Tithing is a second way to acknowledge the community's claim on "our" property and possessions. The tithe represents a voluntary commitment of our property to the life of the community. Traditionally it has been 10 percent of our income.[23] Just as in the days of our Jewish ancestors, tithes are usually given as donations to support faith communities and other nonprofit organizations serving the needs of the community.[24] Paul, referring again to the Jerusalem collection, encourages a regular offering: "On the first day of every week, each of you is to put aside and save whatever extra you earn, so that collections need not be taken when I come" (1 Cor 16:2). Interestingly, the offerings of the Jewish community were not from the extra or surplus grown or earned, like the remnants left in the field for gleaners,[25] but came off the top, from the choicest or best of the "first fruits."[26] Whether our tithe comes as a portion of all of our income, a portion of the best of our property, or simply from the "extra," the offering is for God and the good of the community. It is given out of love of God and neighbor.

Finally, taxes are the third way communities have a claim on "our" property.[27] In Jesus' day, the taxes were imposed by a foreign power: the Roman Empire. Today the taxes we pay are to our own governments who are elected to represent us. Increasingly, however, many experience our own governments as foreign powers antagonistic to our interests and those of the community. This situation has been named a

---

[23] See Lev 27:32; Ron Sider, in *Rich Christians in an Age of Hunger*, 2d ed. (Dallas: Word Publishing, 1997), describes his family's approach to tithing, which includes 10 percent on a base figure and a gradated tithe above that; 193–6.

[24] Num 18:8-32; Deut 12:10-12; 14:22-28; 2 Chron 31:4-12; Neh 10:32-39.

[25] See Lev 19:9, 10; 23:22; Deut 24:19-22.

[26] See Exod 23:15-19; 34:26; Deut 18:4; 26:1-15.

[27] See Rom 13:6-7.

legitimation crisis.[28] People are less and less willing to assent to the claims that communities (local, regional, and national) make on them. Yet, these frail vehicles are the ones we have for building together a house worthy of our God. We must learn to love them so we can care for them and through them all our neighbors in God's beloved creation.

Jesus walked willingly to his death before there were any signs that anyone really understood what he was about or any signs of the success of his ministry. The radical import of Jesus' relinquishment of control in his death becomes transparent as we struggle with the relinquishment of our hard-earned money and our attachment to our property. We relinquish that money for the sake of the community, the children of God, deserving and undeserving, all muddled up together. The freedom of the gospel is the freedom that comes through the cross, through relinquishment of control to God. It is not the freedom attained through property. Almsgiving, tithing, and taxation are three of the ways we acknowledge God's claim on us for the good of the community. They are three ways to practice the etiquette of the banquet table.

[28] Jurgen Habermas, *Legitimation Crisis* (Boston: Beacon Press, 1973).

STATION 7 LITANY:
TABLE ETIQUETTE: ECONOMICS

Voices 1: All that we are, all that we have, all that we cherish,
Comes from you and belongs to you.

Voices 2: We delight in the riches of our inheritance:
the blessings of creation, the gifts of our ancestors, the
fruits of our own industry;

All: **You pour out your grace unstintingly,
We thank you for the extravagance of your love.**

One: For the freedom of life with you:

Voices 1: Freedom from the demands to acquire more, be more,
do more,
In order to be secure, worthy, and satisfied;

One: For the meaning of life with you:

Voices 2: For a center of gravity and purpose,
in the whirl of pressures to keep up;

All: **We thank you for the quality of life with you.**

One: Give us salve for our eyes that we might see,

Voices 1: Instead of price tags, your image stamped on all of creation;
Instead of market opportunities, a web of living relations;

All: **Help us to see Christ's economy—the economy of life.**

One: Open our hands curled from hard work, worry, and
dog-eat-dog competition,

Voices 2: That we might share our property and possessions open-
heartedly, and
find a fair balance between our abundance and others' need.

All: **Free us to fully participate in Christ's economy of overflowing grace for all.**

One: Teach us to translate the language of your heart into the
language of economics,
that all those bank statements, budgets, balance sheets,
and graphs can serve:

Voices 1: to humanize and green our economy, and

create economies of care and community;

Voices 2:   to ensure a place for the least, the last, and the voiceless; and

shape a rich future to the seventh generation.

All: **Touch all the bread and butter issues of our lives with your Spirit,**

That we might reflect your glory in all our relationships.

One: O Economist of all creation,
Garden, jungle, and desert,

Voices 1:   You rekindle our tepid faith,
You unify the separated spheres of our lives,

Voices 2:   You relax the grasp of our hands, and
Reknit relationships of life torn by economies of death.

All: **The very stones sing of the generative power of your love.**
To You be all honor, glory, and praise.

Visual Focus: Money, credit cards, real estate advertisements, stock market reports.

Station 8

"It Is Impossible"

May the God of hope fill you with all joy and peace in believing,
so that you may abound in hope by the power of the Holy Spirit.

—Romans 15:13

Perhaps it is after the first blush of enthusiasm for the journey of the banquet. Perhaps it is after centuries of dust, domestication, and cultural accommodations are blown off the gospel. At some point the enormity of the journey of the banquet becomes clear. If the etiquette of the banquet table were to shape our everyday lives, every dimension of life would be reshaped, from the economy to politics to community life to the intimate details of our relationships. Sarah's laughter, Abraham's incredulity, and Mary's "how can this be?" echo in the space created by the Holy's incredible challenge (Gen 21:6, 7; 17:17; Luke 1:34, 37).

Over history there have been many responses to this challenge. In addition to outright rejection and disbelief, most responses have tried to circumscribe or reduce the scale of the challenge. The etiquette of the banquet is applied to separate communities, not to the whole world. Or it is applied to distinct types of activity with this time or dimension of my life belonging to God and the other parts to Caesar and the demands and etiquette of the secular world. Or it is applied to different roles for different people: one etiquette for religious people, and another for lawyers, teachers, farmers, economists, health and human service practitioners, business people, etc. These responses all make the challenge of the gospel more realistic, more imaginable or conceivable on a human scale. Yet all these well-used responses diminish the gospel. The journey of the banquet is not about that. So, there comes a time of choice: to reject the invitation to the banquet, to manage it as one of many competing claims, or to accept the invitation and go deeper into the story.

VOICES OF THE TRADITION

The enormity of the challenges of the banquet was clear to the first disciples. They encountered the wall between the possible and impossible long before they were all momentarily defeated by the finality of the crucifixion.

There is the account of the earnest inquirer.

> And as he was setting out on a journey, a man ran up and knelt before him, and asked him, "Good Teacher, what must I do to inherit eternal life?" Jesus said to him, "Why do you call me good? No one is good but God alone. You know the commandments: 'You shall not murder; You shall not commit adultery; You shall not steal; You shall not bear false witness; You shall not defraud; Honor your father and mother.'" He said to him, "Teacher, I have kept all these since my youth." Jesus, looking at him, loved him and said, "You lack one thing; go, sell what you own, and give the money to the poor, and you will have treasure in heaven; then come, follow me." When he heard this, he was shocked and went away grieving, for he had many possessions.
>
> Then Jesus looked around and said to his disciples, "How hard it will be for those who have wealth to enter the kingdom of God!" And the disciples were perplexed at these words. But Jesus said to them again, "Children, how hard it is to enter the kingdom of God! It is easier for a camel to go through the eye of a needle than for someone who is rich to enter the kingdom of God." They were greatly astounded and said to one another, "Then who can be saved?" Jesus looked at them and said, "For mortals it is impossible, but not for God; for God all things are possible" (Mark 10:17-27; parallels Matt 19:16-26; Luke 18:18-27).

The story is not set in a context of testing Jesus. The inquirer is a decent man, a good man. He is clearly a person of faith. Yet the radical conditions of the gospel: "go, sell what you own, and give the money to the poor . . . ; then come, follow me," even when offered with all the love of the Holy: "Jesus, looking at him, loved him," deeply "shocked [the inquirer], and he went away grieving, for he had many possessions." The power of wealth is profound. To relinquish its power and security is a huge challenge. Such conditions are not a recipe for easy success. Even the disciples are "perplexed" and "greatly astounded," for they are regular folk who are well grounded in the ways of the world. They can smell failure and a foolhardy agenda just as easily as the next person. Even Jesus is clear. Read against a humanly defined horizon of possibility, of imagination, of action, Jesus states categorically: "it *is* impossible." It is only within the horizon of divine action, when the matter is seen in a different light and moved from a different center, that "all things are possible." Jesus draws a line between humanly defined possibility and divinely defined possibility. There is no attempt to smudge the line between the two. There is no attempt to reduce the scale of the challenge to fit our capabilities or to increase our capabilities to a god-like level.

The story does not rest there. Is that particular wall of wealth indeed impenetrable? Our tradition offers a counterexample. There is the story of the small but rich man. Zacchaeus, a chief tax collector, is very familiar with the ways of money and of the empire. He too has many ill-gotten possessions. He was probably curious, and being short, he climbed a tree to catch a glimpse of Jesus. On being recognized by Jesus and receiving Jesus' invitation, "Hurry and come down; for I must stay at your house today," Zacchaeus does not hesitate. He responds immediately. He hurries down the tree, happy to welcome Jesus. But the crowds were not happy and grumbled about Jesus' open disregard for the table etiquette of the day: "All who saw it began to grumble and said, 'He has gone to be the guest of one who is a sinner'" (Luke 19:7).

Jesus was not bound by the conventions of the possible, the right, who is in and out, or who is or is not deserving. In the unexplained space between one verse and the next, the transformative power of the gospel moves the heart of this small but rich man: "Zacchaeus stood there and said to the Lord, 'Look, half of my possessions, Lord, I will give to the poor; and if I have defrauded anyone of anything, I will pay back four times as much.' Then Jesus said to him, 'Today salvation has come to this house'" (Luke 19:8-9a). Within the Divine horizon of action, change outside human bounds, the healing of human community, indeed salvation is possible. "For mortals it is impossible, but not for God; for God all things are possible" (Mark 10:27).

There is another story that bears on hunger, the market, the banquet, and what is possible. On at least two occasions that differ only in the details,[1] Jesus has compassion on the crowds who have followed him, but are without food.[2] The disciples encourage Jesus to send the crowds away "to buy food for themselves." But Jesus says to his disciples: "you give them something to eat." The disciples respond: it is impossible. They are blinded by an economic rationality that sees only scarcity: "only five loaves and two fish."[3] "Six months' wages [two hundred denarii] would not buy enough food for each of them to get a little" (John 6:7). From their perspective, feeding the multitudes is impossible. Yet the endings of each of these stories are the same: "They all ate and were satisfied" (Matt 14:20a; 15:37a; Mark 6:42; 8:8a; Luke 9:17a; John 6:12a).

And each story records the number of baskets of food fragments left over. There was more than enough for all to eat and be satisfied. The rationality of the gospel is a different rationality than that defined by human logic. Looked at one way, it is impossible. Yet within another horizon of possibility, in another light, can we say it is impossible? Seen with different eyes and a different imagination, set of parameters, or frame of reference, is it impossible that all be fed and satisfied?

There have been many attempts to explain this miracle, to understand it and access its power. What is the power that allows there to be more than enough for all to be fed and satisfied? Is it purely a matter of the redistribution of wealth? Is it a matter of the information, knowledge, or technology to make things happen? Is it a matter of persuasion, a tongue or language that can move all hearts, or even a matter of religious power? Although each of these may play a part, Paul points to the deeper substratum of reality that the power of the banquet draws on:

> If I speak in the tongues of mortals and of angels, but do not have love,
> I am a noisy gong or a clanging cymbal. And if I have prophetic powers,

---

[1] Matt 14:13-21; 15:32-39; Mark 6:30-44; 8:1-10; Luke 9:10-17; John 6:1-15, 25-71.

[2] At the end of the day in the feeding of the five thousand, or after three days of being with Jesus in the feeding of the four thousand.

[3] Or "seven loaves and a few small fish" in the feeding of the four thousand.

and understand all mysteries and all knowledge, and if I have all faith, so as to remove mountains, but do not have love, I am nothing. If I give away all my possessions, and if I hand over my body so that I may boast, but do not have love, I gain nothing (1 Cor 13:1-3).

The spiritual heart of the matter must be in place. The food of the banquet is quite specific. The crowds in one account of the feeding of the five thousand think not of the heart of their own spiritual journeys, but rather that in possessing Jesus they will possess his power. And so Jesus withdrew, for "they were about to come and take him by force to make him king" (John 6:15). But the power at the heart of divine reality is not a power of force or political systems. It cannot be mastered or possessed. Rather, it thrives as it is given away.

The power that defines divine horizons of action and generates incredible possibilities has a different heart, a different logic. Paul offers a description:

> Love is patient; love is kind; love is not envious or boastful or arrogant or rude. It does not insist on its own way; it is not irritable or resentful; it does not rejoice in wrongdoing, but rejoices in the truth. It bears all things, believes all things, hopes all things, endures all things.
> Love never ends (1 Cor 13:4-8a).

This picture of love is virtually the antithesis of most human conceptions of power. In contrast to Paul's quite modest words, another of the great love poems in our tradition, the Song of Solomon, offers a sense of love's indestructible power.

> Love is strong as death,
>   passion fierce as the grave.
> Its flashes are flashes of fire,
>   a raging flame.
> Many waters cannot quench love,
>   neither can floods drown it.
> If one offered for love
>   all the wealth of his house,
>   it would be utterly scorned (Cant 8:6b-7).

Then, beyond all words, the cross became for Christians the ultimate testament to the power of love. The cross could not eradicate the compassion that Jesus had for the crowds. And contrary to all human conceptions of the possible, the tomb could not contain it either. The cross is the statement of the boundless love of God for all of God's creation. The empty tomb testifies to the power of God's love to work through and beyond all humanly defined horizons of action. All things are indeed possible for God.

Jesus' exorcisms are examples of God's power working in situations that we might call impossible. Exorcisms are often understood in terms of our contemporary understanding of mental illness. Yet there is also integrity in the original worldview of possession by a destructive spiritual power. Not every situation can be reduced to a problem of genes, biochemistry, or programming. There are certainly situations today that in their complexity, persistence, or escalating havoc of hatred, destruction, and death seem to have a life of their own well beyond our control. Paul had a clear sense of such situations.

> Finally, be strong in the Lord and in the strength of his power. Put on the whole armor of God, so that you may be able to stand against the wiles of the devil. For our struggle is not against enemies of blood and flesh, but against the rulers, against the authorities, against the cosmic powers of this present darkness, against the spiritual forces of evil in the heavenly places (Eph 6:10-12).

Walter Wink, in his work to recover an understanding of this world-view for us, suggests "that what people in the world of the Bible experienced and called 'principalities and powers' was in fact real. They were discerning the actual spirituality at the center of the political, economic, and cultural institutions of their day."[4] What the ancients named as "powers and principalities" can be seen today in the spiritual ethos at the heart of our institutions, whether corporate, bureaucratic, civil, or religious. This ethos is particularly clear whenever we attempt to change our institutions or way of doing things. As Wink notes: "Only by confronting the spirituality of an institution and its concretions can the total entity be transformed, and that requires a kind of spiritual discernment and praxis that the materialistic ethos in which we live knows nothing about."[5] Although certainly without the blessings of our current scientific understanding, people in Jesus' day were

---

[4] Walter Wink, *Engaging the Powers: Discernment and Resistance in a World of Domination* (Minneapolis: Fortress Press, 1992) 6.

[5] Ibid., 10.

more ready to see the spiritual and material dimensions of reality as inextricably connected. In his whole ministry, but most pointedly in his exorcisms, Jesus addresses these "powers and principalities" and the whole host of realities that hold us captive and block our access to impossible possibilities of a horizon of action defined by the Divine.

In the intimate context of a father's love for his son, Jesus and his disciples again face that seemingly impenetrable wall between the possible and impossible.

> When the whole crowd saw [Jesus], they were immediately overcome with awe, and they ran forward to greet him. He asked them, "What are you arguing about with them?" Someone from the crowd answered him, "Teacher, I brought you my son; he has a spirit that makes him unable to speak; and whenever it seizes him, it dashes him down; and he foams and grinds his teeth and becomes rigid; and I asked your disciples to cast it out, but they could not do so." He answered them, "You faithless generation, how much longer must I be among you? How much longer must I put up with you? Bring him to me." And they brought the boy to him. When the spirit saw him, immediately it convulsed the boy, and he fell on the ground and rolled about, foaming at the mouth. Jesus asked the father, "How long has this been happening to him?" And he said, "From childhood. It has often cast him into the fire and into the water, to destroy him; but if you are able to do anything, have pity on us and help us." Jesus said to him, "If you are able!—All things can be done for the one who believes." Immediately the father of the child cried out, "I believe; help my unbelief!" When Jesus saw that a crowd came running together, he rebuked the unclean spirit, saying to it, "You spirit that keeps this boy from speaking and hearing, I command you, come out of him, and never enter him again!" After crying out and convulsing him terribly, it came out, and the boy was like a corpse, so that most of them said, "He is dead." But Jesus took him by the hand and lifted him up, and he was able to stand. When he had entered the house, his disciples asked him privately, "Why could we not cast it out?" He said to them, "This kind can come out only through prayer" (Mark 9:15-29; parallels Matt 17:14-21; Luke 9:37-43a).

Whose heart would not be moved in pity in the face of the graphic destructive power of the reality that holds the boy captive? Who would not want to help? Yet what can be done? The disciples can do nothing. Even the father is in awe of its destructive power and starts his plea for help: "if you are able. . . ." Jesus hears that "if" and again categorically

asserts: "All things can be done for the one who believes." The response
of the father is the honest cry of the heart when confronted with that
wall of incomprehensibility: "I believe; help my unbelief!" Only a
semicolon marks the dramatic shift from the assertion of belief to the
plea for help. In that surrender of control in his plea for help, the father's
sense of self and the limits of his power are clearly acknowledged.
That cry coming directly from the heart creates the space of possibility for the Holy to act. We need not stand in awe of the destructive
powers, but rather of the shift marked by that mute semicolon.

The horizons of human action, our sense of what is possible and impossible, are vastly different than that of the disciples and this father
of a very ill child. But even with all the power of contemporary science
and technology at our disposal, we too still face tremendous intractable forces of violence, destruction, and death in our world.[6] Why do
as many as twenty-five thousand children die every day from under-
nutrition or related causes?[7] What incapacitates us and keeps us mute?
The disciples' question, "Why could we not cast it out?" is still very
much with us. The location of the line between the possible and the
impossible may have shifted, but it is not gone. It is not a question of
smudging the line but of living into it. Holding in balance the positive,
capable, active declaration "I believe," and the open, receptive, vulnerability of the "help me" position is critical. The open space that exists
between a sense of ability or possibility and a sense of inability or impossibility is the space of prayer: "[Jesus] said to them, 'This kind can
come out only through prayer'" (Mark 9:29). It is the space of faith. It
is an opening to the Holy. In the account of the same event in Matthew,
Jesus responds to the disciples' question: "Why could we not cast it

---

[6] While I suggest only world hunger as an example, Michael Welker proposes any
"situations of individual and collective suffering that are perceived as agonizing and dis-
integrative, but at the same time are stabilized and stubbornly defended. For instance,
addiction, drug problems, epidemic greed, repression of life and self-anesthetization of
consumerist societies on many levels of living, ecological exploitation, and excessive
debt politics call attention to such 'demonic' forms of human persons and human
societies endangering and destroying themselves." *God the Spirit*, trans. John T.
Hoffmeyer (Minneapolis: Fortress Press, 1994) 201–2.

[7] In the context of a theological discussion, see Jurgen Moltmann, "Political Theology and Theology of Liberation," *Liberating the Future: God, Mammon and Theology*,
ed. Joerg Rieger (Minneapolis: Fortress Press, 1998). Otherwise for up-to-date figures,
see the annual human development report of United Nations Development Programme.

out?" with: "Because of your little faith. For truly I tell you, if you have faith the size of a mustard seed, you will say to this mountain, 'Move from here to there,' and it will move; and nothing will be impossible for you" (Matt 17:20). The creative Spirit of God moves into the space created by that cry from the heart—"I believe; help my un-belief"—and brings new life, new possibility, new horizons of action so that, indeed, "nothing will be impossible for you."

All the assets that Paul itemizes as parts of "the armor of God"—perseverance and fortitude, truth, righteousness, gifts for peacemaking, faith, salvation, the word of God, and prayer—are indeed important for any engagement with the powers and principalities of the day (Eph 6:13-17). Yet there is a critical first step that Paul presupposes and without which all comes to naught. As Walter Wink describes it: "One does not become free from the Powers by defeating them in a frontal attack. Rather, one dies to their control . . . by dying out from under [their] jurisdiction and command."[8] In that death the worldview and authority of the powers of the day no longer define our imaginations, hearts, or actions. That first step of faith is the total realignment of the self to the Holy. For Wink that includes not only the egocentricity of individuals, but of cultures, nations, and even our egocentricity as a species. The challenge is that "the ego must be totally reoriented with God at the center, but this is impossible for the ego to do. . . . The task is not ego-conquest by means of the ego, but ego-surrender to the redemptive initiatives of God in God's struggle against the anti-divine powers of the world."[9] This shift from ego-conquest to surrender or from assertion to consent is the letting-go into God that brings life defined on very different terms. It is a fundamental shift of allegiance. This shift is at the heart of Paul's understanding of baptism with its imagery of death and new life: "Therefore we have been buried with him by baptism into death, so that, just as Christ was raised from the dead by the glory of the Father, so we too might walk in newness of life" (Rom 6:4).

Faced with the enormity of the powers and principalities that operate in opposition to the fullness of the banquet, the way may seem impos-sible or completely impassable. And it is impossible for humans on their own. It is only the Spirit that opens a way. And the only way to

---

[8] Wink, *Engaging the Powers*, 157.
[9] Ibid., 159, 161.

the Spirit is surrender, an opening up to, a giving over or transfer of allegiance to the Holy, a consent to move with the Spirit toward fullness of life for all.[10] The gospel promise is that on the other side of the large and small shifts or deaths such a transfer of allegiance requires "newness of life." "Dying to the Powers is only the downside of rebirth. . . . Rebirth is coming home to the universe, the rediscovery of beauty and of delight in creation, the recovery of the capacity to love. . . . It is entry into the values of the society of partnership that is coming."[11] It is the banquet. The hope that springs from this faith is invincible.

Our tradition's witness to this hope in impossible situations is extensive. Two examples come from the experience of the Hebrew people.[12] Hope shines even at the heart of the bitter lamentations after the destruction of Jerusalem and exile of the people (587 B.C.E.).

> The thought of my affliction and my homelessness
> > is wormwood and gall!
> My soul continually thinks of it
> > and is bowed down within me.
> But this I call to mind,
> > and therefore I have hope:
> The steadfast love of the LORD never ceases,
> > his mercies never come to an end;
> they are new every morning;
> > great is your faithfulness.
> "The LORD is my portion," says my soul,
> > "therefore I will hope in him" (Lam 3:19-24).

And there is Job's witness in the depths of his loss, agony, and persecution:

---

[10] For centuries the language of surrender and obedience or a laying down or crucifixion of the ego or self has been used for this shift of allegiance. However, with the long ignoble history of the use of these concepts for purposes of coercive power and domination rather than for the well-being and fullness of life of each person and creation itself, this language has become suspect. It has lost its power to mark the way to "newness of life." Together we must find words to mark the radical but life-giving shift that occurs around that mute semicolon between "I believe" and "help my unbelief."

[11] Wink, *Engaging the Powers*, 164.

[12] Each of the remaining stations consider different aspects of the hope of our tradition in some detail.

O that my words were written down!
    O that they were inscribed in a book!
O that with an iron pen and with lead
    they were engraved on a rock forever!
For I know that my Redeemer lives,
    and that at the last he will stand upon the earth;
and after my skin has been thus destroyed,
    then in my flesh I shall see God,
whom I shall see on my side,
    and my eyes shall behold, and not another (Job 19:23-27a).

Of this hope, Kathleen O'Connor writes: "It is not a simple act of the will, a decision under human control, or a willful determination. It emerges without clear cause, like grace, without explanation, in the midst of despair and at the point of least hope."[13] It is this stance of faith coupled with hope that allows us to stand open-eyed in the face of the impossible and cry "I believe; help my unbelief." Is the banquet an impossible dream? Yes, it is impossible when defined in a human horizon of action. Will the fullness of the banquet happen? Yes, absolutely it will, understood within the horizon of action of the Heart and Wisdom of our Universe.

It is prayer that sustains, deepens, and develops this journey of the banquet in the space between the impossible and the possible. For prayer is our opening to God.[14] Paul's prayer for the early Church is one such example:

> I pray that the God of our Lord Jesus Christ . . . may give you a spirit of wisdom and revelation as you come to know him, so that, with the eyes of your heart enlightened, you may know what is the hope to which he has called you, what are the riches of his glorious inheritance among the saints, and what is the immeasurable greatness of his power for us who believe, according to the working of his great power (Eph 1:17-19).

[13] Kathleen O'Connor, *Lamentations and the Tears of the World* (Maryknoll, N.Y.: Orbis Books, 2002) 57.

[14] See station 4; and Joseph A. Grassi: "Faith is the interior disposition of openness to God in the face of the impossible. Prayer is the outward activation of this faith through the whole body in words and gestures. The essential quality of prayer is absolute confidence, even in the face of impossible obstacles." *Broken Bread and Broken Bodies: The Lord's Supper and World Hunger* (Maryknoll, N.Y.: Orbis Books, 1985) 45.

And so with the "eyes of our hearts enlightened," we too pray that we "may know what is the hope to which we are called," and live with the conviction that "for God all things are possible" (Mark 10:27).

SPIRITUAL CHALLENGE: HOPE

Michael Welker, among a multitude of others, suggests that our "world is threatened in the most massive way."[15] But he argues that the threat is not an external one, but a spiritual one: "the danger to which modern societies expose themselves can be characterized as systematically generated and systematically intensified helplessness."[16] Yet Sharon Welch suggests that we "middle-class people [in North America] can be challenged by the fragile power of love and justice to move from cultured despair to learned hope."[17] This is the agenda of the journey of the banquet. In order for our hope to be reasoned and not naïve, we must take seriously this "systematically generated and systematically intensified helplessness." We must consciously work to counter a culture of despair and cynicism that doubts any possibility of constructive change and erodes any energy to work for a common good.

At the level of world politics, the fall of the Berlin Wall in 1989 marked the end of a Soviet communist alternative to the free market capitalism of the West. Despite the clear limitations of that alternative, in its absence there came a sense that there is no other possibility than what presently exists. It is called the "TINA" syndrome: There Is No Alternative. Indeed some have even claimed an end to history, with changes in time now seen simply as an extension of the present. Jurgen Moltmann calls this foreclosure of the possibility of a future different from the present the "occupation of the future" by the present.[18] From

---

[15] Welker, *God the Spirit*, 32.

[16] Ibid., 32.

[17] Sharon Welch, *A Feminist Ethic of Risk*, rev. ed. (Minneapolis: Fortress Press, 2000) 168.

[18] Jurgen Moltmann, "Liberating and Anticipating the Future," *Liberating Eschatology: Essays in Honor of Letty M. Russell*, ed. Margaret A. Farley and Serene Jones (Louisville, Ky.: Westminster John Knox Press, 1999) 197. See also Jurgen Moltmann, *The Coming of God: Christian Eschatology* (Minneapolis: Fortress Press, 1996), section III, for a more comprehensive discussion of these concepts.

this perspective the current state of affairs will simply be extended over time on its same progressive trajectory limitlessly. For those who do not benefit from our current state of affairs, this is a situation of despair and hopelessness. For those who do benefit, there may be a certain unfocused unease, emptiness, or tediousness, but the dominant sense is of detached complacency. This manifestation of the TINA syndrome is but one of its several faces.

In contrast to the familiarity of a future as the progressive extension of the present, there is the foreboding of a future filled with impending doom. This doom could be an ecological, nuclear, or financial catastrophe, an epidemic, or the disintegration of the social order into violence, terror, and anarchy. In addition to a certain sense of resignation and helplessness in the face of such a future, there is an impulse to forestall such doom with whatever means of control are at hand. "The political and the moral order 'hold back the end of the world' and must therefore be preserved under all circumstances and with every expedient."[19] Attempts to ameliorate current injustices or create an alternative trajectory away from catastrophe upset the ability of the current order to withstand the forces of chaos and are in fact irrelevant to the inevitable outcome. There is not only no reason to act, but it is also counterproductive. Again, there is no alternative to the current state of affairs.

Between these heady alternative ways of narrowing "the space for innovative action in history,"[20] there is also the impenetrable weight of the structures of our contemporary society. The interconnections between the ever differentiating and specializing sectors and subsectors of modern society (education, law, economics, research and development, agriculture, civil society, religion, etc.) have become so complex, tenuous, and changeable as to be unknowable. Even our way of talking about these structures has become dense and obtuse. Yet the various gaps, contradictions, and disassociation among these sectors are constantly generating societal tension and heartache. Our media endlessly fill us with information about these events and their cost in human misery in our world. At the same time as the media convey a sense of activity in corridors of power, they leave us sadly ignorant and powerless. At a commonsense level we are painfully aware that we

---

[19] Moltmann, "Liberating and Anticipating the Future," 193.
[20] Ibid., 197.

"can no longer understand and influence economic processes, intellectual developments, displacements in family life and in morals, and many other things."[21] The possibility of effective action for a common good seems very circumscribed and only really attractive to the young or perpetually idealistic. The majority disengage and "withdraw into private life and pursue their own interests."[22]

In the face of such a culture of despair, to shape our lives around a living hope in the redemptive action of Christ in history is an enormous spiritual challenge. We struggle to find appropriate words and actions to meet our Scripture's challenge: "Always be ready to make your defense to anyone who demands from you an accounting for the hope that is in you; yet do it with gentleness and reverence" (1 Pet 3:15-16). For our hope is not wishful thinking or sunny optimism as if our God was Santa Claus. It is also not based on an immovable conviction that we have privileged access or even ownership of the truth. Nor is our hope that we can predict and control our own future. Rather, our hope is rooted in a living, unfolding relationship with the God revealed to us in Jesus the Christ. The Spirit is our guide, teacher, advocate, and counselor in the ways of this new creation. "The Spirit is the power of the New Age, present in the midst of the old; it is power for moral action in the domain of the new creation, of which it is the pledge."[23] The journey of the banquet is lived in anticipation of the fullness of the new creation, yet fully immersed in the old. We let our "present be determined by the expected future of God's kingdom and God's righteousness and justice."[24] The Spirit is not "a booster in one's capacity to do the will of God under the aegis of the Old Age."[25] The Spirit is of the new age. We do not build this new age. Rather, we align ourselves with it. We make space for the Spirit to empower, direct, and create the possibilities of the new age in which the fullness of banquet is shared by all, and then we follow.

The action of the Spirit is not numinous, mystical, otherworldly, or ghostlike. Rather, in concrete, particular situations of oppression, the disintegration of community, or the diminishment of life potential, the

---

[21] Welker, *God the Spirit*, 34.

[22] Moltmann, "Liberating and Anticipating the Future," 198.

[23] Leander E. Keck, *Paul and His Letters*, 2d ed. (Philadelphia: Fortress Press, 1988) 87.

[24] Moltmann, "Liberating and Anticipating the Future," 203.

[25] Keck, *Paul and His Letters*, 87.

Spirit acts to create possibilities for liberation, for healing and reconciliation, for "the restoration of unimpaired, coherent patterns of life," for hope.[26] It is real human beings, in real time and space, who say yes or no to these possibilities. Are there alternatives? More than can be imagined (Eph 3:20). From this perspective, the TINA syndrome can be considered a denial of God's Spirit, what has traditionally been called "blasphemy against the Spirit."[27] Hope is not about shelving our reason and orienting around wishful thinking and magical promises. It is about maintaining space for "impossible possibilities" and then bringing our best selves into that space. It is about turning toward the sun that rises in a divine horizon of action and orienting by its light. It is about living in the Spirit in this God's beloved creation with our eyes and hearts open.

Spiritual Practice: Humility

To be humble is to be clear-eyed about the line between the possible and impossible. We are not to smudge the line and imagine either that we are completely capable and all is possible or that we are completely incapable and withdraw all the gifts we have been given. To cultivate humility is to cultivate an accurate sense of human limitations and capabilities. Clearly, humility has nothing to do with an inflated sense of our capabilities. It also "has nothing to do with passivity, nor . . . with cultivating a poor self-image. Being a doormat is not being humble . . . nor is daydreaming gentle thoughts while the world's violence goes on around it."[28] But to practice humility is also not to reduce all action to what can be conceivably effective or successful. That way ignores the Spirit. That way leads to paralysis in the face of the complex or intransigent problems of our world. "It seems natural to many people, when faced with a problem too big to be solved alone or within the foreseeable future, simply to do nothing. If one cannot do everything to solve the problem of world hunger, for example, one does nothing

---

[26] Welker, *God the Spirit*, 203.

[27] Ibid., section 4.4.

[28] Roberta C. Bondi, *To Love as God Loves: Conversations with the Early Church* (Philadelphia: Fortress Press, 1987) 54.

and even argues against partial remedies as foolhardy and deluded."[29] Again, to be humble is to be clear-eyed but not paralyzed by the line between the possible and impossible.

In the journey of the banquet, our hope is not based on the likelihood of the success of our ventures, let alone our power to ensure such success. We are not called to be successful, only faithful. In fact, size is not the point.

> [Jesus] also said, "With what can we compare the kingdom of God, or what parable will we use for it? It is like a mustard seed, which, when sown upon the ground, is the smallest of all the seeds on earth; yet when it is sown it grows up and becomes the greatest of all shrubs, and puts forth large branches, so that the birds of the air can make nests in its shade" (Mark 4:30-32; parallels Matt 13:31-32; Luke 13:18-19).

To be humble is to believe in the power of the Spirit acting in mustard seeds. Our hope is not about gaining a power to match that of the forces which restrict access to the fullness of life. It is not about overcoming these forces, but about transforming and liberating them for the banquet.

In the journey of the banquet, we are not required to have the whole answer or a grand plan.[30] We are required only to be a part of the whole that is woven together by the Holy. Humility has everything to do with being one part of a whole. "And again he said, 'To what should I compare the kingdom of God? It is like yeast that a woman took and mixed in with three measures of flour until all of it was leavened'" (Luke 13:20-21; parallel: Matt 13:33). Yeast works when "mixed in with flour." On its own it is inert. That mixing happens in the fine mesh of our everyday lives. The Spirit at work in the silence, the spaces, and the ebb and flow of our conversations and exchanges with others draw each of us into our best selves and into our mutually best possibility. In fact "without working with others . . . it is impossible to maintain the vision and energy necessary to sustain long-term work. If one engages in critique in isolation from those who are the victims of social systems, critique can become despairing and cynical."[31] It be-

[29] Welch, *Ethic of Risk*, 17.
[30] Surely we are clear on the dangers of "final solutions" after our experience of Hitler's "final solution."
[31] Welch, *Ethic of Risk*, 168.

comes an end in itself and therefore "all-encompassing and enervating." It is in our relationships of care and solidarity that the yeast of the Spirit brings life and leavens the whole. Without community we are inert potential and our analysis, however correct, is sterile.

> The journey of the banquet is not a grand, heroic affair. It is in fact quite a humble affair. We are not "building the Kingdom," as an earlier generation liked to put it. We simply lack the power to force the Powers to change. We faithfully do what we can with no illusions about our prospects for direct impact. We merely prepare the ground and sow; the seed grows of itself, night and day, until the harvest (Mark 4:26-29). And God will—this is our most profound conviction—bring the harvest.[32]

Faced with the enormity of the task, hope is about faith in the power of mustard seeds and leaven to transform situations. It is about faith in the power of a "powerless" Jesus who was executed between two common thieves. It is this faith holding hands with hope and inspired by love that moves us past the stuck place of "it is impossible" to the freedom of "the newness of life" that is Christ's unconditional invitation to each of us, each day.

[32] Wink, *Engaging the Powers,* 165.

Station 8 Litany: "It Is Impossible"

Voices 1: For those who have gone before us in the faith,
         For the testimony of their lives to such impossible
           possibilities,

Voices 2: For their resolute commitment and unbounded hope,
         For the fruits of their labor on which we live,

All: **For the cloud of witnesses, we thank You.**

Voices 1: For those who have planted and nurtured the seed of faith
           in our lives,
         For all who have extended hands and wisdom to us in our
           times of need,

Voices 2: For our experiences of love, encouragement, and direction,
         For all the gestures that bring us closer to your Spirit,

All: **For the gifts of faith, hope, and love, we thank You.**

Voices 1: In the face of the powers and principalities of our age,
         Knowing their power to crush, absorb, or deflect any
           resistance,

All: **Re-root us in the power of your love to move mountains
and overturn empires.**

Voices 2: When the way forward seems completely blocked,
         When despair is circling our souls and immobilizing us,

All: **Re-root us in the power of Spirit to unlock doors of
possibility.**

Voices 1: When we stand disabled by the immensity of need before
         us,
         When death, destruction, and simple exhaustion have
           erased our will to act,

All: **Re-root us in the power of mustard seeds and yeast to
create life in the wilderness.**

Voices 2: When all around us share in the laughter of disbelief and
           cynicism;
         When every alternative seems utopian, naïve, or simply
           foolish;

All: **Help us to stand firm in our faith that the last word is always yours.**

Voices 1: For, in the circle of your light,
Horizons stretch past the limits of our imagination;
Voices 2: In the expanse of your heart,
All are accommodated, the hungry are fed, all are satisfied;
Voices 1: In the touch of your presence,
Healing happens; reconciliation is possible.
Voices 2: In the depth of your wisdom,
All ways are known; the opaque becomes transparent.

All: **You are the yes to our every no;**
You are our hope, the bedrock of our faith;
We sing our praise to You:
Source, Power, and Food of the banquet.

Visual Focus: Mustard seeds or yeast.

Station 9

"MY CUP OVERFLOWS"

And God is able to provide you with every blessing in abundance,
so that by always having enough of everything, you may share
abundantly in every good work.

—2 Corinthians 9:8

The journey of the banquet is into the heart of God's impossible possibilities. The banquet is framed within a divine, rather than human, definition of the possible. To move in this landscape requires a reorientation of our imagination. For it is our imagination that has "the power to open us to new possibilities, to discover another way of seeing. . . . While the intention of the will is to a specific project, the imagination is the intention of dominant direction. It is at the level of dominant direction that we are overtaken by the disorienting logic of Jesus."[1] With a shift in our fundamental assumptions, what appears impossible in one light becomes perfectly possible in another. Fluency in this "disorienting logic of Jesus" reorients our imaginations and the dominant direction of our lives. In Christ we glimpse the divine definition of what is truly possible on earth.

What are the noteworthy features or markers that distinguish the divine horizon from our everyday human, culturally defined horizon of action? One significant point of difference is whether a sense of scarcity or abundance dominates our emotional and economic imagination.[2]

[1] Paul Ricoeur, "The Logic of Jesus, the Logic of God," *Christianity and Crisis* (1979) 324–7.

[2] Other differences are taken up in the subsequent stations.

Abundance is of God. Walter Brueggemann names scarcity a myth and contrasts this "myth of scarcity" with "the lyric of abundance [which] asserts that because the world is held in the hand of the generative, generous God, scarcity is not true."[3] He challenges "those of us who care about the lyric of abundance [to] reflect on whether we embrace this claim, and whether it is possible to break free from the claim of scarcity that is all around us, that is the dominant power of politics and the relentless liturgy of TV commercials." He means this "lyric of abundance . . . not as a pious, religious sentiment, but as a claim about the economy" and its real possibilities.[4] The banquet turns on this claim of faith. It is true that "a myth of scarcity will never generate 'bread for the world,' but only bread for us and for ours."[5]

Orienting in a landscape characterized by abundance, by more than enough, by plentitude and fecundity, rather than one defined by scarcity, by never enough and always too little, substantially alters our sense of possibility. It breaks us free of the claim that "unemployment, poverty, pollution, spirit-deadening work and other negative products of our economic order are inevitable 'social costs,' the price we have to pay in this 'best of all possible worlds.'"[6] It says "no" to any sense that scarcity is inevitable and asserts rather that symptoms of scarcity are human constructions. Scarcity is a symptom of our collectively limited human imagination. Within the divine horizon of action there is always more than enough bread for all in the world.

VOICES FROM THE TRADITION

All the accounts of creation in our tradition assert and celebrate the plentitude, fecundity, and fruitfulness of our world. There is the greening of the "dry land" on the third day of God's creative work with its repetitive emphasis on seeds: "Let the earth put forth vegetation: plants yielding seed, and fruit trees of every kind on earth that bear fruit with the seed in it. . . . The earth brought forth vegetation:

---

[3] Walter Brueggemann, "The Truth of Abundance: Relearning Dayenu," *The Covenanted Self: Explorations in Law and Covenant,* ed. Patrick D. Miller (Minneapolis: Fortress Press, 1999) 113.

[4] Ibid.

[5] Ibid.

[6] Roelf Haan, *The Economics of Honour: Biblical Reflections on Money and Property,* trans. Nancy Forest-Flier (Geneva: World Council of Churches, 1988) 9.

plants yielding seed of every kind, and trees of every kind bearing fruit with the seed in it" (Gen 1:11b-12). There is the fifth day's work when again "the earth brings forth," in this case "swarms of living creatures"[7] and birds that God blesses: "Be fruitful and multiply and fill the waters in the seas, and let birds multiply on the earth" (Gen 1:22). And there is the work of the sixth day, when God blesses humankind: "Be fruitful and multiply, and fill the earth" (Gen 1:28a). God sees everything in creation and judges it all very good. Even after the affairs of creation disintegrate, when God's judgment of creation's goodness is reversed and the sweeping destruction of the great flood occurs, God repents. God forswears such rampant loss of life and reaffirms the original blessing of abundance: "Be fruitful and multiply, and fill the earth. . . . Be fruitful and multiply, abound on the earth and multiply in it" (Gen 9:1, 7).

Fruitfulness is at the heart of the promise God makes with our ancestors in the faith. Four times God promises offspring beyond measure to the childless Abram:

> I will make your offspring like the dust of the earth; so that if one can count the dust of the earth, your offspring also can be counted (Gen 13:16).
> [And God] brought [Abram] outside and said, "Look toward heaven and count the stars, if you are able to count them." Then he said to him, "So shall your descendants be" (Gen 15:5).
> [And] "As for me, this is my covenant with you: You shall be the ancestor of a multitude of nations. No longer shall your name be Abram, but your name shall be Abraham; for I have made you the ancestor of a multitude of nations. I will make you exceedingly fruitful; and I will make nations of you, and kings shall come from you (Gen 17:4-6).

Yet this promise is counterintuitive. Not only are Abraham and Sarah childless, but they are "advanced in age; it had ceased to be with Sarah

---

[7] Mary Douglas, in her study of Leviticus, suggests that the codes for the use and avoidance of the creatures of God's creation (as clean/unclean; common and abominable) actually function as "protection" for the creatures named unclean and abominable, rather than a reversal of God's judgment of goodness. She also suggests that "the word which is commonly translated as 'swarming' is closely associated in Hebrew with breeding, bringing forth, and fertility in general. . . . Genesis clearly connects the word with fecundity." And she suggests that the word "teeming" might be more apt. *Leviticus as Literature* (New York: Oxford University Press, 1999) 159, 160.

after the manner of women" (Gen 18:11). Then, before the miraculous
child is even grown, Abraham is challenged to offer this child of promise
back to God. At the moment of Isaac's death, Abraham hears the call
of the angel of mercy, sees the "ram, caught in a thicket by its horns,"
and stays his hand. The impossible possibility of God's creation remains open and the promise is affirmed as a blessing a fourth time:

> I will indeed bless you, and I will make your offspring as numerous as
> the stars of heaven and as the sand that is on the seashore. And your off-
> spring shall possess the gate of their enemies, and by your offspring shall
> all the nations of the earth gain blessing for themselves, because you
> have obeyed my voice (Gen 22:17-18).

The fecundity of God's word is indeed awesome. Through it blessing
comes to all the nations of the earth.

This drama of barrenness becoming fruitful in the faithfulness both
of God to God's promises and of humans in our orientation to God is
enacted throughout our Scriptures in the stories of Isaac and Rebekah
(Esau and Jacob's parents), Jacob and Rachel (Joseph and Benjamin's
parents), Manoah and his wife (Samson's parents); Elkanah and Hannah
(Samuel's parents), and Zechariah and Elizabeth (John the Baptist's
parents). And in Luke's Gospel, Mary's pregnancy is set in the context
of Elizabeth's journey from barrenness to fruitfulness. This fruitfulness is at the heart of Jesus' mission as he summarizes it: "I came that
they may have life, and have it abundantly" (John 10:10b). Life abundant is a fundamental theme of the story of salvation and the journey
of the banquet.

Over and over the Psalms celebrate our hope in the Holy as the
source of the abundance and fecundity of life:

> O God of our salvation;
>   you are the hope of all the ends of the earth
>   and of the farthest seas.
> You visit the earth and water it,
>   you greatly enrich it;
> the river of God is full of water;
>   you provide the people with grain,
>   for so you have prepared it.
> You water its furrows abundantly,
>   settling its ridges,

softening it with showers,
    and blessing its growth.
You crown the year with your bounty;
    your wagon tracks overflow with richness.
The pastures of the wilderness overflow,
    the hills gird themselves with joy,
the meadows clothe themselves with flocks,
    the valleys deck themselves with grain,
    they shout and sing together for joy (Ps 65:5b, 9-13).

In the midst of a poetic retelling of the riches of creation, Psalm 104 reiterates our absolute dependence on God for food, for good things, for life itself.

The earth is satisfied with the fruit of your work.
You cause the grass to grow for the cattle,
    and plants for people to use,
to bring forth food from the earth,
    and wine to gladden the human heart,
oil to make the face shine,
    and bread to strengthen the human heart.
O LORD, how manifold are your works!

In wisdom you have made them all;
    the earth is full of your creatures.
These all look to you
    to give them their food in due season;
when you give to them, they gather it up;
    when you open your hand, they are filled with good things.
When you hide your face, they are dismayed;
    when you take away their breath, they die
    and return to their dust.
When you send forth your spirit, they are created;
    and you renew the face of the ground (Ps 104:13b-15, 24, 27-30).

It is a picture of ever-renewing plenty. It is a picture of satisfaction and fulfillment sung again in Psalm 145 and re-sung in part in Psalm 147.

The eyes of all look to you,
    and you give them their food in due season.
You open your hand,
    satisfying the desire of every living thing.

He fulfills the desire of all who fear him;
    he also hears their cry, and saves them (Ps 145:15-16, 19).

It is a picture of inclusive abundance and delight.

How precious is your steadfast love, O God!
    All people may take refuge in the shadow of your wings.
They feast on the abundance of your house,
    and you give them drink from the river of your delights (Ps 36:7-8).

The bottom line of this generous plentitude is summarized succinctly in the familiar opening affirmation of Psalm 23: "The LORD is my shepherd, I shall not want"; and even more graphically: "my cup overflows" (Ps 23:1, 5a). Brueggemann offers an equivalent bottom line in contemporary language: "creation is primarily an exuberant, lyrical, doxological expression of gratitude and amazement for the goodness and generosity of God. The theme that recurs is generosity and abundance. There is enough! There is more than enough. There is as much as the limitless, self-giving of God can imagine."[8] Even the extravagance of this description of the "lyric of abundance" at the heart of creation is merely a modest echo of that of the psalms.

This "lyric of abundance" is not just a constant refrain in the Hebrew Scriptures, but also resonates throughout Jesus' ministry. There are the miraculous catches of fish (Luke 5:1-11; John 21:1-8); the offer of "water that . . . will become in them a spring of water gushing up to eternal life" to the Samaritan woman at the well (John 4:14b); the gallons and gallons of wonderful wine at the wedding in Cana (John 2:1-11); and the baskets of food left over in the feeding of the multitudes. Like Elijah and Elisha before him,[9] in Christ we glimpse the fullness of God's promises in our midst.

Yet the myth of scarcity is tenacious. Even Jesus' disciples are not free of it, though they are immersed day after day in the presence of Jesus' power for plentitude and human flourishing. In Mark's gospel, after both the feeding miracles and after many healings and a teaching about the goodness of all creation (Mark 7:14ff.), the disciples find themselves without any bread.

---

[8] Brueggemann, "The Truth of Abundance," 108.
[9] 1 Kgs 17:1-16; 2 Kgs 4:1-7, 42-44.

Now the disciples had forgotten to bring any bread; and they had only one loaf with them in the boat. And [Jesus] cautioned them, saying, "Watch out—beware of the yeast of the Pharisees and the yeast of Herod." They said to one another, "It is because we have no bread." And becoming aware of it, Jesus said to them, "Why are you talking about having no bread? Do you still not perceive or understand? Are your hearts hardened? Do you have eyes, and fail to see? Do you have ears, and fail to hear? And do you not remember? When I broke the five loaves for the five thousand, how many baskets full of broken pieces did you collect?" They said to him, "Twelve." "And the seven for the four thousand, how many baskets full of broken pieces did you collect?" And they said to him, "Seven." Then he said to them, "Do you not yet understand?" (Mark 8:14-21; parallel Matt 16:5-12).

It is "the yeast of the Pharisees and Herod" that grows the myth of scarcity. Jesus' bombardment of questions is not about the absence of bread. It is all about the power of this myth of scarcity to harden our hearts and block our ability to see, hear, and appreciate the abundance at the heart of creation. "Do you not yet understand?" Jesus' question remains, always open-ended, at the heart of the journey of the banquet. Even now, do we really understand?

It is against a backdrop of inherent abundance that the struggles of human scarcity and death, that ultimate marker of the limitedness of all that lives, are set. The individual experience of scarcity, of "having no bread," is certainly not a myth. In fact, it is all too real for millions of humans around the globe today. Regina Schwartz, in her insightful study of "the myth of scarcity" from the Cain and Abel controversy on, talks of the "intransigent and tragic scarcities that are part of our condition in the world."[10] These scarcities, however, are humanly created. They are part of the human horizon of action.[11] They are not part of the divine horizon of action. They are not necessary or inherent in

---

[10] Regina M. Schwartz, *The Curse of Cain: The Violent Legacy of Monotheism* (Chicago: University of Chicago Press, 1997) 175–6.

[11] Douglas Meeks, "Economy and the Future of Liberation Theology in North America," *Liberating the Future: God, Mammon and Theology*, ed. Joerg Rieger (Minneapolis: Fortress Press, 1998), suggests that this artificial, humanly created scarcity comes from "a logic of choosing among scarce means." It is not that there are not situations of "natural and human lacks and insufficiencies." It is that we artificially restrict our understanding of a situation of scarcity and thereby unduly restrict the means of addressing the situation so that some are excluded in the distribution of available resources. Amaryta Sen's account of four twentieth-century famines is a dramatic illustration of

the natural order of things. Can we learn to read our world situation with a map of abundance rather than a map of scarcity? That was a significant part of the core curriculum in the forty-year school in the wilderness which formed God's covenant people after their exodus from Egypt.

It was scarcity that brought Jacob's children to Egypt: "There was no food in all the land, for the famine was very severe. The land of Egypt and the land of Canaan languished because of the famine" (Gen 47:13). But in truth there was food. To maximize Pharaoh's power, Joseph had structured "a food monopoly."[12] The all-too-familiar process of humanly created scarcity is outlined in Genesis 47:

> Joseph collected all the money to be found in the land of Egypt and in the land of Canaan, in exchange for the grain that they bought; and Joseph brought the money into Pharaoh's house. When the money from the land of Egypt and from the land of Canaan was spent, all the Egyptians came to Joseph, and said, "Give us food! Why should we die before your eyes? For our money is gone." And Joseph answered, "Give me your livestock, and I will give you food in exchange for your livestock, if your money is gone." So they brought their livestock to Joseph; and Joseph gave them food in exchange for the horses, the flocks, the herds, and the donkeys. That year he supplied them with food in exchange for all their livestock. When that year was ended, they came to him the following year, and said to him, "We can not hide from my lord that our money is all spent; and the herds of cattle are my lord's. There is nothing left in the sight of my lord but our bodies and our lands. Shall we die before your eyes, both we and our land? Buy us and our land in exchange for food. We with our land will become slaves to Pharaoh; just give us seed, so that we may live and not die, and that the land may not become desolate."
>
> So Joseph bought all the land of Egypt for Pharaoh. All the Egyptians sold their fields, because the famine was severe upon them; and the land became Pharaoh's. As for the people, he made slaves of them from one end of Egypt to the other (Gen 47:14-21).

In exchange for food, Pharaoh absorbs all the money, then all the livestock, then the land and the people themselves. All ability to sustain

---

this point: *Poverty and Famines: An Essay on Entitlement and Deprivation* (Oxford: Clarendon Press, 1981).

[12] Brueggemann, "The Truth of Abundance," 112.

life is then at the sole discretion of Pharaoh and the people are captive. They are slaves and landless laborers. This use of food scarcity as a weapon or instrument of domination has a long and ignoble history.[13]

But this is not the end of history. It is only the beginning of the Exodus story of another way. There is "an alternate food policy."[14] The Exodus story is actually an account of "a departure from the myth of scarcity—a liturgical, imaginative, political, economic act of resolve to situate our lives outside this powerful ideological claim" of scarcity. For, as Brueggemann notes, "Pharaoh, then and now, is endlessly powerful in his definitions of reality, and it is not easy to depart."[15] The first chapter of the Exodus story is the geographical departure from Egypt, the battle of the slaves against the empire that culminates in the crossing of the Red Sea and the defeat of the Egyptian army.

The second chapter details the events in the school of the wilderness. There the people learn an alternative food regime. They become a "community of an alternative food policy."[16] Right after the great song of celebration for their physical freedom, there is an account of water scarcity (Exod 15:22-27). Then immediately there is the account of food scarcity:

> The whole congregation of the Israelites complained against Moses and Aaron in the wilderness. The Israelites said to them, "If only we had died by the hand of the LORD in the land of Egypt, when we sat by the fleshpots and ate our fill of bread; for you have brought us out into this wilderness to kill this whole assembly with hunger" (Exod 16:2-3).

To leave Egypt was easy compared to leaving "the myth of scarcity." That lesson took forty years.

To follow Brueggemann's account of this journey: "the first task is leaving; the second task is believing. [The people] are asked to believe that in the wilderness where the ground cannot generate food, food will be given [as rain] from heaven in ways that are strange and inexplicable."[17] But it was more than simply learning to trust God for

---

[13] See Neh 5:1-5. Most contemporary accounts of famine in our world will also include elements of this story.

[14] Brueggemann, "The Truth of Abundance," 114.

[15] Ibid., 113–4.

[16] Ibid., 114.

[17] Ibid., 115.

their daily food and water. At the core of the curriculum of this alternate food policy is God's "trademark requirement":

> "Gather as much of it as each of you needs, an omer to a person according to the number of persons, all providing for those in their own tents." The Israelites did so, some gathering more, some less. But when they measured it with an omer, those who gathered much had nothing over, and those who gathered little had no shortage; they gathered as much as each of them needed (Exod 16:16-18).

Their trust in God for their daily food and water was manifest in a very specific pattern of economic behavior. God's trademark requirement: "gather as much of it as each of you needs," means,

> no hoarding. No storing up. Where there is no scarcity, there is no warrant for hoarding. No member of the community need be threatened by what the neighbor has, no need for greed, no need for brutality, no need for violence, no need for Pharaoh's way with bread, because Yahweh is the giver who keeps on giving, every day, sufficient for the day.[18]

This alternate food policy is rooted in an alternate theology, a different understanding of God. "Israel's second task is believing, believing when you hold this fine flaky substance in your hand, that there will be more, believing that Yahweh is attentive as creator, that Yahweh is powerful in the desert, that Yahweh is unlike Pharaoh and so is perfectly reliable and perfectly generous."[19] God's power is not analogous to Pharaoh's power. God's way is not the empire's way. God's way, the way of the banquet, therefore, has very different implications for our way.

It is the same lesson Jesus tries to communicate to his disciples.

> Do not keep striving for what you are to eat and what you are to drink, and do not keep worrying. For it is the nations of the world that strive after all these things, and your Father knows that you need them. Instead, strive for his kingdom, and these things will be given to you as well (Luke 12:29-31).

Life is not about striving for bread, but about striving for the banquet. The rest is gift. The lessons of the school of the wilderness must

[18] Ibid.
[19] Ibid.

be learned in every generation. In fact, so pervasive are the ways of the empire, God's way must be practiced daily. And so at the very heart of the Lord's Prayer, we find: "Give us this day our daily bread" (Matt 6:11; parallel Luke 11:3). This is the core of the curriculum of the school of the wilderness.

Again, the journey does not end there. The third chapter is life in "the land of milk and honey." It is all about life in the land of abundance.

> On the day after the Passover, on that very day, they ate the produce of the land, unleavened cakes and parched grain. The manna ceased on the day they ate the produce of the land, and the Israelites no longer had manna; they ate the crops of the land of Canaan that year (Josh 5:11-12).

Brueggemann summarizes the shifts from the second to this third chapter: "now instead of a generous heaven, they must rely on a productive earth. Instead of miracle, they are driven to agriculture. Instead of just receiving, they are now into management." The irony of this chapter is that "when Israel—or anybody—thinks about management, it will not be long before there are thoughts about property and ownership and self-sufficiency and greed and we are back to all the circumstances that invite moves to monopoly and thoughts of scarcity."[20] Perhaps abundance can never eliminate a gnawing sense of insecurity. Even in the first garden of plenty, the original humans reached for more. With Qoheleth, we might want to cry: "The eye is not satisfied with seeing, or the ear filled with hearing . . . all human toil is for the mouth, yet the appetite is not satisfied" (Eccl 1:8b; 6:7). Perhaps the experience of scarcity, of not enough or never enough, of a nagging insatiability, of amorphous hungers always prompting a reach for more, of endless desires generated by envy and covetousness (Eccl 4:4), is so much a part of humanity that it necessarily drowns out the lyric of abundance. Perhaps we are trapped in a cage in which we must run ever faster to meet our needs and wants, which are partly, but only partly,[21]

---

[20] Ibid., 116.

[21] Miroslav Volf, "In the Cage of Vanities: Christian Faith and the Dynamics of Economic Progress," *Rethinking Materialism: Perspectives on the Spiritual Dimension of Economic Behavior*, ed. Robert Wuthnow (Grand Rapids, Mich.: Eerdmans, 1995) notes: "the human race did not need to wait for capitalism to infect it with the virus of

manufactured by the economic system that is to meet our desires and from which there is no apparent escape but death. Perhaps we leave captivity in Egypt only to re-create it in the Promised Land. This thinking is the way of "the yeast of the Pharisees and the yeast of Herod." It is a particularly potent, long-lasting yeast.

The terms of the covenant and its codes for the "management" of settled life in the Promised Land of abundance were the ways for the community of an alternative food policy to remember the lessons of the wilderness. Abundance and fruitfulness were imbedded into and made conditional upon observance of the commandments:

> This entire commandment that I command you today you must diligently observe, so that you may live and increase. . . . Remember the long way that the LORD your God has led you these forty years in the wilderness. . . . He humbled you by letting you hunger, then by feeding you with manna, with which neither you nor your ancestors were acquainted, in order to make you understand that one does not live by bread alone, but by every word that comes from the mouth of the LORD. . . . Therefore keep the commandments of the LORD your God, by walking in his ways and by fearing him. For the LORD your God is bringing you into a good land, a land with flowing streams, with springs and underground waters welling up in valleys and hills, a land of wheat and barley, of vines and fig trees and pomegranates, a land of olive trees and honey, a land where you may eat bread without scarcity, where you will lack nothing, a land whose stones are iron and from whose hills you may mine copper. You shall eat your fill and bless the LORD your God for the good land that he has given you.
>
> Take care that you do not forget the LORD your God, by failing to keep his commandments, his ordinances, and his statutes, which I am commanding you today (Deut 8:1-11).

This wonderful picture of abundance is bracketed with the injunctions to remember always the source of these blessings. Yet, as Miroslav Volf

---

insatiability. If this metaphor is appropriate at all, then the virus was there all along. It was active in particular strata of society throughout history, until finally a general epidemic broke out with the rise of capitalism in the West. The inactive virus just needed a change in socioeconomic and cultural [and perhaps religious] conditions to provide it a friendly environment. . . . Cultural acceptance, even encouragement of insatiability is unique to modernity. Insatiability itself is not. . . . The rootedness of insatiability in human nature leads to a very simple but fundamental insight: the economic problem cannot be solved by economic means alone" (172, 174).

reminds us, "the so-called secularizing effects of wealth are proverbial. It cannot suffer a god beside itself."[22] In the land of abundance, the tendency is to forget God or replace God with another god. That is the explicit warning:

> When you have eaten your fill and have built fine houses and live in them, and when your herds and flocks have multiplied, and your silver and gold is multiplied, and all that you have is multiplied, then do not exalt yourself, forgetting the LORD your God. . . . Do not say to yourself, "My power and the might of my own hand have gotten me this wealth." But remember the LORD your God, for it is he who gives you power to get wealth. . . . If you do forget the LORD your God and follow other gods to serve and worship them, I solemnly warn you today that you shall surely perish (Deut 8:12-14, 17-19).

This is the requirement for life in the land of abundance. It is as pertinent now as then.

The challenge in the Promised Land is that "the very possession of the land that should guarantee the identity of the people seems to prompt them to violate the terms of its possession: they are no longer faithful to their God. Possession of the land and idolatry go hand in hand."[23] Possession possesses, distracts, and creates an insidious kind of amnesia. Volf describes the contemporary shape of this process:

> If a person is religious, when he [*sic*] forgets . . . God, he will not simply develop a "self-made-man" style faith with the simple credo "my power and the might of my own hand have gotten me this wealth"; he will also "follow other gods to serve and worship them" (Deut 8:17, 19). Gods that, like the Baal of old, promise to do marvels in stimulating infinite growth and creating boundless prosperity. If not carefully attended to, wealth develops occult powers that erase memories of the one true God and generate new gods that are more congenial to its well-being. [But], what is good for wealth, might not be good for its owners.[24]

Boundless prosperity, a bigger pie, or a bigger piece of the pie become the altar on which we sacrifice ourselves, and the science and technology

---

[22] Ibid., 181.
[23] Schwartz, *The Curse of Cain*, 54.
[24] Volf, "The Cage of Vanities," 184.

that generate the illusion of infinite growth become our new gods. Abundance is no longer a gift from a God of infinite generosity. God's trademark requirement: "gather [only] as much of it as each of you needs," is forgotten. As our material wealth and power grow our sense of God shrinks. God's invitation into the grace-filled freedom, the limitlessness and deep peace of the divine horizon of action given through God's unconditional embrace of the human condition of finitude and scarcity in the cross, seems such a "fine flaky substance." It seems as ephemeral and insubstantial as manna in the wilderness. The third chapter, life in the Promised Land, has proven the most challenging chapter of human history.

SPIRITUAL CHALLENGE: GENEROSITY

How in this third chapter does the "lyric of abundance . . . become more than a pious, religious sentiment"? How does it become a claim about the economy and its real possibilities? At the moment we have great scarcity in the midst of extraordinary abundance. Walter Brueggemann points to the spiritual challenge of generosity that lies at the heart of this contradiction.

> The majority of the world's resources pour into the United States. And as we Americans grow wealthier and wealthier, money is becoming a kind of narcotic for us. We hardly notice our own prosperity or the poverty of so many others. The great contradiction is that we have more and more money and less and less generosity—less and less public money for the needy, less charity for the neighbor.[25]

Although he writes as an American, his observation is true in various degrees for many countries around the globe. Generosity is the impulse at the root of a gift economy. It is our contemporary spiritual challenge. It is at the core of the path of abundant life for all.

The dominant economic logic of the Holy is that of gift. Paul Ricoeur suggests "the logic of Jesus, the logic of God" is a "logic of

---

[25] Walter Brueggemann, "The Liturgy of Abundance, the Myth of Scarcity," *Deep Memory, Exuberant Hope: Contested Truth in a Post-Christian World*, ed. Patrick D. Miller (Minneapolis: Fortress Press, 2000) 69.

generosity" which "clashes head on with the logic of equivalence that orders our everyday exchanges, our commerce and our penal law."[26] The balancing of value in the exchange—I give [or sell] you x for y—is lost in God's logic of "superabundance." This logic of the Holy is not found in the careful balancing of inputs and outputs that lies at the heart of efficiency calculations. Rather, God's logic prizes extravagant gestures of munificence. The clash between Judas and Jesus over the extravagance of the woman's gift of anointing (John 12:1-8) is indeed preparatory to the clash of cultures represented in the unconditional, nothing-held-in-reserve gift of God's self on the cross.[27] Is this inefficient? Is it wasteful? Yes, but it is also the path of abundant life for all. As Paul writes: "For you know the generous act of our Lord Jesus Christ, that though he was rich, yet for your sakes he became poor, so that by his poverty you might become rich" (2 Cor 8:9). Contradicting the familiar logic that it takes money to make money, it is by Jesus' poverty, his renunciation of self-interest, and his participation in the logic of pure gift that the path to true wealth and abundant life is opened for all. By giving away all he had, he created wealth beyond our imagining. Perhaps this is the power that God has given us to get wealth (Deut 8:18). Perhaps it is the lesson the disciples found so hard to understand that day when they sat without any bread (Mark 8:13-21).

What is it about the logic of a gift economy that works to minimize scarcity in the midst of abundance? First, it must be noted that a gift economy is not the kind of reciprocal exchanges we take part in at Christmas, use to honor a birthday, or offer as various forms of tied aid to developing countries. A gift economy includes at a bare minimum three people, so that "no one ever receives [the gift] from the same person he [*sic*] gives it to." As Lewis Hyde describes the circle of a gift economy:

> When I give to someone from whom I do not receive [although I do receive a return elsewhere], it is as if the gift goes around a corner before

---

[26] Ricoeur, "The Logic of Jesus, the Logic of God," 326.

[27] Ibid., 327 notes: "This new thing is that Jesus Christ is himself the 'how much more of God' . . . now Christ is announced as the one who, by the folly of the Cross, breaks the moral equivalence of sin and death. . . . It is in this way that the Church, through the mouth of Paul, gives a name, the name of Jesus Christ, to the law of superabundance."

it comes back. I have to give blindly. And I will feel a sort of blind gratitude as well. The smaller the circle is—and particularly if it involves just
two people—the more a man [sic] can keep his eye on things and the
more likely it is that he will start to think like a salesman.[28] But so long
as the gift passes out of sight it cannot be manipulated by one man or
one pair of gift partners. When the gift moves in a circle its motion is
beyond the control of the personal ego, and so each bearer must be a
part of the group and each donation is an act of social faith.[29]

In a gift economy, "no one by himself controls the cycle of gifts he participates in; each, instead, surrenders to the spirit of the gift in order
for it to move."[30] A gift economy requires a surrender of control, a certain disinterested participation, as well as a basic faith in others and a
faith that there is enough in the economy for the circle to be sustained
over time. Ironically, it is participation in a gift economy that enhances
the faith on which it is based.

Second, there is a paradox at the heart of a gift economy that "when
the gift is used, it is not used up." In fact, "what is given away feeds
again and again while what is kept feeds only once and leaves us hungry."[31] This is the paradox we call a miracle in the feeding of the five
thousand and in the replenishment of the meal and oil jar of the widow
of Zarephath (1 Kgs 17:1-16). The multiplying power of generosity is
captured in Jesus' aphorism: "Give, and it will be given to you. A good
measure, pressed down, shaken together, running over, will be put into
your lap; for the measure you give will be the measure you get back"
(Luke 6:38).

But what is this power of a gift economy to generate more? Following Lewis Hyde, there are at least three types of increase in a gift
economy:

1. people are fed, clothed, warmed, enriched by the gift itself (the
   material dimension);

2. the movement of a gift creates and strengthens community and
   faith in community, (the social dimension); and

---

[28] In the sense of a careful calculation of equivalence, value, return, etc.
[29] Lewis Hyde, *The Gift: Imagination and the Erotic Life of Property* (New York:
Vintage Books, 1979) 16.
[30] Ibid., 128.
[31] Ibid., 21.

3. for people of faith, gift-giving is a practical spiritual discipline
   that deepens our participation in the work of God in Christ in
   our world.[32] It builds up the spiritual dimension of our life together.

The material increase for the individual in the first dimension is accompanied by the social and spiritual increase that accrues to the
whole in the second and third dimensions. Generosity is not just good
for the recipient or for the giver, but is good for the whole. In contrast,
in a market exchange "a commodity is truly 'used up' when it is sold
because nothing about the exchange assures its return. Certainly it can
turn a profit, but that gathers in pools rather than remains freely in
circulation."[33] When gift turns to trade, the material dimension of
increase continues but the social and spiritual dimensions drop away.
The whole is subtly diminished.

It is not that there is no place for the logic of the market. In fact,
much goodness and prosperity has come through market exchanges,
especially when they are free and undistorted by differences of power.
Market exchanges are and will always be a part of our lives. But although useful in many matters, the prosperity that comes with market
exchange relationships creates the contradiction of scarcity in the
midst of plenty. In our current market economy, the exchange "I give
[or receive from] you x for nothing, as an unconditional gift" has been
squeezed into a marginalized corner of our intellectual and practical
lives. Such gift relationships have been domesticated into the philan-
thropic planned-giving industry, or privatized into gestures among intimate friends and family.[34] Are there ways to re-appreciate the logic of
a gift economy and revalue and strengthen our vehicles for collective,
as well as individual, generosity?

---

[32] Hyde refers to this dimension as "a natural-spiritual fact, when gifts are the agents
of a spirit that survives the consumption of its individual embodiments." Ibid., 37. In a
Christian context, the eucharistic elements might be the closest example of such an
"agent."

[33] Ibid., 22.

[34] Leigh Eric Schmidt, "Practices of Exchange: From Market Culture to Gift Economy in the Interpretation of American Religion," *Lived Religion in America: Toward a
History of Practice*, ed. David D. Hall (Princeton, N.J.: Princeton University Press,
1998), begins to explore these changes as they were debated in the nineteenth-century
American culture and as they appear now in contemporary American religious culture.

Fundamental issues are at stake in such an endeavor. For as Hyde suggests: "where we maintain no institutions of [a gift economy], we find ourselves . . . unable to enter gracefully into nature, unable to draw community out of the mass, and, finally, unable to receive, contribute toward, and pass along the collective treasures we refer to as culture and tradition."[35] We depend upon our relationships with creation, each other, and our history in ways the market cannot fully capture. In fact the commodification of these relationships into things bought and sold in the market can change them in very unhelpful, unhealthy ways. Ironically, it is our tradition that keeps us from forgetting how things could be different and, in particular, helps us to remember the source of infinitely renewable abundance for all, the Holy.

But what does a gift economy say to the sense of scarcity generated by the gnawing insatiability of human desiring that leaves us forever unsatisfied, toiling without ceasing, striving always for more? The psalmist writes:

> Unless the LORD builds the house,
>   those who build it labor in vain.
> Unless the LORD guards the city,
>   the guard keeps watch in vain.
> It is in vain that you rise up early
>   and go late to rest,
> eating the bread of anxious toil;
>   for [the LORD] gives sleep to his beloved (Ps 127:1-2).

There is no satisfaction, no ability to rest in and trust the abundance of creation without the gift of faith. Our own efforts cannot create that kind of fulfillment. This is the reason that scarcity, at its root, is a spiritual issue. Egypt's monopolizing power can only be confronted by faith in the one who spoke to Moses from the bush that burned but was not consumed. It is God who can address the anxiety that acts like "Herod's yeast" in our midst: "My God will fully satisfy every need of yours according to his riches in glory in Christ Jesus" (Phil 4:19). This text echoes of the words from the Psalter: "You open your hand, / satisfying the desire of every living thing" (Ps 145:16). Over and over Paul asserts that God offers this satisfaction for free, not in

---

[35] Hyde, *The Gift*, 38–9.

exchange for anything. It is given, not earned: "The wages of sin is death, but the free gift of God is eternal life in Christ Jesus our Lord" (Rom 6:23). In the gift economy of God, all our deaths lead to life, rather than to a dead end. We are a part of an infinite ever-unfolding circle of gift that is always enough for life abundant for all.

These are the faith foundations for living the lyric of abundance, the gift economy of the Holy. And it is a positive feedback loop. Living with a generous heart and hand only enhances our faith, and with faith we are freer and more inclined to "gather only as much as we need." It is generosity rooted in faith that ensures ongoing fruitfulness and abundance for all even in the presence of scarcity:

> Thus says the LORD:
> Cursed are those who trust in mere mortals
>   and make mere flesh their strength,
>   whose hearts turn away from the LORD.
> They shall be like a shrub in the desert,
>   and shall not see when relief comes.
> They shall live in the parched places of the wilderness,
>   in an uninhabited salt land.
> Blessed are those who trust in the LORD,
>   whose trust is the LORD.
> They shall be like a tree planted by water,
>   sending out its roots by the stream.
> It shall not fear when heat comes,
>   and its leaves shall stay green;
> in the year of drought it is not anxious,
>   and it does not cease to bear fruit (Jer 17:5-8).

SPIRITUAL PRACTICE: GRATITUDE

The spiritual practice that undergirds a gift economy is gratitude. A gift requires a response. The response begins with thankfulness. For those who prize self-sufficiency and independence, the indebtedness or obligation to respond that accompanies a gift is its poison.[36] The

---

[36] Schmidt, "Practices of Exchange," 73ff. Also, as Hyde notes, there are gifts that need to be refused because of these obligations, bribes being an obvious example; *The Gift*, 71–73.

tendency for wealth and material abundance is to draw people away from the very sense of interdependence that gift economy generates. Maintaining an everyday practice of thanksgiving counteracts the tendency to forget the Source of all abundance (Deut 8:12-19). When the regenerative source of all life is forgotten, we move to center stage and all the other actors are swallowed up in our shadow. Without gratitude, abundance leads to idolatry, and the cycle of scarcity or fear of scarcity begins again. Our prayers of thanksgiving as we sit at table are more than a simple ritual. They hold a profound transformative capacity if we can access it.

How much we have to be thankful for! Our very life itself is a gift: a gift from God, from our parents, and from all those who nurture us. It is not of our creating. Yet as we grow up and acquire some ability, it is much easier to assume that we are the author of our own successes and blessings. But all life, young and old, is created and sustained in and through a complex web of interactions among microscopic creatures, entities as large as the sun, and everything in between. In fact all life, large and small, human and nonhuman, is sustained through the death of other organisms. We are all a part of the food chain. In addition, living in webs of interdependencies that are unjust, which we all do this side of the fullness of the banquet, means that suffering, our own and others, is also woven into the fabric of every life. Even lives most stubbornly immersed in gift relationships are still sustained through the death and suffering of others.

The burden of obligation and indebtedness that accompanies such an awareness of the true cost of the gift of life and of all the gifts that constitute our daily lives is enormous. We are inclined to look away, to forget or ignore such interdependencies. Such a perspective is depressing and produces an amorphous disconcerting guilt. It is only through the labor of gratitude that we can sustain such awareness. As Mary Jo Leddy points out: "guilt does not nourish giving; it gnaws away at our souls, leaving us consumed. . . . It is those who live out of a sense of gratitude, rather than guilt, who can respond to the world's deep hungers and not get eaten up in the process."[37] Why is this so? If we live rooted in gratitude, we respond from a sense of fullness. "While the guilty person measures life—who has more and who

---

[37] Mary Jo Leddy, *Say to the Darkness, We Beg to Differ* (Toronto: Lester and Orpen Dennys, 1990) 234.

has less, who is better and who is worse—the grateful person does not count the cost because he or she dwells in a sense of the immeasurable."[38]

Through the work of thanksgiving we develop eyes to see the gift economy of abundant life for all. We see gifts and not just deficits; we see opportunities and not just barriers; we see possibilities rather than impossibility. A steady practice of gratitude opens the heavy curtain of sentiment that creates the cry: "Vanity of vanities! All is vanity" (Eccl 1:1), and experiences life as endless, meaningless toil. Through the work of thanksgiving we begin to see how death can lead to life rather than just a dead end. A practice of thanksgiving helps to sustain our hunger for righteousness.[39] It is the alternative to the amnesia, idolatry, and assertion of independence that wealth can generate. It is only in gratitude that we can begin to approach the banquet table of the fullness of God's presence.

What is this practice of gratitude? A gift is given and we receive it, accept it, take it into our lives and our lives change. Our lives are transformed in the twinkling of the eye or over the course of a whole life. The work of thanksgiving is that process of incorporation and transformation. The sign of its completion, the amen to our labor of gratitude, is in the act of passing the gift on. Generosity is born out of the work of thanksgiving. The circle of the gift is sustained and abundance flowers through the practice of gratitude. When our thanksgiving is complete and the gift is passed on, the burden of obligation gives way to "a lingering and generalized gratitude."[40] This is similar to the comfortable satiation and joy that accompanies a delicious meal shared with loved ones. It is a foretaste of the banquet.

This practice of gratitude: of receiving, incorporating, and passing a gift along, is, in our tradition, a contribution to the glory of God.[41] With reason our Scriptures and the songs of our churches are full to overflowing with hymns of thanksgiving.[42] They celebrate the power of the Spirit moving constantly over the face of the deep, drawing life from death, cosmos from chaos, creating abundance in the parched

[38] Ibid., 235.
[39] See Station 10.
[40] Hyde, *The Gift*, 47.
[41] See 1 Cor 10:31; 2 Cor 4:15.
[42] 1 Sam 2:1-10; 1 Chr 29:11-18; Psalms 50; 107; Luke 1:46-55 among many.

barren places of our lives and healing the fissures that gouge our history. Abundance, fecundity, fruitfulness are not anonymous. They bear God's signature. Rooted in the labor of gratitude, in commitment to and participation in the gift economy of the Holy, these hymns are the seeds of the reign of God:

> God is able to provide you with every blessing in abundance, so that by always having enough of everything, you may share abundantly in every good work. As it is written,
>
>> "He scatters abroad, he gives to the poor;
>> his righteousness endures forever."
>
> He who supplies seed to the sower and bread for food will supply and multiply your seed for sowing and increase the harvest of your righteousness. You will be enriched in every way for your great generosity, which will produce thanksgiving to God through us; for the rendering of this ministry not only supplies the needs of the saints but also overflows with many thanksgivings to God (2 Cor 9:8-12).

STATION 9 LITANY: "MY CUP OVERFLOWS"

One: We name and treasure the gifts we have received:

Voices 1: The gift of new life and daily life, food, air, and water, and all the blessings of touch, warmth, light, sound, taste, and smell,

Voices 2: The gestures of love and respect, care and attention, Stories heard, knowledge received, rest enjoyed,

Voices 1: Beauty, wisdom, friendship and goodness,

Voices 2: Healing, reconciliation, justice and peace;

One: Are there other gifts to name today?

[pause]

One: For all the moments of grace that speak of your presence,

All: **With every breath, every day, we offer our thanksgivings to You.**

Voices 1: You shower the earth with your love;

Voices 2: My cup overflows, even my saucer is full;

All: **Grace abounds! Thanks be to You forever!**

One: Free us to be a part of the great circle-giving that sustains life:

Voices 1: Open our hands and hearts, our minds and souls, to receive and extend your grace with abandon;

Voices 2: Liberate our imaginations to see the possibilities you offer; And to cherish the abundance You have created,

All: **That we might know in our bones there is always enough for all, And be free to gather each day only as much as we need.**

Voices 1: Free us from the fear of scarcity and the nagging worry of not-enough; From a dead-end reliance on our own capacity and the illusion of self-sufficiency;

Voices 2: Cure the amnesia of prosperity and the blindness of wealth; Heal insecurity's constriction of our hearts and hands.

Voices 1: Open our minds to value the interplay of the material,
the social, and the spiritual,
And resist the reduction of all things to their economic
value;

Voices 2: Give us discernment to penetrate the wiles of the
marketing industry,
And to see with banquet eyes the genuine worth of things.

Voices 1: Open our hearts to appreciate our place in the whole web
of life,
To will abundant life for all, not just the few;

Voices 2: To live the logic of interdependence, rather than the illusion of independence;
To banish the experience of scarcity and deprivation.

All: **Giver of all good things, unconditional Gift, pure Spirit
of generosity,
You are our life, the ever-flowing stream.
We sing our praise and joy, honor and glory to You, forever and ever.**

Visual focus: An overflowing cup in a full saucer.

Station 10

"LET JUSTICE ROLL DOWN LIKE WATER"

Zion shall be redeemed by justice,
and those in her who repent, by righteousness.

—Isaiah 1:27

Just as abundance bears God's signature, so does justice. "To know God is to know a God of justice."[1] Justice shapes the divine horizon of action. It is part of God's impossible possibility for human history. It is a lode star for the journey of the banquet. Justice is the flavor of the banquet. Without it all is bitter. As Abraham Heschel writes: "in the sight of God even things of beauty or acts of ritual are an abomination when associated with injustice."[2] It is as if the love of God (God's love for us and our love of God) creates patterns of light and shadow, a depth of field or way of seeing that draws attention to structures of justice and injustice in our world. It is as if the world's beauty is marred or distorted by injustice, and out of love for its awesome beauty, every effort is enjoined to restore the fullness of God's glory to every corner of creation. Just as with abundance, the possibility of justice in the face of the monstrosities of injustice reorients our imagination and the dominant direction of our lives. We realize that "to worship God with silence about matters of justice [is] not to worship God at all."[3]

[1] Joseph A. Grassi, *Broken Bread and Broken Bodies: The Lord's Supper and World Hunger* (Maryknoll, N.Y.: Orbis Books, 1985) 26.
[2] Abraham J. Heschel, *The Prophets* (New York: HarperCollins, 1962) 212.
[3] Grassi, *Broken Bread*, 28.

It is our immersion in the reality of abundance that pours from the heart of the God that gives us the courage, strength, and joy to engage the powers and principalities that diminish the abundance of life for all in our day. Rooted in overflowing gratitude, we dare to address the deep hungers of our time and place. For once our roots sink into the abundance that flows from God, the object of our desiring is transformed, not as an act of will or even moral integrity, but as a homecoming to the source of our deep fulfillment:

> If the righteousness of God [God's power for life against death] is present and trusted, then there is enough for God's will to be done. . . . Then it is possible realistically to speak of hungering and thirsting after "more and better" being transformed into hunger and thirst for God's righteousness, which is a deeply satisfying, finite fulfilling.[4]

From this foundation, with this food for the journey, the prophetic demands and vision of justice are compelling. The sweep and urgency of the prophets' rhetoric no longer seems extravagant, but the very object of our desiring: our food, life for all God's beloved creation, in all its fullness, the banquet. We discover the blessedness of those who hunger and thirst after righteousness (Matt 5:6).

VOICES OF THE TRADITION

A prophet not only calls us to hear the heartbeat of God in response to the cries of God's people,[5] but also calls us to account and points the way into the heart of God. Intimacy with God and a closer walk with the Holy involves the work of justice.

> The presence of God in history, the manifestation of His will in the affairs of the world is the object of the prophet's longing. It is not mystical experience he [sic] yearns for in the night, but historical justice. Mystical experience is the illumination of an individual; historical justice is the illumination of all men [sic], enabling the inhabitants of the world to learn righteousness.[6]

[4] M. Douglas Meeks, "Economy and the Future of Liberation Theology in North America," *Liberating the Future: God, Mammon and Theology,* ed. Joerg Rieger (Minneapolis: Fortress Press, 1998) 55–6.

[5] As discussed in Station 3.

[6] Heschel, *The Prophets,* 223.

As we turn toward the light of Christ as our morning star, our imagination and sense of possibility are filled with the vision of God's justice and righteousness.[7] This vision, "this light that shines in the darkness and the darkness did not overcome it," becomes our lode star and we move in that direction (John 1:5).

Amos, speaking in a time of unparalleled prosperity in Israel, calls the people to just such a conversion of heart and life direction. He calls people to the journey of the banquet

> to seek the Lord and live . . .
> [to] hate evil and love good,
>   and establish justice in the gate (Amos 5:6a, 15a).

He speaks in the name of the God of all the grandeur of creation:

> The one who made the Pleiades and Orion,
>   and turns deep darkness into the morning,
>   and darkens the day into night,
> who calls for the waters of the sea,
>   and pours them out on the surface of the earth,
> the LORD is his name,
> who makes destruction flash out against the strong,
>   so that destruction comes upon the fortress (Amos 5:8-9).

He details the charges against those

> that turn justice to wormwood,
>   and bring righteousness to the ground!
> [Who] hate the one who reproves in the gate,
>   and . . . abhor the one who speaks the truth (Amos 5:7, 10).

He speaks judgment and calls for repentance:

> Therefore because you trample on the poor
>   and take from them levies of grain,
> you have built houses of hewn stone,
>   but you shall not live in them;
> you have planted pleasant vineyards,
>   but you shall not drink their wine.

[7] Rev 22:16.

> For I know how many are your transgressions,
>   and how great are your sins—
> you who afflict the righteous, who take a bribe,
>   and push aside the needy in the gate.
> Seek good and not evil,
>   that you may live (Amos 5:11-12a, 14).

And he remarks that "the prudent will keep silent in such a time; / for it is an evil time" (Amos 5:13).

But prudence is not a characteristic of prophets. Silence is not our vocation. Out of an incautious passion for God and God's righteousness, prophets, sometimes reluctantly and often against their better judgment,[8] call to people to see the world with the eyes of God. They invite us to see with the eyes of divine possibility. They do not present tightly reasoned arguments or carefully researched proofs. Their words are often full of outrage and judgment, for they are preoccupied with injustice.

> That justice is a good thing, a fine goal, even a supreme ideal, is commonly accepted. What is lacking is a sense of the monstrosity of injustice. Moralists of all ages have been eloquent in singing the praises of virtue. The distinction of the prophets was in their remorseless unveiling of injustice and oppression. . . . They were not concerned with the definition, but with the predicament of justice, with the fact that those called upon to apply it defied it.[9]

When you have a taste of justice in your mouth, injustice is spit out. It is not justice as a carefully defined abstract concept (as helpful as that can be)[10] that reorients our lives, but it is concrete instances of "the predicament of justice" and a hunger for its remedy or prevention. Although the language of the prophets is biblical, the injustices that they speak about are eerily contemporary.

[8] Consider Moses (Exod 3:11; 4:1, 10); Elijah (1 Kgs 19:9, 10, 13, 14); Isaiah (Isa 6:1-9); Jeremiah (Jer 1:6-10); Amos (Amos 7:14-15); Jonah (Jonah 1:1-3ff.); and even Jesus (John 2:4).

[9] Heschel, *The Prophets*, 260, 261.

[10] See Mary Elsbernd, Reimund Bieringer, *When Love Is Not Enough: A Theo-Ethic of Justice* (Collegeville: Liturgical Press, 2002) for a very clear analysis of contemporary definitions of justice complemented with some very cogent practical examples of justice or banquet work.

Like Amos, Isaiah starts with a picture of abundance, but then the "love-song" goes awry:[11]

> Let me sing for my beloved
>   my love-song concerning his vineyard:
> My beloved had a vineyard
>   on a very fertile hill.
> He dug it and cleared it of stones,
>   and planted it with choice vines;
> he built a watchtower in the midst of it,
>   and hewed out a wine vat in it;
> he expected it to yield grapes,
>   but it yielded wild grapes.
> And now, inhabitants of Jerusalem
>   and people of Judah,
> judge between me
>   and my vineyard.
> What more was there to do for my vineyard
>   that I have not done in it?
> When I expected it to yield grapes,
>   why did it yield wild grapes?
> For the vineyard of the LORD of hosts
>   is the house of Israel,
> and the people of Judah
>   are his pleasant planting;
> he expected justice,
>   but saw bloodshed;
> righteousness,
>   but heard a cry! (Isa 5:1-4, 7).

The question—Why did it yield wild grapes?—remains open-ended. But Isaiah details the how of it: the same monopolization process that Pharaoh had used under Joseph's hand with the same outcome of scarcity.[12]

> Ah, you who join house to house,
>   who add field to field,

---

[11] Just as Phyllis Trible has named her account of the events in the original garden: "A Love Story Gone Awry," *God and the Rhetoric of Sexuality* (Philadelphia: Fortress Press, 1978).

[12] See Station 9.

until there is room for no one but you,
    and you are left to live alone
    in the midst of the land!
The LORD of hosts has sworn in my hearing:
Surely many houses shall be desolate,
    large and beautiful houses, without inhabitant.
For ten acres of vineyard shall yield but one bath,
    and a homer of seed shall yield a mere ephah (Isa 5:8-10).

The blindness and amnesia of luxurious living built on injustice ensues.[13] God's trademark requirement to gather as much as each of you needs for the day is forgotten.

Ah, you who rise early in the morning
    in pursuit of strong drink,
who linger in the evening
    to be inflamed by wine,
whose feasts consist of lyre and harp,
    tambourine and flute and wine,
but who do not regard the deeds of the LORD,
    or see the work of his hands! (Isa 5:11-12).

Exile, scarcity, and misery are the outcome. It is a feast for a ravenous "Sheol."

Therefore my people go into exile without knowledge;
their nobles are dying of hunger,
    and their multitude is parched with thirst.
Therefore Sheol has enlarged its appetite
    and opened its mouth beyond measure;
the nobility of Jerusalem and her multitude go down,
    her throng and all who exult in her.
People are bowed down, everyone is brought low,
    and the eyes of the haughty are humbled (Isa 5:13-15).

But Sheol's feast is in contrast with the fecundity of God's justice and righteousness.

---

[13] See also Isa 56:9-12; Amos 6:4-7; 1 Kgs 4:22-23; and, to a lesser degree, 1 Cor 11:20-22.

> But the LORD of hosts is exalted by justice,
>> and the Holy God shows himself holy by righteousness.
> Then the lambs shall graze as in their pasture,
>> fatlings and kids shall feed among the ruins (Isa 5:16-17).

It is an image of the banquet, a very different feast fed by a different appetite: a hunger and thirst for justice and righteousness.

While "the predicament of justice" can generate passionate concern, it also raises questions of responsibility. Prophets were unrelenting in their preoccupation with "the fact that those called upon to apply [justice] defied it."[14] Then as now, "the concern for justice is delegated to judges as if it were a matter for professionals or specialists. But to do justice is what God demands of every man [*sic*]: it is the supreme commandment, and one that cannot be fulfilled vicariously."[15] Each person is called to the work of justice.

At different times in our history, our call to the work of justice was understood as the fulfillment of the moral codes of the community. The demands of the covenant spelled out what was meant by right living with God in very explicit codes of behavior. The psalmists and prophets called people to obedience to these codes. Ezekiel gives examples of what he means by righteousness.

> If a man is righteous and does what is lawful and right—if he does not eat upon the mountains or lift up his eyes to the idols of the house of Israel, does not defile his neighbor's wife or approach a woman during her menstrual period, does not oppress anyone, but restores to the debtor his pledge, commits no robbery, gives his bread to the hungry and covers the naked with a garment, does not take advance or accrued interest, withholds his hand from iniquity, executes true justice between contending parties, follows my statutes, and is careful to observe my ordinances, acting faithfully—such a one is righteous; he shall surely live, says the Lord GOD (Ezek 18:5-9).

Some of Ezekiel's examples of "what is lawful and right" may seem quaint to us, such as the concern with menstruation or abstention from charging interest, but most are still very much within our contemporary expectations of right action: do not oppress anyone, give

[14] Heschel, *The Prophets*, 261.
[15] Ibid.

bread to the hungry and clothing to those without, work for justice in the midst of conflict, etc. The ongoing interpretation, elaboration, and teaching of codes of behavior is a task for every generation. Indeed morality matters.

In addition to the articulation of expectations for right action, ritual practices were also elaborated to remind people of their relationship with God and reinforce their observance of the prescribed moral codes. These practices included a complex sacrificial system with specified offerings to enact moments of communion with God (feasts, meals, or "sacrifices of well-being"; Lev 3; 7:11-18; Exod 24:9-11); to offer God praise and thanksgiving (whole-burnt offerings, offered daily in the temple after the exile); and to remove barriers to a full (at one) relationship with God (sin-offerings: Lev 4–7; annual rites of the Day of the Atonement: Lev 16; 23).[16] However, over time, this sacrificial system became the vehicle for people to enact their relationship with God and became more important than a right and full relationship with God. As has happened throughout history, the means become the end and the end retreats from view. Our relationship with God becomes something we manage and in the process God is cut down to human scale or domesticated. The prophets are unrelenting in refocusing our attention on what constitutes full relationship with God. The call to justice and righteousness is about more than morality. A living relationship with God involves more than meticulous ritual observance. The means, the rituals or moral codes, are not in themselves problematic; in fact, they are necessary gifts to assist us in our pursuit of justice and right living. Rather, the critique of the prophets is about the inflation of the place of rituals and the structures of institutionalized religion in the life of faith, in the journey of the banquet.

Isaiah provides a classic example of this critique:[17]

> Hear the word of the LORD,
>   you rulers of Sodom!
> Listen to the teaching of our God,
>   you people of Gomorrah!

---

[16] Frances M. Young, *Sacrifice and the Death of Christ* (Philadelphia: Westminster Press, 1975) 25–30.

[17] See also: Isa 66:1-4; Jer 6:20; Hos 8:11–9:4; Amos 5:21-24; Ps 50:16-23; 51:16-19; among many examples of this theme.

What to me is the multitude of your sacrifices?
    says the LORD;
I have had enough of burnt offerings of rams
    and the fat of fed beasts;
I do not delight in the blood of bulls,
    or of lambs, or of goats.
When you come to appear before me,
    who asked this from your hand?
    Trample my courts no more;
bringing offerings is futile;
    incense is an abomination to me.
New moon and sabbath and calling of convocation—
    I cannot endure solemn assemblies with iniquity.
Your new moons and your appointed festivals
    my soul hates;
they have become a burden to me,
    I am weary of bearing them.
When you stretch out your hands,
    I will hide my eyes from you;
even though you make many prayers,
    I will not listen;
    your hands are full of blood.
Wash yourselves; make yourselves clean;
    remove the evil of your doings
    from before my eyes (Isa 1:10-16).

What was intended to nurture the people's relationship with God became a stumbling block that obscured the heart of the matter.

Jesus both honors the codes that define the covenant and demands that they serve our relationship with God. But he also insists that they not become a goal in themselves.

> Do not think that I have come to abolish the law or the prophets; I have come not to abolish but to fulfill. For truly I tell you, until heaven and earth pass away, not one letter, not one stroke of a letter, will pass from the law until all is accomplished (Matt 5:17-18).

He goes on to offer five examples of his understanding of the fulfillment of the law, of what is "to be perfect" (Matt 5:48). Each example starts with: "you have heard it said . . ." (you shall not murder, you shall not commit adultery, you shall not swear falsely, an eye for an eye and a tooth for a tooth, you shall love your neighbor and hate your enemy); and is followed by: "but I say to you. . . ." In each example he moves to the core of the matter and widens rather than narrows its scope and challenge. Yet it is not a slavish perfection he proposes. Over and over in his ministry Jesus' interpretation of the Law conflicts with that of the Pharisees, who were also passionately preoccupied with living by the Law. In conversation with the Pharisees, after his hungry disciples had gathered and eaten grain on the Sabbath despite the Law's prohibitions, Jesus suggests: "If you had known what this means, 'I desire mercy and not sacrifice,' you would not have condemned the guiltless" (Matt 12:7). Jesus' response builds from the prophet Hosea in which God is unhappy with the people:

> What shall I do with you, O Ephraim?
>   What shall I do with you, O Judah?
> Your love is like a morning cloud,
>   like the dew that goes away early.
> Therefore I have hewn them by the prophets,
>   I have killed them by the words of my mouth,
>   and my judgment goes forth as the light.
> For I desire steadfast love and not sacrifice,
>   the knowledge of God rather than burnt offerings (Hos 6:4-6).

The dramatic overturning of the tables in the Temple is in this tradition of refocusing our religious practices on our relationship with God. "It is written, 'My house shall be called a house of prayer'; but you are making it a den of robbers" (Matt 21:13; parallels: Mark 11:17; Luke 19:46). In this, the gospels are but echoing a previous generation of prophets: Isaiah (56:7) and Jeremiah (7:11).

Down through the ages the prophets continue to refocus our attention to the core issue, the very heart of the matter.

> cease to do evil,
>   learn to do good;
> seek justice,
>   rescue the oppressed,
> defend the orphan,
>   plead for the widow (Isa 1:16-17).

> Is not this the fast that I choose:
>   to loose the bonds of injustice,
>   to undo the thongs of the yoke,

to let the oppressed go free,
    and to break every yoke?
Is it not to share your bread with the hungry,
    and bring the homeless poor into your house;
when you see the naked, to cover them,
    and not to hide yourself from your own kin?
If you remove the yoke from among you,
    the pointing of the finger, the speaking of evil,
if you offer your food to the hungry
    and satisfy the needs of the afflicted,
then your light shall rise in the darkness
    and your gloom be like the noonday (Isa 58:6-7, 9b-10).

He has told you, O mortal, what is good;
    and what does the LORD require of you
but to do justice, and to love kindness,
    and to walk humbly with your God? (Mic 6:8).

But let justice roll down like waters,
    and righteousness like an ever-flowing stream (Amos 5:24).

A passion for justice and the work of living justly has deep and un-compromising taproots in our faith tradition. It is not optional or ancillary, but at the very heart of the journey of the banquet.

In our tradition there is a difference between a moral code and the justice ethic proclaimed by the prophets. In comments about Isaiah's claim that God "finds His true exaltation in justice," Heschel notes the difference.

> Isaiah does not pronounce a theory, he proclaims what is to come. He does not teach what ought to be, he predicts what shall be. The impor-tance of moral ideas was known to people everywhere. Yet linked with the awareness of the importance was an awareness of their impotence. The prophets proclaimed that justice is omnipotent, that right and wrong are dimensions of world history, and not merely modes of con-duct. The existence of the world is contingent upon right and wrong, and its secret is God's involvement in history.[18]

Regardless of the appearance of impotence, the assertion is that "jus-tice will decide; righteousness will redeem." The involvement of God

---

[18] Heschel, *The Prophets*, 274–5. See also Station 13 for a more extensive discussion of this claim.

in history changes the nature of moral questions. Moral codes are not just a matter of human choice or cultural appropriateness, but truly are an issue of discernment of the will of God for history.

Just as God's logic of generosity upsets the logic of equivalence that orders our market exchanges, so God's involvement clearly weights the outcome of the careful evenhandedness required for the dispensation of justice in our legal system.[19] "The idea of balancing two sides against one another is expressed in the most common symbol of justice, namely, the scales."[20] Indeed the just path can be discerned with such balancing "when the scales are unimpaired and the judge's eyes sound" and there are no constraints on the search for truth. But, as is most often the case this side of the fullness of the banquet, the scales are unequally weighted, our eyesight is less than perfect, and the constraints of time and money are real.

> When the eyes are dim and the scales unsure, what is required [for justice] is a power that will strike and change, heal and restore, like a mighty stream bringing life to the parched land. There is a thirst for righteousness that only a mighty stream can quench. Righteousness as a mere tributary, feeding the immense stream of human interests, is easily exhausted and more easily abused. But righteousness is not a trickle; it is God's power in the world, a torrent, an impetuous drive, full of grandeur and majesty. [When] the surge is choked, the sweep is blocked, the mighty stream will break all dikes.[21]

For people of faith, "justice is more than an idea or norm." It is the great river pouring from under the altar of the temple in Ezekiel's vision where "everything will live where the river goes"(Ezek 47:1-12). Faith asserts that all the power of the Holy is engaged on the side of justice. In fact, God is the judge of history and therefore the hope of history:

> But the LORD sits enthroned forever,
>   he has established his throne for judgment.
> He judges the world with righteousness;
>   he judges the peoples with equity.

[19] See Lev 19:15 and Exod 23:2-3.
[20] Heschel, *The Prophets*, 271.
[21] Ibid.

> The LORD is a stronghold for the oppressed,
>> a stronghold in times of trouble.
> And those who know your name put their trust in you,
>> for you, O LORD, have not forsaken those who seek you
>>> (Ps 9:7-10).[22]

From Abraham's God as "Judge of all the earth" (Gen 18:25) to the scenes of judgment in the apocalyptic visions of Revelation, God is at the heart of justice as its unfailing source.

But there are two critical caveats to this assertion of God's engagement in history on the side of justice: God's justice is always in the service of God's love, and the human pursuit of justice is always in the service of God's justice, or should be.

First, the power of God's justice is at the service of God's love for creation. God's judgment is woven through and through with a shining irrepressible thread of mercy. From the wonderful account of Abraham's argument with God about the fate of Sodom (Gen 18:22-33), to Hosea's striking imagery of God's compassion for "Ephraim," Israel, in the midst of their apostasy (Hos 11:1-9), to the summary of Jesus' mission offered to Nicodemus in John's gospel (John 3:16-17; see also John 12:47),[23] the thrust of God's justice is always tilted toward redemption, toward transformation, toward life, and not toward destruction, retribution, and condemnation.

Right in the midst of the account of the gift of the Ten Commandments comes this fundamental song of God's love:

> So Moses cut two tablets of stone like the former ones; and he rose early in the morning and went up on Mount Sinai, as the LORD had commanded him, and took in his hand the two tablets of stone. The LORD descended in the cloud and stood with him there, and proclaimed the name, "The LORD." The LORD passed before him, and proclaimed:
>
>> "The LORD, the LORD,
>> a God merciful and gracious,
>> slow to anger,

[22] See also: Pss 7:8-11; 50:4-6; 58:11; 67:4; 75:2; 76:7-9; 82:1-5; 94:2; 96:10-13; 98:9; 105:7; 119:137.

[23] "For God so loved the world that he gave his only Son, so that everyone who believes in him may not perish but may have eternal life; indeed, God did not send the Son into the world to condemn the world, but in order that the world might be saved through him."

and abounding in steadfast love and faithfulness,
keeping steadfast love for the thousandth generation,
forgiving iniquity and transgression and sin,
yet by no means clearing the guilty,
but visiting the iniquity of the parents
upon the children
and the children's children,
to the third and the fourth generation" (Exod 34:4-7).

God's justice for the wronged and oppressed "to the third and fourth generation" is sure, but is balanced in God's extravagant and steadfast love "for the thousandth generation." Paul's assertion of God's unqualified love for us is but a continuation of this song:

Who is to condemn? It is Christ Jesus, who died, yes, who was raised, who is at the right hand of God, who indeed intercedes for us. Who will separate us from the love of Christ? Will hardship, or distress, or persecution, or famine, or nakedness, or peril, or sword? No. . . . For I am convinced that neither death, nor life, nor angels, nor rulers, nor things present, nor things to come, nor powers, nor height, nor depth, nor anything else in all creation, will be able to separate us from the love of God in Christ Jesus our Lord (Rom 8:34-35, 37-39).

The way of God's engagement in history is justice tempered by steadfast love and mercy forever.[24]

This testimony of God's way of mercy is not to negate the witness in Scriptures and history of real consequences to injustice, sin, and idolatry. Those consequences are presented in a variety of ways in the Scriptures. First, and in practice probably the most common, "the wicked are snared in the work of their own hands" (Ps 9:16). Second, for many of the prophets, the Assyrian conquest of northern Israel and Judah's exile to Babylon were a consequence of the people's disregard of God's justice. Third, suffering more generally has been interpreted as a testing, a way to refine away, purify, or prune a people of injustice, sin, and idolatry.[25] Fourth, throughout the Scriptures there is the sense

---

[24] The song of God's steadfast love and mercies for God's beloved creation echoes throughout the Scriptures. See among many others: Gen 9:9-17; 2 Chr 30:1-9; Neh 9; Lam 3:19-33; the whole book of Jonah; Isa 30:15-18; 55:6-9; 2 Cor 1:3-5; Titus 3:3-7; and virtually one third of the psalms sing about God's mercy and steadfast love.

[25] See Ps 66:10; Isa 48:10-11; Mal 3:2-4.

that "the wages of sin is death" in the sense of a dead-end death rather than one that leads to life.[26] Finally, there is the concept of God's wrath, the day of vengeance, the day of the Lord's coming.[27] Although God's mercy does not negate real consequences to injustice, sin, and idolatry, there is also no sense that suffering is always deserved or is the necessary consequences of injustice, sin, and idolatry.[28] Any reflection on the book of Job or the crucifixion leaves that notion forever suspect. The mystery of innocent suffering can only be held within the overall testimony of the ages to God's infinite love and compassion for God's creation. The suffering caused by injustice, sin, and/or idolatry, however, stands forever under God's judgment. The testimony of our tradition is that God will act to address injustice and suffering in creation.

> The LORD is a stronghold for the oppressed,
> a stronghold in times of trouble . . .
> [and] does not forget the cry of the afflicted"[29] (Ps 9:9, 12b).

There is a second critical caveat to the power of God's presence and action for justice. Not only is God's justice always put in the service of God's love, but the human pursuit of justice must also be put in the service of God's justice. The tremendous power—the "torrent, [the] impetuous drive, full of grandeur and majesty" as Heschel describes God's justice—is never ours, as humans, to claim. This side of the fullness of the banquet we see through a veil. "[We] know only in part" (1 Cor 13:12a). Throughout the Scriptures and history, there is evidence of the human inclination to assume the privileged perspective of judge and to assume, sometimes even with the best of intentions, a mantle of self-righteousness or group-righteousness. Jesus struggled throughout his ministry with the blindness, the divisiveness, and refusal of the transformative potential of repentance that such a stance of assumed righteousness creates.

---

[26] See Deut 30:15-20; Ps 1; Jer 17:5-6; Matt 21:33-41; Luke 13:3, 5; John 15:6; Rom 6:23.

[27] Ps 2:1-5; Isa 63:1-6; Zeph 1:14-15; Matt 8:12; 13:41-42, 50; 22:13; 24:51; 25:30; John 3:36; Rom 2:5; see also Station 13.

[28] Nor is it the case that prosperity and health are consequences of our goodness.

[29] See also Station 2.

His parable of the Pharisee and the tax collector captures the insidious dynamic of even a well-intentioned pursuit of righteousness:

> [Jesus] also told this parable to some who trusted in themselves that they were righteous and regarded others with contempt: "Two men went up to the temple to pray, one a Pharisee and the other a tax collector. The Pharisee, standing by himself, was praying thus, 'God, I thank you that I am not like other people: thieves, rogues, adulterers, or even like this tax collector. I fast twice a week; I give a tenth of all my income.' But the tax collector, standing far off, would not even look up to heaven, but was beating his breast and saying, 'God, be merciful to me, a sinner!' I tell you, this man went down to his home justified rather than the other; for all who exalt themselves will be humbled, but all who humble themselves will be exalted" (Luke 18:9-14).

There are clear caution signs posted against judging others:

> Do not judge, so that you may not be judged. For with the judgment you make you will be judged, and the measure you give will be the measure you get. Why do you see the speck in your neighbor's eye, but do not notice the log in your own eye? Or how can you say to your neighbor, "Let me take the speck out of your eye," while the log is in your own eye? You hypocrite, first take the log out of your own eye, and then you will see clearly to take the speck out of your neighbor's eye (Matt 7:1-5; parallel: Luke 6:37-38, 41-42).[30]

And there is clear encouragement for the path of mercy: "Judgment will be without mercy to anyone who has shown no mercy; mercy triumphs over judgment" (Jas 2:13). Love opens the door to transformation. Mercy opens the door to salvation. In the meantime, before the fullness of the banquet, it is not our job to eliminate the weeds in God's garden. "For in gathering the weeds you would uproot the wheat along with them" (Matt 13:29). The final irrevocable judgment is God's.

Judgment is based on a discernment of right and wrong. A line is drawn between good and evil, between the path that leads to fullness of life for all versus the diminishment of life. The privileged perspective of a judge assumes a remove, distance, or set-apartness from wrong,

---

[30] See also Rom 2:1-8 and Jas 4:11-12.

evil, and the structures that diminish life. The invitation of the cross, however, is the invitation to stand with the condemned, in solidarity with the accused, to see the world through their eyes. It is the same invitation that Jesus offered to those accusing the woman caught in adultery: "Let anyone among you who is without sin be the first to throw a stone at her." In the time he was "bent down" in the Temple "writing on the ground," they each chose.

> They went away, one by one, beginning with the elders; and Jesus was left alone with the woman standing before him. Jesus straightened up and said to her, "Woman, where are they? Has no one condemned you?" She said, "No one, sir." And Jesus said, "Neither do I condemn you. Go your way, and from now on do not sin again" (John 8:7-10).

It is critically important to discern right from wrong, good from evil, practices that lead to fullness of life for all versus those that diminish life. The line in the sand matters. Yet it is only by standing with the condemned, by seeing the world through their eyes, that the redemptive power of God's mercy can be fully released in history. It is in our participation in God's mercy, freely poured out in love for the flourishing of all creation, that we find our own wholeness, the restoration of community, and right relations with the Holy. Justice then is not merely discerned but flows. It is a living, creative force that frees the future from the consequences of past actions. God's justice tempered with the life-giving waters of mercy is the foundation of our hope: the power in history that promises life abundant for all, the full redemption of creation from the crushing legacy of our accumulated individual and collective injustices.

SPIRITUAL CHALLENGE: REPENTANCE

The language of justice and judgment brings with it the language of guilt and innocence and questions of responsibility and human freedom. Increasingly it also evokes very ambivalent reactions. At the same time as evidence of rampant injustice accumulates and is communicated virtually instantaneously around the globe, an appreciation of the complexity of the webs of relationships—economic, political, social, psychological, religious—that support that injustice deepens. There is a pervasive sense that things are not right in the world and that we are implicated, complicit, guilty in some way. At the same time, however, there is the sense that we are impotent and unable to effect change in this deeply entrenched path of destruction. Sally McFague's description captures this dynamic:

> The Millennial Edition of State of the World puts it this way: "So far, the world order emerging is one almost no one wants," with its shrinking forests; accumulated greenhouse gases; polluted air and dying species; dwindling fresh water, fisheries, and farmland; and increasing numbers of poor people. But like it or not, we do not seem able to do much about it. Caught as we are in a system so wide and deep that we usually don't see it as *a* system but as *the* system, we despair, even in our moments of awareness, of being able to act differently within it, let alone change it. Paralysis is widespread, a paralysis especially easy for well-off North Americans to endure; in fact, waking up and taking action seems painful by comparison.[31]

Common responses to such a predicament are not often constructive: denial, disengagement, rage, depression, blame. This, however, is exactly the terrain in which faith in a God of justice and mercy requires us to work.

The language of sin, repentance, forgiveness, and salvation is the way our faith speaks to just such a predicament. Our era's attempts to cut God down to human scale and to domesticate the one power in history that orients unwaveringly toward justice and abundant life for all, has so diminished or distorted this language of our faith that it is almost unavailable to us. Yet these concepts point us into paths for the restoration and flourishing of life for all creation.

Through the ages the pervasive sense that things are not right has been labeled as a sense of sin. There are the sins of commission and those of omission. These are the sins that we contribute to through the thoughts, words, or actions that we either do or fail to do. There is also the sin that we participate in simply by living in unjust webs of relationships: economic, political, social, psychological, and religious. This is the sin of the structures and institutions of our collective lives and history. In practice, people who accent the first kind of sin fall into a

---

[31] Sallie McFague, *Life Abundant: Rethinking Theology and Economy for a Planet in Peril* (Minneapolis: Fortress Press, 2001) 74; emphasis in the original.

"full-fault" version of human responsibility; those who accent the second fall into a "no-fault" version of our responsibility for the "not-rightness" of the state of the world.[32] The first version emphasizes human freedom and is often accompanied by language of punishment and just deserts. The second version emphasizes the limits to human choices and is often accompanied by a fatalism that can be softened by sympathetic care. The witness of our tradition is that both kinds of sin are true always and at the same time. We are neither helpless nor completely accountable for all we do.[33]

Our actions are determined by our individual and collective past and by the ways our sense of possibility and vision of the future focus our attention and energy. Yet between past and future lies the present arena of choice, the site of our freedom. "The parameters of freedom may be wide or exceedingly narrow. But the parameters, by definition, are multiple, and therefore force decision making among alternatives."[34] Decisions, actions, words are never completely determined nor completely free. We live in the dynamic, always negotiated, never fully prescribed, gray zone between the stark either/or of a line drawn in the sand. Our actions are neither fully determined, broken, and unredeemable nor fully free, righteous, and whole. They are always a mix.

The reason for attending to the reality of sin as sin is to open the door to a conversation about salvation and the transformative power of faith.[35] Such an open door welcomes rather than resists the Spirit's movement toward fullness of life for all. The path to salvation leads through repentance. Paul's observation conveys a sense of what is at stake: "For godly grief produces a repentance that leads to salvation and brings no regret, but worldly grief produces death" (2 Cor 7:10). The sense that "things are not right" can open the door to change or to

---

[32] Barbara Brown Taylor, *Speaking of Sin: The Lost Language of Salvation* (Boston: Cowley Publications, 2000) 76–7.

[33] Sin and real guilt (in contrast to felt guilt which has a variety of causes) overlap, but are not coterminous. There is sin for which we are not guilty.

[34] Marjorie Hewitt Suchocki, *The Fall to Violence: Original Sin in Relational Theology* (New York: Continuum, 1999) 132–3.

[35] "Sin is our only hope, because the recognition that something is wrong is the first step toward setting it right again. There is no help for those who admit no need of help. There is no repair for those who insist that nothing is broken, and there is no hope of transformation for a world whose inhabitants accept that it is sadly but irreversibly wrecked." Taylor, *Speaking of Sin*, 59.

despair, to transformation or to resignation. What is this repentance that opens the door to the fullness of life for all?

Repentance is about the reorientation of our lives. It is about changing the direction in which we are heading, the objects of our hungering and thirsting. It concerns the deepest yearnings of our heart. Repentance is about turning and then returning, again and again, to the Source of all life, love, and wholeness. It is about giving over more and more of our lives: our thoughts, words, actions, relationships, time and energy and gifts, to God. Repentance involves much more than remorse or feeling badly about something.[36] It is something much more active. It is about actually doing things differently. Repentance is about attending to the voices of the prophets in our midst and discerning the real choices and freedom that we have in any particular situation. It is about valuing the degrees of freedom that we have and choosing the path of abundant life for all. Repentance is all about cultivating the organic parts of life that indeed bear "the fruit that befits repentance."

> And the crowds asked [John the Baptist], "What then should we do?" In reply he said to them, "Whoever has two coats must share with anyone who has none; and whoever has food must do likewise." Even tax collectors came to be baptized, and they asked him, "Teacher, what should we do?" He said to them, "Collect no more than the amount prescribed for you." Soldiers also asked him, "And we, what should we do?" He said to them, "Do not extort money from anyone by threats or false accusation, and be satisfied with your wages" (Luke 3:10-14).

These are concrete actions that could presumably be undertaken within the constraints of daily life and work.

Repentance is about consciously creating space in our lives for the Spirit to work and not over-determining, managing, or controlling every moment.[37] It is a life that maximizes its openness to grace. For, "grace is the mysterious strength God lends human beings who commit themselves to the work of transformation. To repent is both to act from that grace and to ask for more of it, in order to follow Christ into the startling freedom of new life."[38] Repentance is the activity that opens us to

[36] Ibid., 66.

[37] This might be one possible contemporary paraphrase of the thrust of: "The sacrifice acceptable to God is a broken spirit; / a broken and contrite heart, O God, you will not despise" (Ps 51:17).

[38] Taylor, *Speaking of Sin*, 85–6.

the newness in each day of the journey of the banquet. Even at the heart of the Scripture's great collection of lament, we find:

> But this I call to mind,
>   and therefore I have hope:
> The steadfast love of the LORD never ceases,
>   his mercies never come to an end;
> they are new every morning (Lam 3:21-23a).

Grace's gift is the new possibility that each morning brings, and repentance is our turning toward this sun.

Forgiveness is the name our tradition gives to the dynamic that creates the freedom to live every day new, unencumbered by the past and open to the future coming toward us. It is the process of releasing the power of the past to determine the present, letting the past indeed be the past, and opening to the possibility of a future different than today. This process can be a matter of a shake of the head, a blink of the eye, or it can be a healing journey of a lifetime, generation, or several generations. Forgiveness is the process of understanding within our relationships what is self-generated and what is created by another, and then letting the others be other and owning our own contribution. Forgiveness allows us "to accept our God-given place in community and to choose a way of life that increases life for all members in that community."[39] Forgiveness frees us to discern the degrees of freedom that are indeed present to us in any given moment. It opens our imagination to alternative courses of action to reweave our relationships into patterns in which all can flourish. The work of forgiveness is the arena of God's grace. We receive God's gift of forgiveness and extend that gift of forgiveness to others.

At the heart of a faith-based justice agenda is the recovery of God's life-giving, liberating mission given to John the Baptist as summarized by his father, Zechariah:

> You, child, will be called the prophet of the Most High;
>   for you will go before the Lord to prepare his ways,
> to give knowledge of salvation to his people
>   by the forgiveness of their sins.

[39] Ibid., 66.

> By the tender mercy of our God,
>> the dawn from on high will break upon us,
> to give light to those who sit in darkness and in the shadow of death,
>> to guide our feet into the way of peace (Luke 1:76-79).

For "forgiveness, as the active will toward well-being, is the creation of a new human future; and thus forgiveness is the substance of human hope."[40] It is our "yes" to the light at the dawn of the new day that will indeed guide us into the paths of justice and peace. This work of repentance and forgiveness is the lifelong process of becoming disentangled from the life-diminishing realities of "the way things are" and preparing the way for the coming banquet.[41]

SPIRITUAL PRACTICE: COMMUNITIES OF TRANSFORMATION

One of the great barriers to the "godly grief" that "produces a repentance that leads to salvation" is our culture's individualism. "The question is not how each of us can win salvation, but how all of us can give God glory by living together as God's creatures."[42] We are not asked to create justice and fullness of life for all. We are, however, called to participate in that process, to take our place, and only our place, in the community of life. We are not asked to make it right ourselves for ourselves, but rather to orient toward rightness day by day within community. We are called to "prepare the way," not be the way. We are called simply to be a part of that "vast and mighty stream" that is God's justice. And we cannot do that on our own. It requires community. The journey of the banquet is always communal.[43]

[40] Suchocki, *The Fall to Violence*, 153.

[41] "In Christian ethics, earthly justice is not just intended to correspond to the heavenly justice of God. It should also prepare the way for God's coming kingdom." Jurgen Moltmann, "Liberating and Anticipating the Future," *Liberating Eschatology: Essays in Honor of Letty M. Russell*, ed. Margaret A. Farley, Serene Jones (Louisville, Ky.: Westminster John Knox Press, 1999) 205.

[42] McFague, *Life Abundant*, 128.

[43] In fact, "when one strives for individual freedom and personal development alone, freedom becomes empty—a mere absence of outward regulations for individual behavior, and personal development narcissistic. A person is called to freedom and personal

Communities come in many flavors. They exist for many purposes. Communities oriented to the fullness of the banquet for all are communities of transformation. They feast at Christ's table and become what they eat, food for the world. In communities of transformation, people "are expected and supported to be about the business of new life."[44] We journey together. Following Barbara Brown Taylor's analysis, communities of transformation do not "operate like clinics, where sin-sick patients receive sympathetic care for the disease they all share." In such a community, "no one expects anyone to be fully cured . . . [and] no one is responsible because everyone is."[45] New life is not the agenda. At the same time, communities of transformation do not "operate like courts, where both sins and sinners are named out loud, along with punishments appropriate to their crimes. On the whole, the sinners identified by this full-fault theology tend to be people who do not belong to the fold."[46] Restorative justice requires that all gather around the table. Neither of these kinds of communities can foster the repentance that is transformative, that opens to the fullness of God's future. In contrast to "the church-as-clinic, repentance will not make peace with sin. It calls individuals to take responsibility for what is wrong with the world—beginning with what is wrong with them—and to join with other people who are dedicated to turning things around."[47] The repentance of communities of transformation also contrasts with that of communities that operate more like courtrooms, because "repentance is not interested in singling out scapegoats and punishing them. Instead it calls whole communities to engage in the work of repair and reconciliation without ever forgetting their own culpability for the way things are."[48] We are never completely victims without any resources, nor victors with all resources, answers, and assurance. We are broken people in a broken world, fed broken bread

---

development, but if she is not willing to serve others in love, then, in Pauline terminology, she will be using her freedom 'as an opportunity for the flesh' (Gal 5:13). Without being framed by the concern for the common good, freedom and development . . . degenerate into forms of alienation: by being free and developing myself I am alienating myself from my true nature as a being-in-communion." Miroslav Volf, *Work in the Spirit: Toward a Theology of Work* (New York: Oxford University Press, 1991) 186.

[44] Taylor, *Speaking of Sin*, 77.

[45] Ibid., 76.

[46] Ibid.

[47] Ibid., 77.

[48] Ibid.

for the wholeness of the web of life. We are given all the resources we need to play our part in a history that is much bigger and more varied than we can comprehend or imagine.

Although communities of transformation actively resist the havoc of the powers and principalities of our times, they are *not* primarily communities of resistance. They provide support and comfort in the face of injustice, sin, and suffering, but they are not safe, secure enclaves that are "largely protected from the material uncertainties, the political struggles, the moral ambiguities, and especially the spiritual chaos of [our] time."[49] Nor are they about purity or perfection with their attendant attempts to remove all the unjust, sinful, and wounded.[50] Rather, communities of transformation enter deeply into the dynamics of our culture with all of its manifold varieties of victimization, deprivation, and devastation.[51] Communities of transformation accept the radical risk of the gospel and go *into* rather than retreat from the turbulent waters of our times. They go not because they have the answers, but because God has called them there. Communities of transformation are called "to participate humbly and fragilely in the darkness, to experience it as their own without losing heart."[52] In the midst, they witness steadfastly to the hope of our faith in solidarity with all the creatures of creation, our kin.

It is from this place of deep engagement that communities of transformation invite repentance and participation in the journey of the banquet. They call, remind, teach, and inspire people to turn toward and live into the fullness of God's future. There, God's purpose and love for creation is heard in all its hopefulness, challenge, and promise. Communities of transformation are active agents of forgiveness. They are about healing the past and creating possibilities. They are fully engaged in making all that is possible of the present moment's choices. Communities of transformation are places where God's grace is tangible in all the particularities of our time and space.

Yet communities of transformation are also always flawed, marked by sin, and filled with sinners. They are full reflections of the world of

---

[49] Sandra M. Schneiders, *Finding the Treasure: Locating Catholic Religious Life in a New Ecclesial and Cultural Context* (Mahwah, N.J.: Paulist Press, 2000) 324.

[50] The danger of self-righteousness is acute for these types of communities.

[51] Schneiders, *Finding the Treasure*, 324.

[52] Ibid., 327.

which we are a part. Being a part of the "vast and mighty stream" that is God's justice is not just a public agenda that happens out there, for them. As the women's movement of the 1960s claimed, the personal is political, and the political and economic decisions made in the corridors of power in government and corporate institutions have very personal implications. The work of justice is about incarnating, putting flesh and blood, words and touch, to God's love so that our relationships are just, right, and true. All our relationships: human and nonhuman, private and public, past, future, and right here in the present, are open to reformation. There are no places of sanctuary in our lives, places that are always removed or completely separate from the struggles, joys, and hopes of the work of God's justice. In all our relationships, from the most intimate to the most public, there are moments of grace when we experience the movement of the Spirit releasing, healing, liberating, inspiring, encouraging the flourishing of life abundant for all. Communities of transformation have no privileged claim on the Spirit, nor access to a blueprint for social or personal transformation, nor any particular immunity from the brokenness, distortion, and violence of human relating. Rather, communities of transformation are people committed to the journey of the banquet together. Attentive to cries from any corner of God's beloved creation, open always to the call to repentance and engaged in the work of forgiveness both individually and collectively as a community, they work to discern the Spirit and move in that direction. Just as surely the work of justice is part of the spiritual journey, so also it involves the hard work of community: being a part of, building, sustaining, forming and re-forming groups of people oriented to life in its fullness for all.

Station 10 Litany: "Let Justice Roll Down like Water"

Voices 1: For your justice pouring as a mighty river from your heart,
    All: **We thank you.**
           You are the center of our lives, our light and our hope.
Voices 2: Bathed in your grace, fed with the always enough-ness of
           your love,
    All: **We commit ourselves in thanksgiving**
           To address the hungers of your world for the fullness of
           the banquet.

        [pause]

Voices 1: For all who speak the truth in love,
           all who open our eyes, ears, and minds,
           to the cries of your people and your beloved creation;
Voices 2: For all who work in and outside the structures of power
           to create conditions for peace, the just sharing of the
               earth's resources, and
           healthy relationships with each other and creation.
    All: **For all who call us to the banquet, we give you thanks.**

    One: With our reason intact and eyes wide open,
           We face the staggering breadth and depth of suffering in
               our world;
    All: **Give us the compassion and skill, the resilience and**
           courage,
           To be part of communities who incarnate your
           transforming power.

    One: Give us your grace:
Voices 1: To drop the stones in our hands; and
           to take our place in the community of life,
           neither too grand nor too small a place;
Voices 2: To welcome the companions you send to us;
           to discern the degrees of freedom you give,
           and choose the path of abundant life for all.

One: We pray for your mercy,
           for all those times when we swim against the current of
              your heart:

Voices 1:   when we turn away from the anguish of your beloved
              creation,
           when we let the big picture overshadow the near, small,
              and local;

Voices 2:   when we sacrifice the well-being of the parts for the
              well-being of the whole,
           when our righteousness creates barriers rather than
              openings;

Voices 1:   when our structures, practices, and traditions blind us to
              you,
           when our despair or fear, exhaustion, anger, or willfulness
              deafen us to your voice;

Voices 2:   when the lures of security, personal gain, and comfort
              distract us from your path,
           when guilt, a sense of inadequacy, bitterness, or resent-
              ment separate us from you;

All: **Give us your grace**
        to turn and return, again and again, to You,
        to say yes to the new possibilities You offer each day,
        to come home to You.

All: **For You are the path of abundant life for all;**
Voices 1:   You create cosmos from chaos;
           The powers and principalities are nothing in your sight;
Voices 2:   You make the rough places a plain and turn famines into
              feasts;
           In You, all find their true place of dignity and worth;
All: **We sing of your glory,**
        O God of justice, O steadfast Lover;
        And praise your power forever and ever.

Visual focus: A line in the sand with stones.

Station 11

"Abide in Me, As I Abide in You"

*And this is my prayer, that your love may overflow more and more
with knowledge and full insight to help you to determine what is
best, so that in the day of Christ you may be pure and blameless,
having produced the harvest of righteousness that comes through
Jesus Christ for the glory and praise of God.*

—Philippians 1:9-11

The home of all of God's beloved creation is the heart of the Holy. The
kitchen of the banquet is at the center of this home. Like all kitchens,
people are drawn there. It is a place of creativity, sustenance, warmth,
and community. The energy of the hearth or stove of this kitchen of
the banquet inspires, sets the tone, refreshes, nurtures, and ultimately
shapes all those on the journey of the banquet.

The journey of the banquet is filled with danger. Walking, individually
and collectively, the path of abundant life for all is often a strenuous
hike. Transforming our relationships and the institutional structures of
our life together to fully reflect God's justice is an unceasing project.
In the midst of such work, it is easy for our commitment and joy to
shrivel in the face of opposition, defeats, and frustrations. Our vision
can diminish to the scale of our capacity or get clouded by the webs of
pretense, delusion, and sugar-coated lies spun to preserve "the way
things are." Our energy can get diverted to other agendas. Our communities of transformation can implode or explode and become destructive of life and wholeness. We can wake up to find that our love
and compassion have become duty and burden. The hard work of the

199

banquet is fed by deep living communion with the Holy. "Only a life of ever deepening and faithful contemplation can keep the prophet attuned to the Divine."[1] Time spent in the kitchen of the banquet sustains us in the struggles and joys of the journey. It is the Spirit who acts to heal the past as well as to stir up, disturb, crack open, and create ever-new avenues of action and possibility beyond our imagination. It is through the Spirit that all of creation is drawn into the circle of warmth that radiates from the hearth of the banquet.

VOICES OF THE TRADITION

Martha "welcomed Jesus into her home." For all who work in the fields and kitchens of the banquet, the account of Martha's hospitality is salutary. This account follows directly after the parable of the good Samaritan which concludes with Jesus' injunction: "Go and do likewise" (Luke 10:37). As there is no scarcity of those in need, the work of caring for our neighbor is never finished. There is always more to "go and do."

> Now as they went on their way, [Jesus] entered a certain village, where a woman named Martha welcomed him into her home. She had a sister named Mary, who sat at the Lord's feet and listened to what he was saying. But Martha was distracted by her many tasks; so she came to him and asked, "Lord, do you not care that my sister has left me to do all the work by myself? Tell her then to help me." But the Lord answered her, "Martha, Martha, you are worried and distracted by many things; there is need of only one thing. Mary has chosen the better part, which will not be taken away from her" (Luke 10:38-42).

There is a time for everyone to sit at the table of the banquet and be fed. There is a time "to go and do," and a time to deepen our relationship with the Host of the banquet. Contemplation, real time spent listening to the Host, transforms service into gift-giving, anxiety and "distraction by many things" into a steady, focused joy. "I do not call you servants any longer, because the servant does not know what the master is doing; but I have called you friends, because I have made

---

[1] Sandra M. Schneiders, *Finding the Treasure: Locating Catholic Religious Life in a New Ecclesial and Cultural Context* (Mahwah, N.J.: Paulist Press, 2000) 323.

known to you everything that I have heard from my Father" (John 15:15). We are invited to be friends not servants. We are invited to know the master chef of the banquet. To do that we must spend real time at the hearth "listening to what he says."

At another dinner table, Martha is again serving and Mary again attends to the one who is the Host of the banquet.

> They gave a dinner for [Jesus]. Martha served and Lazarus was one of those at the table with him. Mary took a pound of costly perfume made of pure nard, anointed Jesus' feet, and wiped them with her hair. The house was filled with the fragrance of the perfume. But Judas Iscariot, one of his disciples (the one who was about to betray him), said, "Why was this perfume not sold for three hundred denarii and the money given to the poor?" (He said this not because he cared about the poor, but because he was a thief; he kept the common purse and used to steal what was put into it.) Jesus said, "Leave her alone. She bought it so that she might keep it for the day of my burial. You always have the poor with you, but you do not always have me" (John 12:2-8).

Mary's attention fills the whole house with the atmosphere of gracious pleasure, beauty, and intimacy. This time it is Judas who is distracted by many things. He translates the extravagant generosity of Mary's attention into financial terms and cannot smell the scent of transformation. He understands only scarcity, cannot draw near to the source of abundant life, and so excludes himself from the fullness of the table. What he sees as contradiction, love for Jesus and love for the poor, is actually complementary.[2] For the depth of our connection with the overflowing generosity of the Sacred is directly related to our capacity to be generous.

Another banquet and another kind of distraction lie at the heart of the parable of the two brothers: the prodigal son and the faithful son. The prodigal son, having "come to himself," repents of his profligate ways and the squandering of all his "property in dissolute living," and returns home.

> But while he was still far off, his father saw him and was filled with compassion; he ran and put his arms around him and kissed him. Then

---

[2] Although, as has happened too often in history, love for a humanly made, non-authentic image of Jesus can be in contradiction to love for the poor.

the son said to him, "Father, I have sinned against heaven and before you; I am no longer worthy to be called your son." But the father said to his slaves, "Quickly, bring out a robe—the best one—and put it on him; put a ring on his finger and sandals on his feet. And get the fatted calf and kill it, and let us eat and celebrate; for this son of mine was dead and is alive again; he was lost and is found!" And they began to celebrate (Luke 15:20b-24).

The father's delight is palpable. His embrace, his hospitality is as extravagantly expansive as a prairie sky. The richness of the banquet is an expression of the father's free unconditional joy in his child's return.

This is just half of the story. The parable continues with the story of the other brother, the faithful, responsible son.

Now his elder son was in the field; and when he came and approached the house, he heard music and dancing. He called one of the slaves and asked what was going on. He replied, "Your brother has come, and your father has killed the fatted calf, because he has got him back safe and sound." Then he became angry and refused to go in. His father came out and began to plead with him. But he answered his father, "Listen! For all these years I have been working like a slave for you, and I have never disobeyed your command; yet you have never given me even a young goat so that I might celebrate with my friends. But when this son of yours came back, who has devoured your property with prostitutes, you killed the fatted calf for him!" Then the father said to him, "Son, you are always with me, and all that is mine is yours. But we had to celebrate and rejoice, because this brother of yours was dead and has come to life; he was lost and has been found" (Luke 15:25-32).

The expansive generosity of the father's love is constant. Again he goes out to meet his son where he is. Again his embrace is full: "you are always with me, and all that is mine is yours." Yet the brother, this wonderful, faithful son, is distracted by many things. In his distraction, he cannot hear his father and he refuses to go in to the celebration. He cannot participate in the joy of the banquet. How hard it is for a rich person (whatever the form of the riches) to enter the fullness of the banquet. "Indeed, it is easier for a camel to go through the eye of a needle than for someone who is rich to enter the kingdom of God" (Luke 18:25; parallels Mark 10:25; Matt 19:24). Why is that so?

Two sisters: Mary and Martha, two disciples: Mary and Judas, two brothers: the prodigal and the faithful, each separated from the other, each with different responses to the banquet. God's invitation stands, regardless, offered to all, always, unconditionally, with great joy:

> Abide in me as I abide in you. Just as the branch cannot bear fruit by it-self unless it abides in the vine, neither can you unless you abide in me. I am the vine, you are the branches. Those who abide in me and I in them bear much fruit, because apart from me you can do nothing. As the Father has loved me, so I have loved you; abide in my love. If you keep my commandments, you will abide in my love, just as I have kept my Father's commandments and abide in his love. I have said these things to you so that my joy may be in you, and that your joy may be complete. This is my commandment, that you love one another as I have loved you (John 15:4-5, 9-12).

We belong together: God and humans. We are of one being. Separated "we can do nothing." The sap, the life force, the nourishment that moves between us is love and joy.

> Beloved, let us love one another, because love is from God; everyone who loves is born of God and knows God. Whoever does not love does not know God, for God is love. No one has ever seen God; if we love one another, God lives in us, and his love is perfected in us. By this we know that we abide in him and he in us, because he has given us of his Spirit. God is love, and those who abide in love abide in God, and God abides in them (1 John 4:7-8, 12-13, 16b).

It is in love that we see, know, reflect, and dwell in God. Love is the fuel of the hearth of the banquet. We are invited to warm ourselves, to be transformed and sustained by the hearth's fire, and then to bear it, share it, let it grow and flourish.

Jesus, toward the end of his extended prayer of farewell with his disciples, deepens this invitation to abide in the Heart and Wisdom of the Universe. He prays:

> All mine are yours, and yours are mine; and I have been glorified in them. And now I am no longer in the world, but they are in the world, and I am coming to you. Holy Father, protect them in your name that you have given me, so that they may be one, as we are one. I ask not only on behalf of these, but also on behalf of those who will believe in me through their word, that they may all be one. As you, Father, are in me and I am in you, may they also be in us, so that the world may believe

that you have sent me. The glory that you have given me I have given
them, so that they may be one, as we are one, I in them and you in me,
that they may become completely one, so that the world may know that
you have sent me and have loved them even as you have loved me (John
17:10-11, 20-23).

Then Jesus' disciples were gathered around a table just before his
crucifixion and now we are scattered around the globe speaking every
language but still gathering around his table. Jesus' prayer, then and
now, is that his disciples "may be one, as we are one," in love, in God's
protection, to God's glory.

From the totalitarian option of the tower of Babel to the mystery of
Pentecost, we have been bewildered in our understanding of this "oneness." Not surprisingly, our tradition has many ways of describing this
oneness. One fundamental approach is Trinitarian, although, ironically,
it has caused deep dissension in the Church throughout the ages as
well as considerable confusion for those looking in. In this approach,
the template for our relationships with each other and with God is
Christ's relationship with his "Abba": "As you, Father, are in me and I
am in you, may they also be in us" (John 17:21). Through the centuries,
theologians have struggled to apprehend this mystery of Christ's relationship with his "Abba." In all the theological argumentation, one
point of agreement is that the oneness of the Holy is differentiated. It
is not the oneness of fusion or sameness. It includes differences. Contemporary theologian Catherine LaCugna borrows a Greek word,
perichoresis, to describe the relationship among the persons of the
Trinity: Father, Son, and Spirit. Its translation is "being-in-one-another,
permeation without confusion," union without absorption, a communion based on mutuality and interdependence.[3] We are invited into this
way of relating with the Holy. Some have turned to analogies to image
this relationship:[4] as the light of more than one lamp or perfume
sprayed into the air mingles; as every physical object can exist in three

[3] Catherine Mowry LaCugna, *God for Us: The Trinity and Christian Life* (New
York: HarperCollins, 1991) 270–2, 275, 277. Also see Jurgen Moltmann, *God in Creation: An Ecological Doctrine of Creation* (London: SCM Press, 1985) 358–62.

[4] Other theologians have stressed the visible work of the Trinity in our salvation history as described in the condensed theological language of the early Christian community: 2 Cor 13:13; 1 John 4:9-16; Rom 1:1-7; Eph 1:3-14; and the earliest versions
of the creeds to come: 1 Cor 15:3-7; Phil 2:6-11; 1 Tim 3:16; 1 Pet 3:18-22.

very different states: liquid, solid, and gas; or as source-stream-river, or root-trunk-branch are connected; or as in a divine dance; as the Godhead is and so we are invited to relate with God.[5] Each of these analogies are images of oneness which includes difference. However we come to understand it, through Christ in the Spirit, we are invited to participate in and abide in this mystery of the life of God in all its fullness.[6]

In fact, just as Jesus is son, so we too in Christ become daughters and sons of God. As God sent Jesus into creation to be one with us, so Christ brings us into the Holy as God's adopted children. In a world in which one's identity and possibilities are defined by family, being part of God's family, bearing God's name as a surname, carries even more meaning than in our culture of self-made or self-defined people. "But to all who received him, who believed in his name, he gave power to become children of God, who were born, not of blood or of the will of the flesh or of the will of man, but of God" (John 1:12-13). Just as Martha welcomed Jesus into her home, we welcome Christ into our homes. In that welcome, through our believing, we become "children of God." Blood politics and willpower are not the path of faith. The Spirit comes to meet us while we are still far off. We need only respond with a "yes."

> For all who are led by the Spirit of God are children of God. For you did not receive a spirit of slavery to fall back into fear, but you have received a spirit of adoption. When we cry, "Abba! Father!" it is that very Spirit bearing witness with our spirit that we are children of God, and if children, then heirs, heirs of God and joint heirs with Christ—if, in fact, we suffer with him so that we may also be glorified with him (Rom 8:14-17).[7]

Family is not only about belonging, it is also about property inheritance and legacies. Led by the Spirit, we come into the wealth of Christ. We too can hear: This is my beloved son, my beloved daughter, in whom I am well pleased (Matt 3:17; parallels: Mark 1:11; Luke 3:22). We too can know God's embrace. And not just us individually, but indeed all of creation is invited into this communion (Rom 8:20-23).

[5] LaCugna, *God for Us*, 275, 277.
[6] See Eph 3:16-19.
[7] See also Gal 3:26; 4:4-7; Eph 2:5.

Our Hebrew ancestors used different imagery for the sense of intimacy or communion with the Holy. One understanding was of being at table and sharing food with God.

> Moses took the blood and dashed it on the people, and said, "See the blood of the covenant that the LORD has made with you in accordance with all these words." Then Moses and Aaron, Nadab, and Abihu, and seventy of the elders of Israel went up, and they saw the God of Israel. Under his feet there was something like a pavement of sapphire stone, like the very heaven for clearness. God did not lay his hand on the chief men of the people of Israel; also they beheld God, and they ate and drank (Exod 24:8-11).[8]

There is the more ambiguous account of Abraham and Sarah's three visitors who herald the arrival of Isaac, the child of God's promise of blessing for all nations.[9]

> The LORD appeared to Abraham by the oaks of Mamre, as he sat at the entrance of his tent in the heat of the day. He looked up and saw three men standing near him. When he saw them, he ran from the tent entrance to meet them, and bowed down to the ground. He said, "My lord, if I find favor with you, do not pass by your servant. Let a little water be brought, and wash your feet, and rest yourselves under the tree. Let me bring a little bread, that you may refresh yourselves, and after that you may pass on—since you have come to your servant." So they said, "Do as you have said." And Abraham hastened into the tent to Sarah, and said, "Make ready quickly three measures of choice flour, knead it, and make cakes." Abraham ran to the herd, and took a calf, tender and good, and gave it to the servant, who hastened to prepare it. Then he took curds and milk and the calf that he had prepared, and set it before them; and he stood by them under the tree while they ate (Gen 18:1-8).

It is no surprise that part of the dictation of the extraordinary figure who is "like the Son of Man" in Revelation includes the invitation to just such a feast: "Listen! I am standing at the door, knocking; if you hear my voice and open the door, I will come in to you and eat with you, and you with me" (Rev 3:20). This is the invitation of the banquet: the invitation to share table with the Holy.

[8] With a less dramatic parallel: Exod 18:12.
[9] See Station 9.

Moses lived his life in intimate dialogue with God. The account of Moses bringing the commandments of God to the people for the second time gives a sense of this relationship:

> Moses came down from Mount Sinai. As he came down from the mountain with the two tablets of the covenant in his hand, Moses did not know that the skin of his face shone because he had been talking with God. When Aaron and all the Israelites saw Moses, the skin of his face was shining, and they were afraid to come near him. But Moses called to them; and Aaron and all the leaders of the congregation returned to him, and Moses spoke with them. Afterward all the Israelites came near, and he gave them in commandment all that the LORD had spoken with him on Mount Sinai. When Moses had finished speaking with them, he put a veil on his face; but whenever Moses went in before the LORD to speak with him, he would take the veil off, until he came out; and when he came out, and told the Israelites what he had been commanded, the Israelites would see the face of Moses, that the skin of his face was shining; and Moses would put the veil on his face again, until he went in to speak with him (Exod 34:29-35).

The tremendous energy of life lived in conversation with God is reflected in the radiance of Moses' face for all to see. In Christ, we too are invited to become "children of light." Like Moses we are called to radiate with the brilliance of the light in our midst.[10]

The covenant codes were the guidelines or manual for the relationship of God's people with God. Like all codes, it was easy to reify them. What was intended to sing of relationship became instead a dry dusty distant object of devotion. In contrast, the prophets speak to renew a living, intimate connection.

> Surely, this commandment that I am commanding you today is not too hard for you, nor is it too far away. It is not in heaven, that you should say, "Who will go up to heaven for us, and get it for us so that we may hear it and observe it?" Neither is it beyond the sea, that you should say, "Who will cross to the other side of the sea for us, and get it for us so that we may hear it and observe it?" No, the word is very near to you; it is in your mouth and in your heart for you to observe (Deut 30:11-14).[11]

[10] See Matt 5:15-16; John 12:36; Phil 2:14-15; Eph 5:8; 1 Thess 5:5.
[11] Psalm 139 echoes this closeness from a different perspective.

The commandments are to be as our heartbeat, our breath, or words forming in our mouths. For Jeremiah the covenant is not an external phenomenon but one deeply embedded in the structure of our hearts:

> But this is the covenant that I will make with the house of Israel after those days, says the LORD: I will put my law within them, and I will write it on their hearts; and I will be their God, and they shall be my people. No longer shall they teach one another, or say to each other, "Know the LORD," for they shall all know me, from the least of them to the greatest, says the LORD (Jer 31:33-34a).[12]

The invitation is to know God. Hosea extends this knowing to the commitment and intimacy of marriage: "And I will take you for my wife forever; I will take you for my wife in righteousness and in justice, in steadfast love, and in mercy. I will take you for my wife in faithfulness; and you shall know the LORD" (Hosea 2:19-20). It is a path to restore the essential unity and intimacy of the garden when God walked "in the garden at the time of the evening breeze" and "the man and his wife were both naked and were not ashamed" (Gen 3:8; 2:25).

Finally, in the trajectory of the story between the original garden and the final city, the new Jerusalem, there are the architectural images of God's dwelling place or God's house. The ark of the covenant and later the temple or "house of the Lord" symbolized God's presence with the people and the longing of the people "to dwell in the house of the Lord forever" (Ps 23:6). Yet even Solomon, the builder of the first temple, knew the inadequacy of such imagery: "But will God indeed dwell on the earth? Even heaven and the highest heaven cannot contain you, much less this house that I have built!" (1 Kgs 8:27). But the psalmists still sing their longing:

> One thing I asked of the LORD,
>   that will I seek after:
> to live in the house of the LORD
>   all the days of my life,
> to behold the beauty of the LORD,
>   and to inquire in his temple (Ps 27:4).

---

[12] See also Ezek 11:19-20.

Although the Temple in Jerusalem became a clear focus or address for the Holy, the tradition is clear that God is simultaneously beyond any particular space or time and connected in love to every particular:

> For thus says the high and lofty one
>   who inhabits eternity, whose name is Holy:
> I dwell in the high and holy place,
>   and also with those who are contrite and humble in spirit,
> to revive the spirit of the humble,
>   and to revive the heart of the contrite (Isa 57:15).

The prophets are relentless in their insistence that dwelling with God is contingent on living by the commandments:

> Thus says the LORD of hosts, the God of Israel: Amend your ways and your doings, and let me dwell with you in this place. Do not trust in these deceptive words: "This is the temple of the LORD, the temple of the LORD, the temple of the LORD."
>   For if you truly amend your ways and your doings, if you truly act justly one with another, if you do not oppress the alien, the orphan, and the widow, or shed innocent blood in this place, and if you do not go after other gods to your own hurt, then I will dwell with you in this place, in the land that I gave of old to your ancestors forever and ever (Jer 7:3-7).

Temple devotional practices are not different from the practices of justice, for God is a God of justice and steadfast love. For the prophets the dwelling of God "in this place" is all about right relationships as described in the covenant codes.

For Paul, the extraordinary gift of the gospel is that "God proves his love for us in that while we still were sinners Christ died for us" (Rom 5:8). And not just sinners; he adds: "if while we were enemies, we were reconciled to God through the death of his Son, much more surely, having been reconciled, will we be saved by his life" (Rom 5:10). It is not that the covenant codes are superseded in the gospel.[13] They are still operative. Rather, through Christ, we know that the love of God in the form of God's grace active in our lives enables their fulfillment. God comes to us in Christ unbidden, unearned, as pure unconditional

---

[13] See Station 10 and Jesus' discussion of fulfillment of the Law.

gift. The journey starts in love, blessing, and affirmation. It is only for us to turn, to say yes. In the Spirit we are given the grace to turn and become "members of God's household."

> So then you are no longer strangers and aliens, but you are citizens with the saints and also members of the household of God, built upon the foundation of the apostles and prophets, with Christ Jesus himself as the cornerstone. In him the whole structure is joined together and grows into a holy temple in the Lord; in whom you also are built together spiritually into a dwelling place for God (Eph 2:19-22).

Through Christ in the Spirit we become "a dwelling place for God." We become God's temple.[14] "Do you not know that you are God's temple and that God's Spirit dwells in you?" (1 Cor 3:16). In all our physicality, we dwell with the Holy and the Holy with us: "Do you not know that your body is a temple of the Holy Spirit within you, which you have from God, and that you are not your own?" (1 Cor 6:19). It is out of God's unconditional love for this God's beloved creation that we are invited to abide in God. We are invited to be part of God's family, God's house.

There in its kitchen, at the hearth of God's house, we are formed and re-formed by the Spirit, until collectively the rivers of life flowing out from the temple of Ezekiel's vision become the river that flows through the center of the New Jerusalem of John's vision.[15]

> On the banks, on both sides of the river, there will grow all kinds of trees for food. Their leaves will not wither nor their fruit fail, but they will bear fresh fruit every month, because the water for them flows from the sanctuary. Their fruit will be for food, and their leaves for healing (Ezek 47:12).

Intimacy with the Holy brings life in all its fullness for all. "Everything will live where the river goes" (Ezek 47:9b).[16] There will be good food for the flourishing of all of creation.

---

[14] Paul also elaborates this idea as "the body of Christ": Eph 4:13-16 and 1 Cor 12. See also Station 6.

[15] See Rev 22:1-2 and Station 12.

[16] See also Station 10.

SPIRITUAL CHALLENGE:
SANCTIFICATION

Simply saying it is so does not make it so. We must actually set out on the journey. The invitation is open. Then in trust that all the necessary grace will be provided, we take the steps.[17] Though Sandra Schneiders writes of those in religious orders, the same is true for any on the journey of the banquet:

> However long the struggle [and it may well outlast one's own life], however deep the darkness, however violent the engagement, the Religious continues to cling, like Jacob, to a God who is often invisible but who alone can offer the blessing we crave. This perseverance and fidelity are not based on an expectation of solutions or victory but on a naked faith and love born of contemplative intimacy with God in prayer.[18]

This journey into intimacy with God, "the blessing we crave," has variously been called: sanctification, divinization *(theosis)*, or deification. As Christ came from God in the Spirit to the full life of a day-six creature, so we in all our humanness are drawn through Christ in the power of Spirit into the fullness of God.[19] The journey of sanctification is the inverse of the journey of incarnation: God's self-communication to us in love in Christ and God's drawing us in the power of the Spirit into God's very heart. In the process we become fully embodied spirits and inspired bodies. We approach the oneness that Christ knew with his "Abba." This journey of sanctification is fueled by grace and lived with "naked faith and love born of contemplative intimacy with God in prayer."

Given the violent and virtually catastrophic trajectory of humanity's will to power and glory, talk of sanctification, divinization, or deification can seem ill-advised. Another objection to such concepts is that they reduce the differentiation between God and creation, and lessen the transcendence, the more-than-anything-human, that God is always and forever. Perhaps, however, one of the root problems of the industrial age is that God was sent so far away, both intellectually and theologically, that we stepped into the God-sized hole that was left with

[17] 1 Cor 10:13, among many.
[18] Schneiders, *Finding the Treasure*, 327.
[19] See John 1:14-16; Eph 1:22-23; 3:19; Col 2:9-10.

disastrous consequences to ourselves and creation.[20] It is only with the cross as the image of God's power and presence with us that talk of sanctification can be life-giving rather than death-promoting. God's power is that of infinite love broken and poured out for all. Sanctification is a journey into a radically different kind of power and glory than our culture knows; one which inverts our understanding of power and glory.

> Consider your own call, brothers and sisters: not many of you were wise by human standards, not many were powerful, not many were of noble birth. But God chose what is foolish in the world to shame the wise; God chose what is weak in the world to shame the strong; God chose what is low and despised in the world, things that are not, to reduce to nothing things that are, so that no one might boast in the presence of God. He is the source of your life in Christ Jesus, who became for us wisdom from God, and righteousness and sanctification and redemption, in order that, as it is written, "Let the one who boasts, boast in the Lord" (1 Cor 1:26-31).

God's power is not ours. It cannot be possessed. It can only be given away. Even the aphorism "use it or lose it" must be qualified to "gift it or lose it." The path of sanctification is the path of the cross.

Sanctification, or our participation in the divine nature, is a process of transformation by the Spirit.[21] Moses spoke face-to-face with God, but then veiled the shining of his face after such conversations. So Paul writes:

> When one turns to the Lord, the veil is removed. Now the Lord is the Spirit, and where the Spirit of the Lord is, there is freedom. And all of us, with unveiled faces, seeing the glory of the Lord as though reflected in a mirror, are being transformed into the same image from one degree of glory to another; for this comes from the Lord, the Spirit (2 Cor 3:16-18).

The journey of sanctification is an emptying or making room for the movement of the Spirit in and through us that we might be perfect reflections of God's glory.

---

[20] We usurp God's rightful place and/or turn God into a patriarchal, judgmental, dependency-inducing dominating reality that has been our experience of power.

[21] 2 Pet 1:4.

> For it is the God who said, "Let light shine out of darkness," who has shone in our hearts to give the light of the knowledge of the glory of God in the face of Jesus Christ. But we have this treasure in clay jars, so that it may be made clear that this extraordinary power belongs to God and does not come from us (2 Cor 4:6-7).

Just as God created light in that first day of creation, so our earthiness is being created anew to fully incarnate the image of God. Sanctification is the work of the new creation.

Paul describes this process as the enlightenment of the eyes of our hearts through a spirit of wisdom or revelation as we come to know Christ (Eph 1:17-18a), or more simply "the renewing of our minds": "Do not be conformed to this world, but be transformed by the renewing of your minds, so that you may discern what is the will of God—what is good and acceptable and perfect" (Rom 12:2). Sanctification then is the transformation that allows us to discern and align our wills with the will of God, so that our deepest desiring is for God. As Jesus said to his disciples who had gone to buy food while he talked with the Samaritan woman at Jacob's well: "My food is to do the will of him who sent me and to complete his work" (John 4:34). And so we are taught to pray: "Your will be done, / on earth as it is in heaven" (Matt 6:10).

Lest anyone think that this transformation comes as effortlessly as the Lord's Prayer to our lips, there is Jesus' prayer in Gethsemane as he prepared for his death: "Father, if you are willing, remove this cup from me; yet, not my will but yours be done" (Luke 22:42; parallels Matt 26:39, 42; Mark 14:36; and John in another context: 5:30; 6:38). Such "perseverance and fidelity is [truly] based . . . on a naked faith and love born of contemplative intimacy with God in prayer."[22] Time spent communing with God and opening to the wonder and love that graces our world is at the heart of the journey of sanctification. It is there that we learn to distinguish God's Spirit from all the spirits of our age. It is there that drop by drop, decision by decision, day by day, the Spirit teaches us the will of God and gives us the grace to melt, surrender, join, move more completely in that direction. It is the Christ who invites us to be one with the Source of all life, the One who spins the interconnections of life, love, beauty, truth, and justice in God's beloved universe. It is the Spirit at work in us that allows us to will one

---

[22] Schneiders, *Finding the Treasure*, 327 and above; see also Station 4.

thing: that God's will be done here on earth in the midst of all the principalities and powers of our age.

The nub of the challenge lies in the considerable ambiguity in our understandings of will. Gerald May highlights the ambiguity in his use of the categories of willingness and willfulness. To be one with or abide in the Holy requires a willingness to act with the Spirit that contrasts with a willful assertion of our own will in a separate direction from, ignoring, or denying the movement of the Spirit.[23] The question is "whether we engage the deepest levels of our lives in willing or in willful ways."[24] This is not, however, about specific situations, for certainly there is much that diminishes fullness of life for all that must be actively resisted. Rather,

> Willingness implies a surrendering of one's self-separateness, an entering-into, an immersion in the deepest processes of life itself. It is a realization that one already is a part of some ultimate cosmic process and it is a commitment to participation in that process. In contrast, willfulness is the setting of oneself apart from the fundamental essence of life in an attempt to master, direct, control, or otherwise manipulate existence. More simply, willingness is saying yes to the mystery of being alive in each moment. Willfulness is saying no, or perhaps more commonly, "yes, but. . . ."[25]

Willingness to participate as one part of the "ultimate cosmic process" of which we are not the author is the commitment of faith. It is the fundamental dynamic of life in God. It is not the renunciation, surrender, or elimination of our wills per se. They are God's good gift given to resist what is destructive and choose what is good. Our willingness to be one with the Holy is, however, all about the direction of our will. It is not the denial of freedom; it is the door to extraordinary freedom. Talk of obedience in this regard is in fact fraught with danger. It leaves

[23] For the application of these distinctions to the contemplative prayer tradition see Cynthia Bourgeault, "Centering Prayer as Radical Consent," *Sewanee Theological Review* 40:1 (1996) 46–54. For a thoughtful reflection of the tension between these concepts and those of the women's movement which emphasize autonomy, see Carol Lee Flinders, *At the Root of This Longing: Reconciling a Spiritual Hunger and a Feminist Thirst* (New York: HarperCollins, 1999) esp. ch. 6.

[24] Gerald May, *Will and Spirit: A Contemplative Psychology* (San Francisco: Harper and Row, 1982) 4–6.

[25] Ibid.

open the door to mastery: self-mastery, mastery over others, and the cultivation of our willfulness. Rather, the journey of sanctification is about the union of will and Spirit.[26] These moments of union are moments of grace that, added together, can become a life of grace, a reflection of the pure glory of God.

After centuries of holiness projects built on a spirit/body dualism, talk of abiding with God or the journey of sanctification, divinization, or deification may sound like a project of withdrawal rather than engagement with the world. Actually, it frees and deepens the "eyes of our hearts" to see the fullness of life God intended for all of creation and to labor for its birth.[27] Just as Christ became fully human in the mystery of the incarnation, so we with all creation, with our bodies not in spite of them, are oriented toward the full "freedom of the glory of the children of God" (Rom 8:21).

What is that glory? "The glory of God is every creature fully alive."[28] The path of sanctification is the path of this glory.[29] It is what Catherine LaCugna has called our "vocation to glory." For "we were created for the purpose of glorifying God by living in right relationship, by living as Jesus Christ did, by becoming holy through the power of the Spirit of God, by existing as persons in communion with God and every other creature."[30] Yet over time, as the divide deepened between spiritual and material matters in our culture, this vocation to glory was understood as a spiritual project separate from the economic and scientific projects, public and private, that sustain our material lives.[31] That was never the intent. Followers of Christ have always been "enjoined to

---

[26] Much of May's work elaborates the psychological aspects of this journey.

[27] Gal 4:19; John 16:19-22; Rom 8:20-23.

[28] Sallie McFague, *Life Abundant: Rethinking Theology and Economy for a Planet in Peril* (Minneapolis: Fortress Press, 2001) 128; quoting Ireneaus, third century C.E.

[29] Isa 43:7; Phil 1:9-11; Eph 1:11-14; 3:16-21; 1 Cor 10:31; 2 Cor 3:15-18; John 17:22; Rom 5:1-2.

[30] Earlier she describes this process as deification: "The vocation of every human being is to be deified by the Spirit of God, to become holy, to become more and more conformed to Christ, in order to give glory and honor to God"; or, more simply: "to be redeemed means to be caught up in Christ, caught up in the path of glory." LaCugna, *God for Us*, 337, 338, 342.

[31] The resources developed to support these projects over the centuries: all the different spiritual disciplines and guides as well as the bodies of knowledge developed in ethics, medicine, ecology, for instance, have also been separated into very separate domains of specialization.

give glory to God not only in prayer but with our whole lives."[32] All our relationships, all our dreams, memories, ideas, creations and life projects are to be seen in the light of the glory of God as part of our vocation to glory.[33] This is the journey of sanctification, our invitation to participate in the life of God in history for God's glory and honor.

SPIRITUAL PRACTICE: PRAISE

Praise is offering with all of ourselves all glory and honor to God. It is no coincidence that the presentation of our gifts of money, time, and talent is often accompanied by a doxology, a song of praise.[34] In praise we "remember Who owns the house,"[35] to whose house we belong, whose name we bear. With the eyes of our hearts enlightened, we see the glory of God permeating all of creation and respond in awe, wonder, and praise. In silence or song, with tears or laughter, on our knees or swirling in dance, we offer our "yes," our "alleluia," our "amen" to God, the Source of all that is, the Breath of Life, the path of abundant life for all. Indeed, "God is made our God when creation and humanity render praise to God."[36]

This seemingly simple movement of our spirits to praise is actually quite radical in its implications. Praise calls the powers and principalities of our day "to abdicate all pretensions to absoluteness" and acknowledge the true power at the heart of the universe. Praise "preserves the harmony of the whole by preventing usurpation of the whole by its parts. Praise is the ecological principle of divinity whereby every creature is subordinated to its organic relationship with the Creator. Praise is the cure for the apostasy of the Powers."[37] Regardless of the particu-

---

[32] LaCugna, *God for Us*, 342.

[33] In fact, "traditionally, the doctrine of sanctification has provided the context for theological reflection on the problem of work." Miroslav Volf, *Work in the Spirit: Toward a Theology of Work* (New York: Oxford University Press, 1991) 71ff.

[34] In some traditions the bread and wine are presented by the congregation as symbols of the fruits of creation and their labor. Their subsequent consecration and distribution back to the assembly is an enactment of the process of sanctification.

[35] Walter Wink, *Engaging the Powers: Discernment and Resistance in a World of Domination* (Minneapolis: Fortress Press, 1992) 160.

[36] LaCugna, *God for Us*, 338.

[37] Wink, *Engaging the Powers*, 167.

lar manifestations of the powers and principalities, whether in multinational institutions, specific political situations, or the actions of individuals in localized roles, in praise we assert that they

> do not exist as ends in themselves, but for the humanizing [life-giving] purposes of God as revealed in Jesus. We do not have to relate them to God. They are already, by virtue of their creation, related to God. We simply have to remind them that they exist in and through and for God.[38]

In praise we reassert right relations in creation and breathe life into the journey of the banquet. In theological language then, it is possible to assert that, "since sin is the absence of praise, then salvation is the restoration of praise."[39] Praise allows us to see things in their full and true light and to commit ourselves to live in that light.

For our praise to be indeed to the glory of God, it is important to note that praise does not contradict the lament of Station 3. To participate in the life of God includes participation in both the delight and the pathos of the Holy. God is acknowledged and honored in our protests as well as our hymns of joy. Without expression of both delight in the right relatedness and blessings of creation as well as lament for its fractures, suffering, and destruction, we "end either in denial of self and reality for the sake of God or in self-indulgence which trivializes God into our therapist or whipping boy."[40] To bring all of ourselves to God includes both praise and lament. "Either of these alternatives, taken alone, precludes the kind of liveliness and honesty that properly belongs to this relation [between God and ourselves]."[41] Our praise is a free gift of ourselves to God. Our lament is for all that destroys or diminishes that freedom to truly see the glory of God shining in every corner of creation. Therefore, it is in praise that acknowledges lament that we anticipate "the freedom of the glory of the children of God," the fullness of the reign of God, the banquet, that time when "God's will, will be done on earth as in heaven," and we move in that direction.

---

[38] Ibid.

[39] LaCugna, *God for Us*, 343.

[40] Walter Brueggemann, "The Daily Voice of Faith: The Covenanted Self," *The Covenanted Self: Explorations in Law and Covenant* (Minneapolis: Fortress Press, 1999) 19.

[41] Ibid.

STATION 11 LITANY:
"ABIDE IN ME, AS I ABIDE IN YOU"

One: We give You thanks for our home in your heart,
For a permanent address;
Voices 1: May we always find our way home.

One: We give You thanks for our family name,
For our identity as a child of God: your son, your daughter;
Voices 2: May we always hear You when you call our name.
All: **We belong to You, You are our home,**
We give You thanks for the welcome of your embrace.

Voices 1: You are the center, we rest in You,
Everything else is derivative, subordinate, and partial.
In You, all find their fullness.
Voices 2: Your Spirit warms the hearth and
Irresistibly draws us into the creative, nourishing energy
of the kitchen of the banquet.
All: **We thank You for the depth of our life in You.**

Voices 1: We stand naked before the fire of your love,
Voices 2: Barefoot on holy ground.
Voices 1: Dissolve all our distractions and preoccupations,
Voices 2: Transform our lives to perfectly reflect your light,
All: **That your will be done on earth as in heaven,**
And the full fruits of intimacy with You be available for all.

One: Keep us from splitting apart what is woven together in
your Spirit;
All: **Teach us to move seamlessly between:**
Action and contemplation,
Silence and song,
Work and rest,
Gathering in and pouring out;
One: For in you all coheres;
All: **You are the music of the ages, and we are your dance**
partners.

One: Lost in wonder and awe, adoration and praise,
All creation cries: "Glory!"

Voices 1: We move in a tidal ebb and flow, from and to, your glory.
It is our origin and our destination.

Voices 2: We live in your grace, with your breath,
Part of the community of life of your beloved creation.

All: **We radiate your glory as creatures fully alive.
All praise, honor, and glory are Yours,
O Heart and Wisdom of the Universe.**

Visual Focus: A vine, tree, or plant with multiple branches.

Station 12

THE BANQUET

He also allured you out of distress
into a broad place where there was no constraint,
and what was set on your table was full of fatness.

—Job 36:16

The journey starts with the eating of "the fruit of the tree in the middle of the garden," and its destination is the banquet: "Then people will come from east and west, from north and south, and will eat in the kingdom of God" (Luke 13:29; parallel Matt 8:11). Or, as Jesus said in his Last Supper with his disciples: "I confer on you, just as my Father has conferred on me, a kingdom so that you may eat and drink at my table in my kingdom" (Luke 22:29-30a). Isaiah gives us a word picture of this banquet:

> On this mountain the LORD of hosts will make for all peoples
>   a feast of rich food, a feast of well-aged wines,
>   of rich food filled with marrow, of well-aged wines strained clear.
> And he will destroy on this mountain
>   the shroud that is cast over all peoples,
>   the sheet that is spread over all nations;
>   he will swallow up death forever.
> Then the Lord GOD will wipe away the tears from all faces,
>   and the disgrace of his people he will take away from all the earth,
>   for the LORD has spoken.

It will be said on that day,
> Lo, this is our God; we have waited for him, so that he might save
> us.
> This is the LORD for whom we have waited;
> let us be glad and rejoice in his salvation (Isa 25:6-9).

The banquet, a feast, a table gathering is the destination of our journey.

What is this banquet that lies at the heart of the reign of God? What is this feast that is the destination of our journey? How does this eating and drinking reconfigure the realities described in that first eating at the foot of "the tree in the middle of the garden"? We finished the twentieth century with more people fed and more people hungry than ever before in human history, and with the human capacity to heal and to destroy life on this planet precariously balanced. How does the light from this banquet table illuminate these realities that we face at the start of the twenty-first century?

VOICES OF THE TRADITION

Unlike the simplicity and clarity of a story with a beginning, middle and an end, God's creative activity cannot be so neatly summarized. Right in the middle of the story, talk of God's new creation begins. Ironically, this talk of the new creation begins in a time of endings, uncertainty, insecurity, and loss. The third part of Isaiah with its vision of God's creative activity in history was written out of Israel's Babylonian exile experience. In 587 B.C.E. Israel was conquered and forced to leave the Promised Land. "For ancient Israel, it was the end of privilege, certitude, domination, viable public institutions, [and] a sustaining social fabric. Not to overstate, it was the end of life with God which Israel had taken for granted."[1] Later in that century Babylon itself was conquered, and a remnant returned to Jerusalem and began the work of reconstruction. Isaiah's vision of God's agenda comes out of this time of radical dislocation and challenge.

---

[1] Walter Brueggemann, "Four Indispensable Conversations Among Exiles," *Deep Memory, Exuberant Hope: Contested Truth in a Post-Christian World* (Minneapolis: Fortress Press, 2000) 60.

For I am about to create new heavens
>and a new earth;
the former things shall not be remembered
>or come to mind.
But be glad and rejoice forever
>in what I am creating;
for I am about to create Jerusalem as a joy,
>and its people as a delight.
I will rejoice in Jerusalem,
>and delight in my people;
no more shall the sound of weeping be heard in it,
>or the cry of distress.
No more shall there be in it
>an infant that lives but a few days,
>or an old person who does not live out a lifetime;
for one who dies at a hundred years will be considered a youth,
>and one who falls short of a hundred will be considered accursed.
They shall build houses and inhabit them;
>they shall plant vineyards and eat their fruit.
They shall not build and another inhabit;
>they shall not plant and another eat;
for like the days of a tree shall the days of my people be,
>and my chosen shall long enjoy the work of their hands.
They shall not labor in vain,
>or bear children for calamity;
for they shall be offspring blessed by the LORD—
>and their descendants as well.
Before they call I will answer,
>while they are yet speaking I will hear.
The wolf and the lamb shall feed together,
>the lion shall eat straw like the ox;
>but the serpent—its food shall be dust!
They shall not hurt or destroy
>on all my holy mountain,
>>says the LORD (Isa 65:17-25).

God's new heaven and earth is filled with joy and delight. Intimacy with God is immediate. There will be no suffering or untimely death, no weeping or distress. Work will be redeemed for "people shall enjoy the work of their hands." Even the competitive relations of creation will be reordered and the possibility of destruction, discordance, and disease (represented by the snake) banished.[2] It is a new creation, a new Jerusalem and a new Jerusalem people, that God is creating.

In the midst of the Roman Empire's persecution of the new Christian communities, with time enough since Jesus' ministry to grapple with the historical implications of the kingdom he talked about so much, John writes his vision of God's creative activity in history. It is somehow fitting to end the Bible with an account of the new beginning:

> Then I saw a new heaven and a new earth; for the first heaven and the first earth had passed away, and the sea was no more. And I saw the holy city, the new Jerusalem, coming down out of heaven from God, prepared as a bride adorned for her husband. And I heard a loud voice from the throne saying,
>
>> "See, the home of God is among mortals.
>> He will dwell with them as their God;
>> they will be his peoples,
>> and God himself will be with them;
>> he will wipe every tear from their eyes.
>> Death will be no more;
>> mourning and crying and pain will be no more,
>> for the first things have passed away."
>
> And the one who was seated on the throne said, "See, I am making all things new" (Rev 21:1-5a).

Creation was not once long ago, but is open-ended and on a trajectory toward union with the Holy.

John continues with a detailed and grand description of the new Jerusalem as befits "the glory of God." After a description of its walls, gates, and foundations with their measurements and jewels, he notes that at the heart of the city:

> I saw no temple in the city, for its temple is the Lord God the Almighty and the Lamb. And the city has no need of sun or moon to shine on it, for the glory of God is its light, and its lamp is the Lamb. The nations will walk by its light, and the kings of the earth will bring their glory into

---

[2] In an earlier vision, during the time when Israel was facing the military might of the Assyrian Empire, Isaiah foresaw a time when military weapons would be converted into agricultural implements (Isa 2:4). This vision is echoed by Micah 4:3 and inverted by Joel 3:10 in his vision of the end times (see Station 13).

it. Its gates will never be shut by day—and there will be no night there. People will bring into it the glory and the honor of the nations. But nothing unclean will enter it, nor anyone who practices abomination or falsehood, but only those who are written in the Lamb's book of life (Rev 21:22-27).

The vision encompasses human history with talk of nations, kings, and people; religious history with the temple obviated by the full indwelling of God; and the cosmos itself with the night, sun, and moon replaced with the light of the Holy. The integrity of the relationship between matter and spirit, creation and creator is restored. Heaven and earth are married and "the home of God is among mortals."

> Then the angel showed me the river of the water of life, bright as crystal, flowing from the throne of God and of the Lamb through the middle of the street of the city. On either side of the river is the tree of life with its twelve kinds of fruit, producing its fruit each month; and the leaves of the tree are for the healing of the nations. Nothing accursed will be found there any more. But the throne of God and of the Lamb will be in it, and his servants will worship him; they will see his face, and his name will be on their foreheads (Rev 22:1-4).

Access to the tree of life growing on either side of the river of life is restored. As in Isaiah's vision, even the potential for destruction, discordance, and disease is banished. It is a vision of ever-renewable abundance, diversity, and "healing of the nations." The glory of God will be seen face-to-face. Praise, offering, and gift-giving will be the practice.

Our tradition is full of talk of newness. We are encouraged to sing, to see, to be named anew, to be new. Isaiah abounds with talk of the new:

> See, the former things have come to pass,
>   and new things I now declare;
> before they spring forth,
>   I tell you of them.
> Sing to the LORD a new song,
>   his praise from the end of the earth! (42:9-10).
> Do not remember the former things,
>   or consider the things of old.
> I am about to do a new thing;
>   now it springs forth, do you not perceive it? (43:18-19b).

You have heard; now see all this;
   and will you not declare it?
From this time forward I make you hear new things,
   hidden things that you have not known.
They are created now, not long ago;
   before today you have never heard of them,
   so that you could not say, "I already knew them."
You have never heard, you have never known,
   from of old your ear has not been opened (48:6-8a).
You shall be called by a new name
   that the mouth of the LORD will give (62:2b).

The Psalms are often "singing a new song to the Lord" (33:3; 40:3; 96:1; 98:1; 144:9; 149:1; with echoes in Rev 5:9; 14:3). There is talk of new covenants (Jer 31:31; 1 Cor 11:25; Heb 8:8ff.), new hearts and spirits (Ezek 11:19; 18:31; 36:26), new selves (Eph 4:24; Col 3:10), new names (Rev 2:17; 3:12), and Paul almost shouts: "So if anyone is in Christ, there is a new creation: everything old has passed away; see, everything has become new!" (2 Cor 5:17; see also Gal 6:15). What does it mean to acknowledge such a creative force in history?

With such talk of the new, it is easy to skip over the wisdom of Qoheleth's invitation to stop and consider what we mean by new:

What has been is what will be,
   and what has been done is what will be done;
   there is nothing new under the sun.
Is there a thing of which it is said,
   "See, this is new"?
It has already been,
   in the ages before us.
The people of long ago are not remembered,
   nor will there be any remembrance
of people yet to come
   by those who come after them (Eccl 1:9-11).

Is the "new" of which our tradition sings the same as the "new" that our culture so idolizes? Is it progress and/or wishful thinking writ large? Is newness simply a lack of memory, shallow roots, or a superficial understanding into the fundamental dynamics of life? T. S. Eliot writes:

We shall not cease from exploration
and the end of all our exploring
will be to arrive where we started
and know the place for the first time. . . .[3]

Does that knowing "for the first time" count as new knowing? Is history a spiral or a closed circle? Is there an arc or a direction to history? Is the Creator bound by the creation or free to create a new thing? How do we live open to the new, to what perhaps cannot be known, to an always remaining, reconfiguring question mark on the horizon, to a possibility beyond our imagining, predicting, and engineering? Are we open to a new thing?

Again, in the middle of the story, when the Romans had occupied the land, Jesus came teaching, healing, "proclaiming the good news of God, and saying, 'The time is fulfilled, and the kingdom of God has come near; repent, and believe in the good news'" (Mark 1:15; parallels Matt 4:17; Luke 4:43). The kingdom, the reign of God, is what Jesus taught and revealed in all he did. It was the purpose for which he was sent (Luke 4:43). It was the promise of Isaiah fulfilled:[4]

"The Spirit of the Lord is upon me,
    because he has anointed me to bring good news to the poor.
He has sent me to proclaim release to the captives
    and recovery of sight to the blind,
        to let the oppressed go free,
to proclaim the year of the Lord's favor."
And [Jesus] rolled up the scroll, gave it back to the attendant, and sat down. The eyes of all in the synagogue were fixed on him. Then he began to say to them, "Today this scripture has been fulfilled in your hearing" (Luke 4:18-21).

The promise was fulfilled not only in word, but in deed.

When the men had come to him, they said, "John the Baptist has sent us to you to ask, 'Are you the one who is to come, or are we to wait for another?'" Jesus had just then cured many people of diseases, plagues, and evil spirits, and had given sight to many who were blind. And he

[3] T. S. Eliot, "Little Gidding," *The Complete Poems and Plays* (New York: Harcourt, Brace and Co., 1972) 145.
[4] Isa 61:1-4.

answered them, "Go and tell John what you have seen and heard: the blind receive their sight, the lame walk, the lepers are cleansed, the deaf hear, the dead are raised, the poor have good news brought to them" (Luke 7:20-22).

The newness was not separate from all that was before. It was in continuity with what had gone before, a fulfillment and extension of its trajectory. It was an invitation to understand and engage history anew, with new eyes.

What was promised was experienced in history by real flesh and blood people in their particular time and place. Jesus healed both in the sense of a restoration to physical wholeness (the lame, bent, and paralyzed walk tall, the blind see, the mentally ill are free and at peace) and to the wholeness of community (lepers and the menstruating woman healed, tax collectors belonging, sins forgiven, children and outsiders included). With Jesus there was enough and even an abundance for all.[5] With Jesus, tears of grief were turned to tears of joy. Jesus invites people into Sabbath rest and refreshment.[6] In Jesus, there is reconciliation and full communion with God.[7] In the events of Easter, we see the possibility of life transformed, rather than extinguished, in death. Our tradition holds that in Christ's time after death before his resurrection, he journeyed to hell to redeem even its denizens. Indeed, then and now, people "were all amazed, and they kept on asking one another, 'What is this? A new teaching—with authority!'" (Mark 1:27a). This "new teaching" was all about the reign of God. It was and is the heart of Jesus' work. This reign of God is full of the great reversals longed for by all who have suffered. It is a place, a time, and a way of being where:

> Blessed are the poor in spirit, for theirs is the kingdom of heaven.
> Blessed are those who mourn, for they will be comforted.
> Blessed are the meek, for they will inherit the earth.
> Blessed are those who hunger and thirst for righteousness, for they will be filled.
> Blessed are the merciful, for they will receive mercy.
> Blessed are the pure in heart, for they will see God.

[5] See Stations 6 and 9.
[6] Matt 11:28-29; Acts 3:19-20; and Heb 4:1-11.
[7] See Stations 4 and 11; and Col 1:19-20; Eph 2:15-20; 2 Cor 5:18-19.

Blessed are the peacemakers, for they will be called children of God.

Blessed are those who are persecuted for righteousness' sake, for theirs is the kingdom of heaven.

Blessed are you when people revile you and persecute you and utter all kinds of evil against you falsely on my account. Rejoice and be glad, for your reward is great in heaven, for in the same way they persecuted the prophets who were before you (Matt 5:3-12; parallel Luke 6:20-28).

In Jesus' presence, this reign of God or kingdom of heaven was experienced by real people. This is the banquet.[8] For this, people left everything and followed Jesus. As Jesus counsels those who are distracted by many things, "Strive for [God's] kingdom, and these things will be given to you as well" (Luke 12:31; parallel Matt 6:33). This is the heart of the matter, the heart of the Holy. The trajectory of the arc of history is to the banquet. The great love song of our tradition describes the intention of our Lover, "He brought me to the banqueting house, / and his intention toward me was love" (Cant 2:4). The fullness of the banquet is the reign of God.

If this were all, it could be dismissed as interesting history or food for dreamers. But a cross is etched into the banquet table and the empty tomb floodlights the feast. These two events create a depth and reality to the banquet that invites the kind of "exploration without ceasing" that Eliot describes. The cross means that the banquet is never present in ignorance, denial, fantasy, or distance from the reality and costs of suffering and injustice in individual lives, cultures, and the very earth, air, and water itself. The cross is God's commitment to be with us, with God's beloved creation, in the very midst. God's commitment to the banquet is unqualified, then, now, and forever. The cross says unequivocally that the power of the reign, its life force, is love. The empty tomb says that this power cannot be contained, eliminated, or disappeared.[9] Jesus' resurrection is the beginning of the new creation: life that death cannot diminish. The claim of faith is that

---

[8] For a brief sketch of the secular community's description of the banquet see Appendix 2.

[9] See Julia Esquival, *Threatened with Resurrection: Prayers and Poems from an Exiled Guatemalan*, 2d ed. (Elgin, Ill.: Brethren Press, 1994), for a contemporary glimpse of the power of the resurrection as experienced in the midst of the death and disappearances of the Guatemalan struggle of the 1970s and 80s.

Jesus, who really lived in first-century Palestine and really died on the cross, is alive with God in the full integrity of his humanity . . . and is interactively present in and among us now and forever. . . . He is not dead; he is not absent; he is, on the contrary, alive, present, and active and, when he chooses to be so, active within history or in relation to people within history.[10]

The cross and empty tomb illuminate the creative energy at the heart of history: earth and heaven as one,[11] God's will done in love on earth as in heaven for life abundant for all. Taken together, they are a window into the new creation that God is creating. This new creation is present tense, not a memory or teaching from two thousand years ago. This reality, however, was too fantastic, perhaps also too earthy and certainly too challenging a "new teaching" for those lovers of the new, the Athenians, to hear in their day (Acts 17). It is still so for many today. Yet for those who believe, it becomes the word of life.

It took time for even the first disciples to understand the power of the empty tomb. After Jerusalem and the death of Jesus, they returned to Galilee to their nets and their work as fishers. After an unproductive night of fishing, "just after daybreak," they listened to a man on the beach whom they didn't recognize and they cast their net one more time. With the signature of the One of abundance, "they were not able to haul [the net] in because there were so many fish." When they got to shore "they saw a charcoal fire there, with fish on it, and bread," and Jesus said to them: "Come and have breakfast" (John 21:1-19). That is the invitation of the banquet: "Come and have breakfast." It is the invitation of faith that comes with the dawn of a new day. It comes in the context of work that bears abundant fruit through the Word of Life. It is offered by the Holy One who continues to bear the marks of suffering and death, of involvement in creation,[12] and whose invitation is to become "like one of us," but by eating a very different meal than that eaten at the foot "of the tree in the middle of the garden" (Gen 3:22).[13]

---

[10] Sandra M. Schneiders, "The Resurrection of Jesus and Christian Spirituality," *Christian Resources of Hope* (Collegeville: The Liturgical Press, 1995) 104, 106, 107.

[11] Rev 11:15.

[12] This is the third and last resurrection account in John's gospel. The second account includes Jesus' invitation to faith to Thomas: "Put your finger here and see my hands. Reach out your hand and put it in my side. Do not doubt but believe" (John 20:27).

[13] See Stations 2 and 4.

After breakfast, that first taste of the banquet of the new creation, Jesus turns to the disciple who had disowned him three times a few days before. He points again to the path of redemption, reconciliation, and the fullness of life intended for all from before time. Jesus asks him three times: "Simon, son of John, do you love me more than these? . . . Simon, son of John, do you love me? . . . Simon, son of John, do you love me?" (John 21:15a, 16a, 17a). And each time, after Peter's, "Yes, Lord; you know that I love you," Jesus commands: "Feed my lambs, . . . tend my sheep, . . . feed my sheep" (John 21:15b, 16b, 17b). Love of the Lord is inseparable from the journey of the banquet. An unconditional "yes" to God is an unconditional commitment to the fullness of the banquet for all. There is no heaven without earth; no holiness without breakfast.

Ezekiel is very clear about what "feed my sheep" means:

> For thus says the Lord GOD: I myself will search for my sheep. . . . I will rescue them from all the places to which they have been scattered on a day of clouds and thick darkness. . . . I will feed them on the mountains of Israel, by the watercourses, and in all the inhabited parts of the land. I will feed them with good pasture, and the mountain heights of Israel shall be their pasture . . . ; there they shall lie down in good grazing land, and they shall feed on rich pasture on the mountains of Israel. I myself will be the shepherd of my sheep, and I will make them lie down, says the Lord GOD. I will seek the lost, and I will bring back the strayed, and I will bind up the injured, and I will strengthen the weak, but the fat and the strong I will destroy. I will feed them with justice.
>
> I will make with them a covenant of peace and banish wild animals from the land, so that they may live in the wild and sleep in the woods securely. I will make them and the region around my hill a blessing; and I will send down the showers in their season; they shall be showers of blessing. The trees of the field shall yield their fruit, and the earth shall yield its increase. They shall be secure on their soil; and they shall know that I am the LORD, when I break the bars of their yoke, and save them from the hands of those who enslaved them. They shall no more be plunder for the nations, nor shall the animals of the land devour them; they shall live in safety, and no one shall make them afraid. I will provide for them a splendid vegetation so that they shall no more be consumed with hunger in the land (Ezek 34:11-12, 13b-16, 25-29a).

A "yes" to Christ's query, "Do you love me?" is not only a "yes" to the invitation to the feast of reconciliation offered to the prodigal son.[14] It is not only reunion with the Holy, a coming home to God, but it is also a "yes" to "feed my sheep." It is a "yes" to the journey of the banquet where not only will the injured be treated, the weak strengthened, the bound and burdened freed, but justice, peace, and security will be food for all, and there will be showers of blessing, and "they shall no more be consumed with hunger." Participation in the fullness of the banquet is inseparable from the "yes" of discipleship. "Come and have breakfast. . . . Do you love me? . . . Feed my sheep. . . . After this, Jesus said to [Peter]: 'Follow me'" (John 21:12, 15-17, 19). The journey of the banquet is life with the risen Christ.

Earlier, in the conversation after Jesus' Last Supper with his disciples in which Jesus had mentioned that he would leave them, Peter had said to him: "'Lord, where are you going?' Jesus answered, 'Where I am going, you cannot follow me now; but you will follow afterward'" (John 13:36). Jesus continued to talk about his imminent absence, so Thomas asked:

> "Lord, we do not know where you are going. How can we know the way?" Jesus said to him, "I am the way, and the truth, and the life. No one comes to the Father except through me. If you know me, you will know my Father also. From now on you do know him and have seen him" (John 14:5-7).

The way of the banquet is the gospel Jesus proclaimed in word and deed. In a unique way, he embodied a way of knowing the Heart and Wisdom of the Universe, and so became an invitation into that power. But in incomprehension, even having walked the journey with Jesus, the original disciples arrive at the place where they started,[15] and Philip asks Jesus: "'Lord, show us the Father, and we will be satisfied.' Jesus said to him, 'Have I been with you all this time, Philip, and you still do not know me?'" (John 14:8-9). So Jesus summarizes the challenge and promise of the Christian path—the core of the new covenant.

> Believe me that I am in the Father and the Father is in me; but if you do not, then believe me because of the works themselves. Very truly, I tell

[14] See also John 20:22-23.

[15] Philip was the one who, right at the beginning of the story, had gone to Nathanael and said: "We have found him about whom Moses in the law and also the prophets wrote, Jesus son of Joseph from Nazareth" (John 1:45).

you, the one who believes in me will also do the works that I do and, in fact, will do greater works than these, because I am going to the Father. I will do whatever you ask in my name, so that the Father may be glorified in the Son. If in my name you ask me for anything, I will do it (John 14:11-14).

On the other side of the cross, they come to discipleship, the place where they started, and know it for the first time. Jesus is not only the Messiah, the longed-for Savior in a way they could not have imagined before the journey began, but Jesus reveals the path into the creative life-generative force of the universe, the very Source and Power of the banquet. "In a little while the world will no longer see me, but you will see me; because I live, you also will live. On that day you will know that I am in my Father, and you in me, and I in you" (John 14:19-20). It is the living, active presence of the glorified Christ, with the power of the Spirit,[16] that enables us to live creatively and constructively in the midst of all the tensions of the new creation that is begun but is also not yet. We live into all the grand reversals of the banquet. Christ's ongoing presence and action "within history and in relation to people in history" is the proof and possibility of the new creation that God is about and that we are about as contemporary followers of Christ.

SPIRITUAL CHALLENGE: DISCIPLESHIP

What does discipleship mean for us today? Frederick Herzog's phrase for discipleship is "walking," walking with God; hence the title of his book: *God-Walk*. "Walking *[peripatein]*, often translated as 'following,' 'leading a life,' or 'conducting oneself,' in the Christian Scriptures always indicates a way of life, an ethos: 'walk as children of light.'"[17] Walking is a lively, active image that brings all sorts of questions to mind. What path are we walking? Is it the path of abundant life for all? Is it the

---

[16] Catherine Mowry LaCugna, *God For Us: The Trinity and Christian Life* (New York: HarperCollins, 1991): "Knowledge of God is given by the Spirit, apart from whom we cannot acknowledge Jesus Christ to the revelation of God" (362).

[17] Frederick Herzog, *God-Walk: Liberation Shaping Dogmatics* (Maryknoll, N.Y.: Orbis Books, 1988) xxxi; and Eph 5:8.

journey of the banquet? What is the etiquette of the journey? Whose company do we keep on this walk? Are we walking the walk we talk?

Argumentatively one could ask, why not talk about driving or flying or surfing the net in this twenty-first century? Why still talk of walking when we have the technology to alter time (speeding it up seemingly without limit) and space (reducing distance to almost nothing)? Just as walking is clearly earth-bound, we too are still shaped from earth, eat from the earth, and return to the earth. We live the particularities of our place and moment in history. Salvation is enacted in the particulars of our lives: at home, in nonprofit community organizations, as helpers and helped, as tradespeople and professionals, in the business world and government bureaucracies, at the local, national, and global levels. Though open to and drawn by the universal, the path we walk is particular. It is unique to our place and time and the gifts God has given us. The walk, the journey of the banquet, starts in the garden, for "God is still walking in the garden, our beautiful planet earth, asking all of us: 'Where are you?' (Gen 3:8-9)."[18] Although the "you" can be read in the plural (Where are you humans?), the response of faith is always in the singular: "Here I am." And it is always a response. The initiative belongs to God. We choose to say yes. The path is God's. We walk it.

Who is this "I" that responds? In another garden, Mary has gone looking for Jesus. "They have taken away my Lord, and I do not know where they have laid him" (John 20:13). It is only when she is named, with all the love and knowledge of the Jesus she knew, that she can recognize the risen Christ in the one she had mistaken for the gardener. The new creation is like that. There is a sense of being known, found, loved, named as a child of God, an "I" created in the image of God. There is also at the same time a sense of not knowing, of encountering a reality that is beyond our grasp. It is true that "one always commits oneself before fully knowing what one is committing to. . . . Commitment is based not on facts, but on desire—and the root meaning of desire is to follow a star."[19] Like Mary in the garden surprised by God on that first day of the new creation, we turn and in joy commit to the one who names us and the journey unfolds.

---

[18] Herzog, *God-Walk*, xxxii.

[19] Norman Fischer, Joseph Goldstein, Judith Simmer-Brown, *Yifa, Benedict's Dharma: Buddhists Reflect on the Rule of Saint Benedict*, ed. Patrick Henry (New York: Riverhead Books, 1991) 8.

We are drawn on in our desiring, for "every act of knowing God both satisfies and engenders human curiosity; every encounter with God both quenches and deepens human thirst."[20] The satisfactions of this God-walk are so different from those offered by "the endless stream of new goods and services that has become a cornucopia of mystery, protection, and salvation we call progress."[21] Wants are certainly created and satisfied by the engines of "progress," but at what cost? We consume the very substance that gives us life, leave suffering and destruction in our wake, and can never rest. As Amos predicted, we wander from sea to sea; run to and fro, seeking the word of God, but unable to find it (Amos 8:12).[22] In contrast, our walk with Jesus, whom we do not fully know and cannot contain, is always new and oriented to life abundant for all. It is always more than we can imagine. Walking in the company of "the infinite being of God, the incessant movement of the human spirit begins to arrive at its final rest."[23] This is the rest of completeness, wholeness, belonging, of life lived rightly from the center. It is the rest that leads to life rather than death.

> Have you not known? Have you not heard?
> The LORD is the everlasting God,
>   the Creator of the ends of the earth.
> He does not faint or grow weary;
>   his understanding is unsearchable.
> He gives power to the faint,
>   and strengthens the powerless.
> Even youths will faint and be weary,
>   and the young will fall exhausted;
> but those who wait for the LORD shall renew their strength,
>   they shall mount up with wings like eagles,
> they shall run and not be weary,
>   they shall walk and not faint (Isa 40:28-31).

It is a rest that engages rather than detaches us from life.

---

[20] Miroslav Volf, "In the Cage of Vanities: Christian Faith and the Dynamics of Economic Progress," *Rethinking Materialism: Perspectives on the Spiritual Dimension of Economic Behavior*, ed. Robert Wuthnow (Grand Rapids, Mich.: Eerdmans, 1995) 190.

[21] Ibid., 190.

[22] See Station 3.

[23] Volf, "In the Cage of Vanities," 190.

In that place of wholeness that we cannot own, grasp, or manage, that place of pure grace, we know the counterintuitive truth of the beatitudes as the wisdom of our hearts. We know that the fullness of the reign, of the banquet, is more accessible to those whose lives, hearts, and hands are not already filled up with possessions, attachments, achievements, or accomplishments; who live lives of compassion, who work for justice, who cultivate peace. So we orient to those truths much as a plant turns to follow the sun's movement across the sky. Then, in the midst of the daily round of work, of loving, of producing and consuming, organizing and creating, living and dying, when that surprising gardener turns up with opportunities for us to release the captives, offer sight to the blind, free the oppressed and usher in the time of the jubilee, we respond "yes." It is not because it is we who build the kingdom of God. In any given situation we live into the banquet as potential, as seed buried in the soil of our lives.[24] In the power of the Spirit, the seed bears the fruit of discipleship, our participation in the journey of the banquet.

But Jesus' beatitudes also talk of times of persecution and hate. Certainly the cross testifies to the cost of discipleship. In our day, discipleship is challenged on a variety of fronts.

First, its particularity is an offense in this time of religious pluralism. When understanding and respect among faith traditions is critical for global peace and justice, it seems counterintuitive to commit to a particular faith tradition. Krister Stendahl poses one of the questions of contemporary discipleship: "How can I sing my song to Jesus fully and with abandon without feeling it necessary to belittle the faith of others?"[25] By analogy, he suggests, singing one's love to one's marriage partner does not belittle others to whom one is not committed. In fact an appreciation for others may grow out of a deep commitment to one. Ironically, a syncretistic or simple "taste and see" approach to different faith traditions does not do justice to the integrity of each tradition and the real diversity among traditions. Deep roots in a particular tradition allow for a full, fruitful, respectful conversation with those deeply rooted in another tradition. The challenges to those called on the Christ-walk is "to find our right place, our peculiar and particu-

---

[24] See Stations 8 and 13.

[25] Krister Stendahl "Christ's Lordship and Religious Pluralism," *Meanings: the Bible as Document and as Guide* (Minneapolis: Fortress Press, 1984) 233.

lar place as faithful witnesses to Jesus Christ, leaving the result of the witness in the hands of God." Salvation, the new creation, the banquet is God's project. It is not about our waving "the Christ-flag."[26]

A second challenge in this information age is that the walk of faith is always with the Gardener who is more than we can comprehend or even imagine. This keeps us humble, unable to claim absolute certitude about the path, and always open and attentive to surprise and corrective. Or it should.[27] The knowing and learning of faith is not the same as the dominant instrumental scientific rationality of our day. It is not a simple cause and effect, objective, externally verifiable knowing. It participates in a kind of communicative rationality, but includes the Sacred as an active participant.[28] This is to say that the knowledge arising from faith has a rationality, but like all human knowledge, it is also limited and finite. Faith claims are open to reasoned exploration and yet cannot ever be fully circumscribed, defined, or owned by any one person or group. Faith is not antithetical to reason or the intellectual, scientific, technological enterprise. We are asked to bring all of ourselves, including our gift of reason, to the walk of faith. But faith always asks us to take a step into the unknown. Faith leads beyond knowledge to wisdom and wisdom is a goal worthy of the human enterprise.

For Jesus, for the prophets, and for many since then, a third challenge is that a God-walk often leads to conflict with those who promote and defend a much smaller, more distant, less accessible banquet table than the one Jesus proclaimed. Discipleship is about feeding the hungry, releasing the captives, offering sight to the blind, healing the sick, reconciling the estranged, welcoming the stranger, freeing the oppressed, and working for the jubilee time when the structural injustices

[26] Ibid., 243.

[27] Our history has too many examples of religious ideologies. As Miroslav Volf has written, "Though I must be ready to deny myself for the sake of *the* truth, I may not sacrifice the other at the altar of *my* truth. Jesus, who claimed to be the Truth, refused to use violence to 'persuade' those who did not recognize his truth. The kingdom of truth he came to proclaim was the kingdom of freedom and therefore cannot rest on pillars of violence." *Exclusion and Embrace: A Theological Exploration of Identity, Otherness, and Reconciliation* (Nashville: Abingdon Press, 1996) 272; emphasis in original.

[28] Delineating this communicative rationality is at the heart Jurgen Habermas' work. Introducing the Sacred as a participant alters the conception of an ideal speech situation, but the same base for analyses of speech claims in a communicative ethics can pertain to the interpretation of human claims about the walk.

that accumulate in any society are corrected. Resistance to such work will emerge. In the midst of such conflict, the Christ-walk is bound by the logic and etiquette of the banquet table. The peacemakers have a special place at the table along with those who hunger and thirst after righteousness or right relations among God, humans, and creation. The strategies in preparing the banquet are inseparable from its message. The banquet is not cut to human scale or designed to be feasible or achievable. It is God who is making all things new. We are merely the seeds, Christ's disciples.

Spiritual Practice: Joy

At the beginning of the twenty-first century, discipleship, our God-walk along the path of abundant life for all, is challenging in many respects. Yet Jeremiah's description of the heart of the banquet from 2500 or so years ago is still accurate. In conversation with God he says:

> Know that on your account I suffer insult.
> Your words were found, and I ate them,
>   and your words became to me a joy
>   and the delight of my heart;
> for I am called by your name,
>   O Lord, God of hosts (Jer 15:15b-16).

Joy—the heart delighted—is at the very core of discipleship. Just as Mary recognized the One mistaken for the gardener in her naming, we are named with God's true name. We become the word we eat: children of God. The snake said eat the fruit of the tree in the middle of the garden and you will become like God. God says eat of the banquet and you will become fully who you are: children of God, one with the Holy.

Despite the Hollywood caricatures of Christians as earnest, dour, or fiercely moralistic, discipleship springs from joy and feeds joy. Joy is one of the fruits of the Spirit (Gal 5:22) and it is one of the signs of the kingdom: "For the kingdom of God is not food and drink[29] but

---

[29] This was written in the context of dissension about food rules about what was good and right to eat and what should be avoided.

righteousness and peace and joy in the Holy Spirit" (Rom 14:17). In Jesus' farewell conversation with his disciples he says: "I have said these things to you so that my joy may be in you, and that your joy may be complete" (John 15:11). "The joy Jesus offers his disciples is his own joy, which flows from his intimate communion with the One who sent him."[30] As St. Aelred has said: "Joy is the echo of God's life in us." It is a true mark of our life in Christ in the power of the Spirit.

Witness to the joy of life with God bubbles up throughout our Scriptures:

> Surely God is my salvation;
>   I will trust, and will not be afraid,
> for the LORD GOD is my strength and my might;
>   he has become my salvation.
> With joy you will draw water from the wells of salvation (Isa 12:2-3).

> You show me the path of life.
>   In your presence there is fullness of joy;
>   in your right hand are pleasures forevermore (Ps 16:11).

> Your decrees are my heritage forever;
>   they are the joy of my heart.
> I incline my heart to perform your statutes
>   forever, to the end (Ps 119:111-112).

> The law of the LORD is perfect,
>   reviving the soul;
> the decrees of the LORD are sure,
>   making wise the simple;
> the precepts of the LORD are right,
>   rejoicing the heart;
> the commandment of the LORD is clear,
>   enlightening the eyes;
> the fear of the LORD is pure,
>   enduring forever;
> the ordinances of the LORD are true
>   and righteous altogether.
> More to be desired are they than gold,
>   even much fine gold;

---

[30] Henri J. M. Nouwen, *Lifesigns: Intimacy, Fecundity and Ecstasy in Christian Perspective* (Garden City, N.Y.: Doubleday & Co., 1986) 98–9.

> sweeter also than honey,
>> and drippings of the honeycomb (Ps 19:7-10).

This delight-full sense of joy in the path of life and in the decrees, laws, or road map for our God-walk is not always associated with the life of faith. Sometimes the somber severity of mourning has seemed a more appropriate image than a festive feast. When "the book of the law of Moses" was first read to the people after the return from the Babylonian exile, there was a struggle between the two responses.

> So they read from the book, from the law of God, with interpretation. They gave the sense, so that the people understood the reading.
> And Nehemiah, who was the governor, and Ezra the priest and scribe, and the Levites who taught the people said to all the people, "This day is holy to the LORD your God; do not mourn or weep." For all the people wept when they heard the words of the law. Then he said to them, "Go your way, eat the fat and drink sweet wine and send portions of them to those for whom nothing is prepared, for this day is holy to our LORD; and do not be grieved, for the joy of the LORD is your strength." So the Levites stilled all the people, saying, "Be quiet, for this day is holy; do not be grieved." And all the people went their way to eat and drink and to send portions and to make great rejoicing, because they had understood the words that were declared to them (Neh 8:8-11).

Heard from the outside as an external code without understanding, the path can generate tears, grief, and fear. Heard from the inside, from a place of connection with God, heard as an invitation "to draw water from the wells of salvation," it is all about the joy of the banquet.

This joy is not the same as a "made in the world" happiness. As Nouwen notes:

> Much money and energy is spent trying to make people happy and relaxed by offering a moment of artificial bliss. This happiness is as contrived as the good meal given to a man on death row before his execution. It tastes good but does not keep him alive. . . . It is neither lasting nor deeply satisfying.[31]

Such happiness is often in spite of, or in contradiction to, the truth of our lives. In contrast, the joy at the heart of discipleship comes from sharing intimately every day with the Holy.

[31] Ibid., 97.

[It] does not separate happy days from sad days, successful moments from moments of failure, experiences of honor from experiences of dishonor, passion from resurrection. This joy . . . does not leave us during times of illness, poverty, oppression or persecution. . . . For Jesus, joy is clearly a deeper and more truthful state of life than sorrow.[32]

This joy is like a subterranean spring or aquifer that allows the potential, the seeds and gifts of life, to flourish. It is replenished from the Heart of the Holy. It is not transitory. It is infinitely renewable and offered as pure gift for free, for everyone, forever. Artificial sweeteners have different origins and always have a different taste from honey.

Joy is all about the coming of the new heaven and new earth. It is a sign of the creative, generative force of God's love active in creation and human history. The birth process is the analogy that Jesus uses in his farewell conversation with his disciples:

Very truly, I tell you, you will weep and mourn, but the world will rejoice; you will have pain, but your pain will turn into joy. When a woman is in labor, she has pain, because her hour has come. But when her child is born, she no longer remembers the anguish because of the joy of having brought a human being into the world. So you have pain now; but I will see you again, and your hearts will rejoice, and no one will take your joy from you (John 16:20-22).

The agenda of the struggle is new life. And it is not just human life. As Paul writes: "The whole creation has been groaning in labor pains until now" (Rom 8:22). Isaiah in his image of this birthing process reaffirms God's presence in the struggle:

For a long time I have held my peace,
    I have kept still and restrained myself;
now I will cry out like a woman in labor,
    I will gasp and pant.
I will lay waste mountains and hills,
    and dry up all their herbage;
I will turn the rivers into islands,
    and dry up the pools.
I will lead the blind
    by a road they do not know,

[32] Ibid., 99.

by paths they have not known
    I will guide them.
I will turn the darkness before them into light,
    the rough places into level ground.
These are the things I will do,
    and I will not forsake them (Isa 42:14-16).

In the midst of the struggle, when the path is not clear and there is no map, there is the light of faith. There is God's presence with us. This is the difference between the transitory joy of the seed that falls on rocky ground, which "cannot endure when trouble or persecution arises on account of the word" (Mark 4:17b, 20-21), and the joy that comes with the harvest of the seed that was well-rooted in the soil of faith. The joy of this God-walk that is at the heart of discipleship is rooted and grounded in faith in the love of God for us and for God's beloved creation.

Fear and its related passion for certainty, foreknowledge, and security is antithetical to the joy of discipleship. As William Blake wrote:

He who binds to himself a joy
Doth the winged life destroy
But he who kisses the joy as it flies
Lives in eternity's sunrise. . . .[33]

Joy is always present tense. It cannot be bottled, contained, or stored up. It can only be experienced with an open hand. For "joy is always connected with movement, renewal, rebirth, change—in short, with life."[34] This life is not in spite of or in denial of death, but is the life that includes death, that knows the death that leads to life, the life that death cannot eliminate, destroy, or disappear, indeed eternal life, "eternity's sunrise." The joy at the heart of discipleship comes from our participation in God's agenda for creation and its trajectory toward abundant life for all, the fullness of the banquet.

---

[33] William Blake, "Eternity," *The Complete Poetry and Prose of William Blake*, rev. ed., ed. David V. Erdman (Berkeley: University of California Press, 1982) 470; also quoted in Gerald May, *Will and Spirit: A Contemplative Psychology* (San Francisco: Harper and Row, 1982) 210.

[34] Nouwen, *Lifesigns*, 88.

STATION 12 LITANY: THE BANQUET

Voices 1: At the beginning of the day, we join you at the breakfast table;

Voices 2: We sing our thanksgivings to you for all the blessings of the banquet.

One: O Host of the wedding feast, who calls each of us by name,

Voices 1: You welcome the poor, the weeping, the lost, exiled, rejected, and reviled,
the hungry and thirsty, the bullied and victimized;
and in your mercy, the bullies and victimizers.

Voices 2: You welcome the humble, the peace-makers,
the patient, the faithful, and the resolute;
and in your steadfast love, the tentative, the impatient, and the proud.

Voices 1: You welcome the eccentrics, the wild ones and
those who dance to drummers we don't yet hear;
and in your great love, the upright and respectable.

Voices 2: You welcome the great hearts and the scared hearts,
the wise ones and the simple ones;
and in your compassion, the misguided and the angry.

All: **All the creatures are welcomed to your table**
Indeed all of creation has a place at your table.

Voices 1: The joy of your welcome is perfect peace;

Voices 2: The company you keep is love's full harvest;

All: **We come each day to the feast of your grace,**
With hearts full of wonder and thanksgiving.

One: O Source and Power of Salvation,

Voices 1: Banish scarcity, destruction, and fear from our midst;

Voices 2: Banish the ravenous and aching hungers of your beloved creation.

One: Feed us with the abundance of your table:

Voices 1: The food of justice and truth,
The food of reconciliation and solidarity,

Voices 2: The food of healing and wholeness,
The food of freedom and peace,

All: **That we ourselves might become food for all.**

One: Source of all wisdom and compassion,

All: **You open the door to the new creation,
And accompany us as friend, challenge, and surprising
provider;
Lead and we will follow.**

[pause]

One: Deep current of everlasting joy,

Voices 1: All our striving, reaching, consuming, and restless searching
find fulfillment in you.

Voices 2: You are the well that satisfies all thirst.

All: **We sing of the glory, splendor, and joy of the banquet,
And praise your name forever. Amen. Alleluia!**

Visual focus: Bread, fish, and/or a broken chain.

Station 13

"YOUR KINGDOM COME!"

I will not leave you orphaned; I am coming to you.

—John 14:18

Time is an extraordinarily dominant reality in our culture. It matters to us. We have too little of it no matter how fast we go, or we have too much of it and it weighs heavily on us. How much time do we have? What do we have time for? What is our point of reference?

One simple way we structure our experience of time is around three days: yesterday, today, and tomorrow. All our conversations reflect this structure in the tenses of the verbs we use: past, present, and future. Our past (memory, history, family legacies) and our future (plans, visions, sense of possibility) shape our present, and vice versa: our present reinterprets the past and creates a trajectory into our tomorrow. Yet time-bound as we are, the thought of eternity, of existence outside of, beyond, behind, or before time, is also part of human history. How does God's time relate to, or intersect with, our time? If matter and spirit are inseparable, if heaven and earth touch, if the banquet is more than metaphor or dream, the question "when?" (and its cousin: "where?") must be addressed.

This "when" question is raised in time. Our understanding of time is shaped by the particularities of our times. Scientific explorations are opening up the earliest milliseconds of the universe and detailing the intricacies of the twists and turns of the history of life, both non-human and human, that have brought us to this now. Never before have we had

such an extraordinary window of understanding into our past. That
same science shapes our future in radical ways. It has led to the creation of technologies that could exterminate all life on the planet, either
quickly and noisily, as in a nuclear holocaust, or slowly and silently,
through pollution and disintegration of the regenerative capacity of
our planet. Never before have humans had such capacity to end life on
the planet. The image of earth from space has given us a visual icon of
earth's integrity and its vulnerability that has shaped our sense of ourselves and our shared future. At the same time, the structures we have
to generate, integrate, and direct these developments are very diffuse.
They are diverse and global in their impact. We have tremendous wealth
of knowledge and of power. Yet danger grows along with the growth of
this power and its progressive concentration. As constructive opportunities increase, destructive opportunities increase as well. How we
will use this knowledge and power, for what ends, for what future, for
whom, are the open-ended questions of our times.

Our faith does not remove us from this dynamic of history, nor give
us privileged access to its resolution. Our tradition, however, does
position the questions and answers that it offers in a particular way.
Jurgen Moltmann delineates that position:

> Christian theology is not a theology of universal history. It is a historical
> theology of struggle and hope. It therefore does not teach the secular
> millenarianism of the present, as does the naïve modern faith in progress,
> maintaining that in the future everything will get better and better. Nor
> does it teach that in the future everything will get worse and worse, like
> equally naïve modern apocalypticism. But it does warn that in the fu-
> ture of this world things are going to become more and more critical.[1]

We do not stand outside history in some privileged space. The future
is undetermined, critical, and open to human choice. Human decisions
matter in creating the balance between "better and better" and "worse
and worse." As people of faith, we root ourselves in our tradition as
the wisdom of the ages and as the foundation of our hope. We understand God's engagement in love in creation and we accept God's invitation to us to participate in that love-making. As disciples we are fed
at the banquet table and orient toward abundant life for every last lost

---

[1] Jurgen Moltmann, *The Coming of God: Christian Eschatology* (Minneapolis: Fortress
Press, 1996) 200.

sheep and fragment of suffering in creation. Yet the question of timing remains: When? How much of salvation is here and now, and how much there and then?

VOICES OF THE TRADITION

To talk of a "new heaven and a new earth" raises the question of the status of the original heaven and earth.[2] Do the original and new co-exist or are they sequential: one ends and the other begins? If sequential, how is the transition visualized? Almost every option to those questions that can be imagined has been imagined, with various justifications and implications for our here and now arena of struggle and hope.[3] To take a less speculative tack, the very compact summary of faith: "Christ has died, Christ is risen, Christ will come again," suggests that it is in Christ that our past, present, and future are woven into a whole. Each thread has a meaningful place.

OUR PAST: CHRIST HAS DIED

To consider the past through the lens of "Christ has died" is to say, first, that the past consists of given historical events, irreversible and unrepeatable, but not over. Our past enters our present through our active remembering.[4] From the time of the early Church until now, we enact this history in our worship, explicitly in the Eucharist, and every year on Good Friday. We remember, and in remembering also proclaim or make present God's revelation in Christ. Paul writes:

> For I received from the Lord what I also handed on to you, that the Lord Jesus on the night when he was betrayed took a loaf of bread, and

---

[2] For an extended discussion of why it is a new heaven and a new earth see Jurgen Moltmann, *God in Creation: An Ecological Doctrine of Creation* (London: SCM Press, 1985) ch. 7, pp. 158ff.

[3] For a succinct review of the options, see Peter C. Phan, *Eternity in Time: A Study of Karl Rahner's Eschatology* (Cranbury, N.J.: Associated University Presses, 1988) 15–18, 26–31.

[4] The formal term for this "active remembering" is *anamnesis*.

when he had given thanks, he broke it and said, "This is my body that is for you. Do this in remembrance of me." In the same way he took the cup also, after supper, saying, "This cup is the new covenant in my blood. Do this, as often as you drink it, in remembrance of me." For as often as you eat this bread and drink the cup, you proclaim the Lord's death until he comes (1 Cor 11:23-26; parallel: Luke 22:19; 1 Cor 1:23).

This constant doing of our remembering makes the truth of the historical event ever available for present participation. It continually shapes our perception of present choices. As George Santayana reminds us: "Those who cannot remember the past are condemned to repeat it." In proclaiming Christ's death, we remember the present possibility of our rejection of salvation. At the same time, we remind ourselves of God's love, God's solidarity with the rejected, and God's suffering with us. This enactment shapes our very identity. We internalize this mystery, it lives in us and we become what we eat. Indeed, we become the living present body of Christ ourselves today. That at least is the invitation, the possibility.[5]

What can make the difference between memory as simple recollection of a past event and memory that transforms the present? What generates a subversive memory that is oriented to the grand reversals of the banquet in real time in the public and private dimensions of our lives? The Scriptures provide direction into this question. In the context of a polemical discussion about resurrection, Jesus uses the Scriptures: "Have you not read in the book of Moses, in the story about the bush, how God said to him: 'I am the God of Abraham, and the God of Isaac and the God of Jacob'? He is God not of the dead, but of the living" (Mark 12:26-27; parallels: Matt 22:31-32; Luke 20:37-38). In God, these historical figures are indeed living, not dead. In God, the past is not a closed book. In God, the continuity of the past into the present is assured. That continuity is maintained in God's memory, God's remembering, God's faithfulness. God's faithfulness to the covenant—to Noah, Abraham, the Hebrew people in the desert and

---

[5] As Bruce Morrill rightly adds, this is an ideal: "Theology has failed to grasp that religion no longer belongs to the social constitution of the identity of the subject, but is rather added to it." If Christ is to shape present and future, he cannot be a side dish added to the stew of our lives. He must be the main meal. Bruce T. Morrill, *Anamnesis as Dangerous Memory: Political and Liturgical Theology in Dialogue* (Collegeville: The Liturgical Press, 2000) 20.

Christians in Christ—is sung over and over in the Scriptures.[6] God is a God of steadfast love and faithfulness. God remembers God's people, hears our cries, and is committed to us and God's beloved creation for all time. In God, memory stretches across the ages. Nothing is lost.

If Susan Griffin's intuition is correct, the same is true, consciously or unconsciously, of human memory. She writes:

> It is said that the close study of stone will reveal traces from fires suffered thousands of years ago. . . . Perhaps we are like stones; [with] our own history and the history of the world embedded in us, we hold a sorrow deep within and cannot weep until that history is sung.[7]

Our individual and collective history is part of our present. To be free in the present to love, create, grow the fullness of the banquet, all of our history must be sung. Remembering, singing, celebrating Christ's death is an invitation and reminder to do the work of our past for the sake of our future.

History, tradition, memory is the soil, substratum, or foundation into which we are born. The fertility of the seed depends on the soil and how deeply the plant is rooted in this soil. The flourishing of the kingdom, the fullness of the harvest, depends on these dynamics, as the parable of the sower describes.[8] For memory to become subversive and transformative, the soil must be rich and prepared. It must be living, truthful, deep, indeed "sung." The corrosive, hardened, life-poisoning elements must be broken open and redeemed. This is the hard work of truth-telling, repentance, forgiveness, and reconciliation; the work of healing the scars of the past. Then we must actually connect with it, enter into it, and be open to the soil. Suffering, our own as well as, through empathy, others' suffering, is often the reality that cracks open the protective shells of the seeds of our lives. It is possible, then, to sink deep roots in soil that is rich and prepared. With our tears, the tears of others and tears of God as water for the seed and with the radiance of God's grace, the past yields life abundant, a good harvest for the banquet. The future not only cannot be divorced

---

[6] Among many others, see: Exod 2:23-25; Luke 1:54-55; Rom 8:37-39; Pss 36; 89; 100; 105:7-10; 117; 136; 145.

[7] Susan Griffin, *A Chorus of Stones: The Private Life of War* (New York: Doubleday, 1992) 8.

[8] Matt 13:1-9, 18-23; Mark 4:1-9, 13-20; Luke 8:4-8, 11-15.

from the past, but its full flourishing is predicated on the past. So, we do the work of the past today. We continue "to proclaim the Lord's death until he comes." If we are silent or silenced then "the stones would shout out" (Luke 19:40).

OUR FUTURE: CHRIST WILL COME AGAIN

What does it mean to say that God is coming toward us in our future? There have always been whole industries to "tell the future." Knowing the future is important to people. So we turn to astrology, almanacs, calendars, or computer models which measure and extrapolate current trends into the future.

But this information is important in different ways for people. For the privileged and those with power, the information is used to prolong and extend the present situation into the future. "Their future is [a] planned and projected future, for only the person who has the power to implement and enact can plan and project."[9] For others with fewer resources to influence their futures, the response can be fatalism, resignation, cynicism, or disillusionment. Timelines shrink and the future has more the character of a bad dream or nightmare than the extension of a victorious present. The possible meanings of "Christ will come again" vary greatly depending upon a person's present social context and resources.

At a minimum, to claim that "Christ will come again" says that there are alternatives, even if they are not perceptible in their entirety or open to definition in achievable time frames.[10] The future is open. It is not just an extrapolation of the present or past. The element of surprise, the unknown, the decisively unpredictable, the question mark cannot be erased or contained. The future includes something that we cannot engineer or manage. It is coming toward us.

Our tradition has seen two components in our future. One is judgment and the other is the fullness of the banquet. The scriptural testimonies to judgment are many. Sometimes they are quite fearsome and apocalyptic, full of images of destruction and God's anger.[11] This thread

[9] Moltmann, *The Coming of God*, 45.

[10] See Station 8.

[11] Abraham J. Heschel has a thoughtful analysis of "the meaning and mystery of wrath" in the Hebrew Scriptures in *The Prophets* (New York: HarperCollins, 1962) ch. 5, pp. 358–82.

runs throughout the Scriptures. God judges in the initial years of creation:

> The LORD saw that the wickedness of humankind was great in the earth, and that every inclination of the thoughts of their hearts was only evil continually. And the LORD was sorry that he had made humankind on the earth, and it grieved him to his heart. So the LORD said, "I will blot out from the earth the human beings I have created—people together with animals and creeping things and birds of the air, for I am sorry that I have made them" (Gen 6:5-7).

God's judgment continues through the destruction of Sodom and Gomorrah (Gen 18:16–19:29); the slaughter following the worship of the golden calf in the wilderness (Exod 32:9-10, 26-29); the terrible visions of the prophets;[12] to Matthew's chilling refrain at the end of some of the judgment parables ("where there will be weeping and gnashing of teeth"), coupled to furnaces of fire (13:41, 49), outer darkness (22:13, 25, 30), or dismemberment (24:51); to the time of swords, fire, hate, and division;[13] and the gospel apocalypses,[14] which are amplified in the great visions of judgment in Revelation,[15] and culminate in a "great supper of God"—a terrible feast of birds prey upon the powerful (Rev 19:17-20). These are texts of terror and meant to be so.[16] But, as Moltmann notes, "better an end with terror than a terror without end."[17] For many whose present is one of endless terror, times of judgment cannot come too soon. In fact, read against the contemporary scenarios of economic, ecological, and nuclear horror, the terrors of the judgment texts do not seem at all fantastic. Our tradition is clear that our actions have consequences; if not immediately, then certainly in the time that is coming.

Our tradition is also absolutely clear that the times of judgment are linked inseparably with times of restoration and the wholeness of the

---

[12] For example: Isaiah 13; 24; Jeremiah 19; Ezekiel 21; Hosea 13; Amos 7; 8.

[13] Matt 10:34-38; parallels Luke 12:49-53; 14:26.

[14] Matt 24:4-29; Mark 13:5-25; Luke 21:9-26.

[15] See chapters 6, 8, 9, 11, 14, 16, 18 in particular.

[16] This borrows from the title of Phyllis Trible's consideration of the terror in the biblical stories of Hagar, Tamar, Jephthah's daughter, and the unnamed woman of Judges 19: *Texts of Terror: Literary-Feminist Readings of Biblical Narratives* (Philadelphia: Fortress Press, 1984).

[17] Moltmann, *The Coming of God*, 135.

new heavens and new earth. This linkage of judgment and restoration is clear in the prophets. As Abraham Heschel writes: "Others may be satisfied with improvement, the prophets insist upon redemption. . . . Together with condemnation, the prophets offer a promise . . . a promise of 'the day of the Lord,' a day of judgment followed by salvation, when evil will be consumed and an age of glory will ensue."[18] In Isaiah's visions, this time of redemption is a time of gathering, when all the nations come and

> [God] shall judge between the nations,
>   and shall arbitrate for many peoples;
> they shall beat their swords into plowshares,
>   and their spears into pruning hooks;
> nation shall not lift up sword against nation,
>   neither shall they learn war any more (Isa 2:4).

> The spirit of the LORD shall rest on [the Righteous One],
>   the spirit of wisdom and understanding,
>   the spirit of counsel and might,
>   the spirit of knowledge and the fear of the LORD.
> His delight shall be in the fear of the LORD.
> He shall not judge by what his eyes see,
>   or decide by what his ears hear;
> but with righteousness he shall judge the poor,
>   and decide with equity for the meek of the earth;
> he shall strike the earth with the rod of his mouth,
>   and with the breath of his lips he shall kill the wicked.
> Righteousness shall be the belt around his waist,
>   and faithfulness the belt around his loins.
> The wolf shall live with the lamb,
>   the leopard shall lie down with the kid,
> the calf and the lion and the fatling together,
>   and a little child shall lead them.
> The cow and the bear shall graze,
>   their young shall lie down together;
>   and the lion shall eat straw like the ox.
> The nursing child shall play over the hole of the asp,
>   and the weaned child shall put its hand on the adder's den.

---

[18] Heschel, *The Prophets*, 231.

> They will not hurt or destroy
>> on all my holy mountain;
> for the earth will be full of the knowledge of the LORD
>> as the waters cover the sea (Isa 11:2-9).

It is a time of judgment linked with an image of shalom,[19] when even the order of the food chain is rewritten, and the serpent is no longer dangerous. It is a time when God's reign of peace among us and within all of creation is established. And so the time of judgment is linked with joy:

> Worship the LORD in holy splendor;
>> tremble before him, all the earth.
> Say among the nations, "The LORD is king!
>> The world is firmly established; it shall never be moved.
>> He will judge the peoples with equity."
> Let the heavens be glad, and let the earth rejoice;
>> let the sea roar, and all that fills it;
>> let the field exult, and everything in it.
> Then shall all the trees of the forest sing for joy
>> before the LORD; for he is coming,
>> for he is coming to judge the earth.
> He will judge the world with righteousness,
>> and the peoples with his truth (Pss 96:9-13; 98; 75).

It is the time of salvation.

> Surely his salvation is at hand for those who fear him. . . .
> Steadfast love and faithfulness will meet;
>> righteousness and peace will kiss each other.
> Faithfulness will spring up from the ground,
>> and righteousness will look down from the sky (Ps 85:9-11).

It is a time when heaven and earth will embrace.

This is the moment that was prefigured in the incarnation of the fully divine with the fully human one. "With all wisdom and insight [God] has made known to us the mystery of his will, according to his good pleasure that he set forth in Christ, as a plan for the fullness of

---

[19] See also Zeph 3:8, 9; Joel 3:11-18; Isaiah 65.

time, to gather up all things in him, things in heaven and things on earth" (Eph 1:8b-10). In Christ, in the middle of the story, we catch a glimpse of the "mystery of God's will—God's plan for the fullness of time." We see the reign, the fullness of the banquet shared by all.[20] We see the love of God poured out for God's beloved creation, but we see it in the midst of opposition, resistance, rejection, and persecution. "The light shines in the darkness, and the darkness did not overcome it" (John 1:5). In that window of time that Christ opened for us, we see the time that is coming when "there will be no more night; they need no light of lamp or sun, for the Lord God will be their light and they will reign forever and ever" (Rev 22:5). But that time is not yet.

Throughout the ages, the question of the delay has continued to haunt us. Why is the banquet still not yet? Surrounded by the agonies of so many and so much in creation, there is "the apocalyptic cry: what is God waiting for?"[21] The psalms urge God to act in judgment:

> God has taken his place in the divine council;
>> in the midst of the gods he holds judgment:
> "How long will you judge unjustly
>> and show partiality to the wicked?
> Give justice to the weak and the orphan;
>> maintain the right of the lowly and the destitute.
> Rescue the weak and the needy; deliver them from the hand of the
>> wicked."
> They have neither knowledge nor understanding;
>> they walk around in darkness;
>> all the foundations of the earth are shaken.
> Rise up, O God, judge the earth;
>> for all the nations belong to you! (Ps 82:1-5, 8).

And Job cries: "Why are times not kept by the Almighty, / and why do those who know him never see his days?" (Job 24:1). Then he goes on to detail the suffering of his day, and our day, in heartrending poetry.

The early Church also struggled with the delay, yet the people were urged to "regard the patience of our Lord as salvation" (2 Pet 3:15a). But in the face of the enormity of suffering in our world, how can God's patience be considered salvation? Can we imagine this "pa-

---

[20] See Station 12.

[21] Morrill, *Anamnesis*, 25.

tience of the Lord" as the gift of time for our perfection, our becoming? Does God delay the day to create the "opportunity to turn hurt into forgiveness, anger into compassion, hatred into love?"[22] Perhaps God waits because we have not learned yet to love every last fragment of creation as God does—unconditionally, unto death. Or perhaps it is for the fullness and completeness of the gathering.[23] Perhaps it is time to ensure the "joy in the presence of the angels of God" that is like the joy of the shepherd who finds his lost sheep or the woman her lost coin, or the parent who cries: "Let us eat and celebrate; for this son of mine was dead and is alive again; he was lost and is found!" (Luke 15:10, 23b-24a). As Jesus said: "This is the will of him who sent me, that I should lose nothing of all that he has given me, but raise it up on the last day" (John 6:39). Moltmann gives an image of just how radical and inclusive Jesus' work of redemption is:

> In the divine Judgment all sinners, the wicked and the violent, the murderers and the children of Satan, the Devil and the fallen angels will be liberated and saved from their deadly perdition through transformation into their true, created being, because God remains true to himself, and does not give up what he has once created and affirmed, or allow it to be lost. . . . It is a source of endlessly consoling joy to know, not just that the murderers will finally fail to triumph over their victims, but that they cannot in eternity even remain the murderers of their victims.[24]

The vision is that evil itself will be redeemed. Perhaps the delay is in the service of redemption.

But it is certain that the Last Judgment is always in the service of the fullness of the banquet. It is never simply vindication for the righteous. And in the meantime, as Paul cautions, it is not ours to act as God's surrogates: "Therefore do not pronounce judgment before the time,[25] before the Lord comes, who will bring to light the things now hidden in darkness and will disclose the purposes of the heart. Then each one

---

[22] Ronald Rolheiser, *The Holy Longing: the Search for a Christian Spirituality* (New York: Doubleday, 1999) 224. See also Jurgen Moltmann, "God's Kenosis in the Creation and Consummation of the World," *The Work of Love: Creation as Kenosis*, ed. John Polkinghorne (Grand Rapids, Mich.: Eerdmans, 2001) 148–51.

[23] See Rev 6:11

[24] Moltmann, *The Coming of God*, 255.

[25] This echoes the injunction against judging others in the Sermon on the Mount/ Plain: Matt 7:1-5; Luke 6:37-42; see Station 10.

will receive commendation from God" (1 Cor 4:5). Rather, until "the Lord comes" we live in the posture of faith: waiting with longing.

> I will stand at my watchpost,
>> and station myself on the rampart;
> I will keep watch to see what he will say to me,
>> and what he will answer concerning my complaint.
> Then the LORD answered me and said:
> Write the vision;
>> make it plain on tablets,
>> so that a runner may read it.
> For there is still a vision for the appointed time;
>> it speaks of the end, and does not lie.
> If it seems to tarry, wait for it;
>> it will surely come, it will not delay.
> Look at the proud!
>> Their spirit is not right in them,
>> but the righteous live by their faith (Hab 2:1-4).

Our faith asserts plainly that the future that we are walking into in- cludes God coming toward us in the fullness of God's rectifying and compassionate power.[26]

And so through the ages, from the midst of history, people have longed for the day of the Lord's coming:

> My soul waits for the Lord
>> more than those who watch for the morning,
>> more than those who watch for the morning.
> O Israel, hope in the LORD!
>> For with the LORD there is steadfast love,
>> and with him is great power to redeem (Ps 130:6-7).

Every time we pray the Lord's Prayer, we voice this faith and our long- ing: "Your kingdom come" (Matt 6:10a; parallel: Luke 11:2b). The Christian Scriptures end with the promise of Christ's coming and our "yes" of expectant longing: "'It is I, Jesus, who sent my angel to you with this testimony for the churches. I am the root and the descen- dant of David, the bright morning star.' The one who testifies to these things says, 'Surely I am coming soon.' Amen. Come, Lord Jesus!"

---

[26] See Leander E. Keck, *Who Is Jesus? History in Perfect Tense* (Columbia: University of South Carolina Press, 2000) 81, 150.

(Rev 22:16, 20). The Christ of our ancestors, the Christ of history, is the Christ of the brightness of the dawn of the new day that is coming toward us. In response, we sing "O come, O come, Emmanuel"; come and usher in the time of restoration and fullness.

Like children waiting for Christmas, disciples then and now ask: When? How long will it be? "Tell us, when will this be, and what will be the sign of your coming and of the end of the age?" (Matt 24:3b; parallels: Mark 13:4; Luke 21:7). Even at the very last time Christ was visibly present before his ascension, his disciples are still asking: "Lord, is this the time when you will restore the kingdom to Israel?" (Acts 1:6). Christ's response is clear. It is decisive. "About that day and hour no one knows, neither the angels of heaven, nor the Son, but only the Father" (Matt 24:36; Mark 13:32); and "It is not for you to know the times or periods that the Father has set by his own authority" (Acts 1:7). We are not the lords of history. In fact, Christ warns against even the question. In the chaos of the times, he suggests, many will use such a question to lead seekers astray (Matt 24:4-5; Mark 13:5-6; Luke 21:8). Indeed, ideological promises of salvation in our time bloodied the history of much of the twentieth century. Just as the "why" of suffering is held in God's wisdom, so is the "when" of the end of history.

Yet we are not helpless in our ignorance of the time. Jesus offers a parable: "Look at the fig tree and all the trees; as soon as they sprout leaves you can see for yourselves and know that summer is already near. So also, when you see these things taking place, you know that the kingdom of God is near" (Luke 21:29-31; parallels Matt 24:32-33; Mark 13:28-29). His answer to the place of judgment is analogous: "Where the corpse is, there the vultures will gather" (Luke 17:37; parallel Matt 24:28). These are natural signs of life and death that we can all understand. Yet we do not seem to understand the times.

> When you see a cloud rising in the west, you immediately say, "It is going to rain"; and so it happens. And when you see the south wind blowing, you say, "There will be scorching heat"; and it happens. You hypocrites! You know how to interpret the appearance of earth and sky, but why do you not know how to interpret the present time? (Luke 12:54-56).

Qoheleth, after piling up image after image of our sense of time and the natural ebb and flow of activities in time, underlines our incomprehension: "He has made everything suitable for its time; moreover he has put a sense of past and future into their minds, yet they cannot find out what God has done from the beginning to the end" (Eccl 3:11). There is such a simplicity and concrete earthiness to these examples of interpreting the times. They argue against the extravagant complexities of speculative millenarianism and apocalyptic scenarios. Rather, everyone can be engaged in discernment of the times in the regular activities of our lives. Since the very beginning when the original people and the snake had a discussion about what it meant when God said, "You may freely eat of every tree of the garden; but of the tree of the knowledge of good and evil you shall not eat, for in the day that you eat of it you shall die" (Gen 2:16b-17), we each and together have been engaged in remembering and interpreting the meaning of what God is doing. Reading the signs of our times is part of our God-walk toward the fullness of the banquet.

Our Present: Christ Is Risen

The arena of our struggle and joy is this present time: between the time when Christ has died and when the glorified Christ will come again. We live in the time lit by the risen Christ. When Jesus of Nazareth walked the earth, many went to see, hear, and be touched by him. Two of these, on the first day of the week after the Sabbath following the crucifixion, were leaving Jerusalem.

> While they were talking and discussing, Jesus himself came near and went with them, but their eyes were kept from recognizing him. And he said to them, "What are you discussing with each other while you walk along?" They stood still, looking sad. Then one of them, whose name was Cleopas, answered him, "Are you the only stranger in Jerusalem who does not know the things that have taken place there in these days?" He asked them, "What things?" (Luke 24:15-19a).

A stranger comes to them and the travellers review their history for this stranger. They explain their hope "that Jesus was the one to redeem Israel," their disappointment, and their mystification by the resurrection accounts. Then the three of them settle into a discussion of the Scriptures and "he interpreted to them all the things about himself in all the scriptures."

As they came near the village to which they were going, [the stranger] walked ahead as if he were going on. But they urged him strongly, saying, "Stay with us, because it is almost evening and the day is now nearly over." So he went in to stay with them. When he was at the table with them, he took bread, blessed and broke it, and gave it to them. Then their eyes were opened, and they recognized him; and he vanished from their sight. They said to each other, "Were not our hearts burning within us while he was talking to us on the road, while he was opening the scriptures to us?" That same hour they got up and returned to Jerusalem; and they found the eleven and their companions gathered together. They were saying, "The Lord has risen indeed, and he has appeared to Simon!" Then they told what had happened on the road, and how he had been made known to them in the breaking of the bread (Luke 24:28-35).

This is the geography of the present time, the time of the resurrection, when our future comes to meet us in love. The Christ we do not know walks with us. We experience his presence sharp and clear for a time. In his presence, the wisdom of the tradition opens to us as a sturdy, subversive memory that can set our hearts on fire. Then, in the simplicity and concreteness of bread broken with the stranger, the now moment of salvation, the kairos moment, expands around us. Our disappointments, discouragement, and frustrations drop to the ground and in that unique opening into the future, "that same hour," the dance turns and we turn and return to Jerusalem, the place of our beginning, the site of our hope, in the joy of a present transformed. Our past is fully present, healed, with sins forgiven. It is available as "dangerous memory." Our future is reconfigured in the presence of Christ. Our hope is renewed. We are fully alive in the Spirit in the present moment of holy time. For these are God's moments, God's time, time out of time, time at the very heart of time, in which we are offered the kingdom and we can reach for the food of the banquet. These are the moments when we learn how to love creation, each other, and ourselves as God does. These are moments of decision—moments in real time and space, for individuals as well as communities and nations,[27] when the path of abundant life for all can be chosen.

[27] See the *kairos* documents created in South Africa, Central America, and among majority world theologians compiled by Robert McAfee Brown, *Kairos: Three Prophetic Challenges to the Church* (Grand Rapids, Mich.: Eerdmans, 1990).

This time at the heart of time, God's time, is always present tense. It is always an event in the now. Life in its fullest, the banquet, is always lived in the present. Right at the beginning of Mark's gospel is the proclamation: "The time *[kairos]* is fulfilled, and the kingdom of God has come near; repent, and believe in the good news" (Mark 1:15). This nearness, the presentness of "the kingdom of God" or the banquet, is the heart, the slogan even, of the mission Jesus gives the disciples:

> Whenever you enter a town and its people welcome you, eat what is set before you; cure the sick who are there, and say to them, "The kingdom of God has come near to you" (Luke 10:8-9). [Or:] As you go, proclaim the good news, "The kingdom of heaven has come near." Cure the sick, raise the dead, cleanse the lepers, cast out demons. You received without payment; give without payment (Matt 10:7-8).

Whether the table (in Luke) or the restoration to wholeness (in Matthew) is stressed, the core message is the same: the kingdom has come near! When? Where? "Look at the fig tree and all the trees; as soon as they sprout leaves you can see for yourselves and know that summer is already near. So also, when you see these things taking place, you know that the kingdom of God is near" (Luke 21:29-31; parallels Matt 24:32-33; Mark 13:28-29). The signs of its nearness are analogous to the signs of the nearness of summer: leaves sprouting on the fig tree, the signs of life. And so Paul urges the church in Rome to wake up and attend to this presence: "Besides this, you know what time it is, how it is now the moment for you to wake from sleep. For salvation is nearer to us now than when we became believers; the night is far gone, the day is near" (Rom 13:11-12a). Attention, alertness, preparation are needed, for it is all too possible to miss the moment (the kairos) or to misread the times with devastating consequences.[28] So Paul, building on Isaiah's witness, seems virtually to shout the nowness of the kingdom to the church in Corinth: "'At an acceptable time I have listened to you, / and on a day of salvation I have helped you.' See, now is the acceptable time; see, now is the day of salvation!" (2 Cor 6:2).

---

[28] See: Luke 21:8; Matt 24:42-44; Luke 12:42-46; Matt 25:1-13; Luke 19:41-44; Matt 25:31-46; Mark 13:32-42.

The banquet is not somewhere else in time or space, it is near. It is present. "What comes about the day of which Paul is speaking is the kairos of salvation through the call of the gospel and the rebirth in faith."[29] These times of the in-breaking of God and explosion of time in the midst of our lives are different than the end of historical (chronos) time which is in God's future coming toward us. In these moments our eyes are opened, we can glimpse the banquet and we too can choose to return to Jerusalem in hope. Moses' great speech of decision and challenge to the people before they crossed the Jordan into the Promised Land culminates in just such a moment of choice: "I have set before you life and death, blessings and curses. Choose life so that you and your descendants may live, loving the LORD your God, obeying him, and holding fast to him" (Deut 30:19-20a). Building on that speech, Paul writes:

> But the righteousness that comes from faith says, "Do not say in your heart, 'Who will ascend into heaven?'" (that is, to bring Christ down) "or 'Who will descend into the abyss?'" (that is, to bring Christ up from the dead). But what does it say?
>
> > "The word is near you,
> > on your lips and in your heart"
>
> (that is, the word of faith that we proclaim) (Rom 10:6-8; following Deut 30:11-14).

This is the word of life—Christ near, present, in the here and now, at the very center, not the margins of space and time. These are moments in the midst of the journey when Christ invites us to the banquet and we can choose to move in that direction. They are times of opportunity, challenge, decision, and great blessing.

---

[29] Note Moltmann's distinction: "What is meant is a present with a clearly recollected past and distinctly expected future. Any interpretation of this 'present' as 'eschatological moment' puts too great a strain on it and destroys it. What happens on 'the day of salvation' is not the 'sudden' transformation of time into eternity, for it is not yet the raising of the dead in that eschatological moment which does not belong at all to time any longer." *The Coming of God*, 293. It is in this light that Paul's injunction to work, and in fact for food to be withheld from those unwilling to work, can be understood: 2 Thess 3:7-11. The "rest" of the end times is not now. See also the redemption of work as part of Sabbath spiritual practice.

In the midst of all the complexities, entanglements, seductions, and distractions of our unique here and now, we are not orphans. Christ comes to us (John 14:18). In living the tension of the banquet reality in the midst of our specific historical situation, we are not without teachers or guides. In addition to each other and "the prophets,"[30] the Spirit is our counselor, guide, and teacher. In the moment of his leave-taking as he moved into another dimension of his life with us, Jesus assures his disciples of God's presence:

> When the Spirit of truth comes, he will guide you into all the truth; he will declare to you the things that are to come (John 16:13). [And:] You will receive power when the Holy Spirit has come upon you; and you will be my witnesses in Jerusalem, in all Judea and Samaria, and to the ends of the earth (Acts 1:8).

This same creative, generative Spirit of God that moved over "the formless void and darkness [that] covered the face of the deep" at the beginning of time, moves over the deeps of our time and over the deeps of our hearts (Gen 1:1). The Spirit heals our pasts and sweeps open doors of possibility into the fullness of the banquet time. The Spirit is the breath of life, the energy of the new creation, the way God's love touches creation in compassion, healing, and reconciliation. Until the time when Christ will come again, the Spirit guides Christ's disciples along the paths of wisdom and compassion and prompts our hearts, wills, and minds to "choose life" in those moments of *kairos*.

SPIRITUAL CHALLENGE: PATIENCE

Our now, our present, is sandwiched between the legacies of our history, with all its accumulated weight of tradition and suffering, and the yearnings of our hearts for the fullness of the future. It is so easy to miss this now, either lost in or crushed by our pasts or in an impatient rush into the future. In the twenty-four hours a day, seven days a week reality of electricity and availability of services, time can be totally unrelenting. Like a train, once out of the station we follow its steel tracks until it stops. The future becomes fate, the past what we have left

---

[30] See Station 2 and 10.

behind, and our task is to endure, to cope, to survive. Or we can take control of time and define the value of time by what we do with it, what we make of it, by our achievements. Or we can be defined by our work and when we can no longer contribute or be useful, our time is worthless and so are we. We are expendable and time hangs very heavy. In this culture dominated by time and devoted to speed, our spiritual challenge is patience. This is not a patience that advocates submission to the implacable realities of time, nor denies the urgencies of present action. Rather, it is a patience which is acutely attentive to the movement of God's Spirit in our time and is prepared to follow that Spirit into the very thick of life. With this patience, the fullness of each now and all its possibility is brought into focus without premature reduction or blurring in a rush to solutions. Patience opens the door to the future that comes to meet us in love.

The word of God needs patience to bear its fruit. "But as for that [seed] in the good soil, these are the ones who, when they hear the word, hold it fast in an honest and good heart, and bear fruit with patient endurance" (Luke 8:15). "Patience makes us realize that the Christian who has entered into discipleship with Jesus Christ lives not only with a new mind but also in a new time."[31] Patience focuses our eyes and tunes our ears to the heartbeat of God, so that we can experience in each moment, whether joyful or agonizing, the fullness of all that is.

> When patience prevents us from running from the painful moment in the false hope of finding our treasure elsewhere, we can slowly begin to see that the fullness of time is already here and that salvation is already taking place. . . . In and through Christ, all human events can become divine events in which we discover the compassionate presence of God.[32]

Ronald Rolheiser calls this "pondering." "To ponder," he writes, "is less a question of intellectually contemplating something than of patiently holding it inside one's soul, complete with all the tension that it brings. . . . [It is to] carry tension without giving in to premature resolution. . . . It is the gestation time."[33] It is the time in which new

[31] Donald P. McNeill, Douglas A. Morrison, Henri J. M. Nouwen, *Compassion: A Reflection on the Christian Life* (Garden City, N.Y.: Doubleday, 1983) 96.

[32] Ibid., 100.

[33] Rolheiser, *The Holy Longing,* 220, 223, 224.

life, healing, and reconciliation are conceived and grown. It is the pregnant, rich, fruitful time of the Spirit. It is not clock time. It is not time filled up with junk food, but rather a space, a cup or bowl deep in our souls which we hold open and ready for the food of the banquet.

This posture of faith requires a very active, alert, awake, expectant, open-to-the-moment kind of patience. This is the watchfulness, the active waiting for the *kairos* moment, of which our Scriptures speak.

> Be dressed for action and have your lamps lit; be like those who are waiting for their master to return from the wedding banquet, so that they may open the door for him as soon as he comes and knocks. Blessed are those slaves whom the master finds alert when he comes; truly I tell you, he will fasten his belt and have them sit down to eat, and he will come and serve them (Luke 12:35-37).

These moments are large and momentous or transitory and scarcely perceptible. They can happen anywhere, with anyone. We cannot rush toward them, earn them, create them, or simply clench our teeth and endure for them. These moments come as gift. We do not know the hour of their coming, for if we did we could not live fully in the moment and it is in the moment that salvation comes. In that moment, time stands still, then expands in another dimension, and we catch a whiff, a hint of the taste of the banquet.

There are two related aspects to the cultivation of this active patience. There are practices to awaken the heart and practices to dismantle structures that harden the heart. They are flip sides of the same coin, the left foot/right foot beat of walking with the living Christ.

First, the practices to cultivate an awakened heart develop eyes that see and ears that hear; a heart that welcomes the stranger; hands that offer food to the hungry, healing to the wounded and hurting, and freedom to the captive and enslaved; a mind that discerns the path of truth and wisdom, that is wise as a serpent yet innocent as a dove (Matt 10:16); and a soul that trusts in the infinite love and always-enoughness of God.

Second, there are practices to dismantle the structures that harden the heart, kill the body, poison the mind, and shrink the soul. These structures are legion. There are all the threads of addiction; of hate, envy, violence, resentment; of attachments, acquisitiveness, greed; of patterns of discrimination, prejudice, racism, sexism, and individualism; of justifications for inequality, injustice, scarcity, and exclusion; and all the practices that harm the integrity of creation and create terrible legacies for the generations to come.

The cultivation of patience is active work. It happens in clock time and is sustained by grace. It is patience or sustained pondering that keeps us walking in time with Christ and ready for those times of *kairos*.

SPIRITUAL PRACTICE: SABBATH

In a culture of impatience how do we cultivate patience? How can we reorient our focus, the cycle of our days, the patterns of our actions, thoughts, and habits of the heart to the fullness of the banquet? How can we continue to stand fully present to our past but not a victim of it; to live in anticipation of God's coming toward us and opening futures beyond our grasp, yet fully alive in the moment we are in? What sustains us in an awareness of God's non-clock time, of the eternal in the now? How do we continue to stay tuned to the rhythm of Jesus' walk? Surely it is only possible if we can hear the music of God's heart —God's tears, God's tenderness, God's laughter and joy—if we spend real time waiting in the cool of the evening breeze to meet God in the garden of God's creation (Gen 3:8).

At the heart of the answer of our tradition is the fourth commandment: "Remember the Sabbath day and keep it holy" (Exod 20:8; parallel Deut 5:12-15). The Sabbath is the seventh day of creation, the day of God's rest and delight in its goodness. It is the day that God blessed and sanctified (Gen 2:2-3; Exod 20:11). God hallows not just a time of rest, but also a place of rest. The great journey of the peoples' liberation was to the Promised Land, a place of rest (Josh 1:13; Deut 5:12-15). The twin gifts of God, creation and liberation, are the foundations of the Sabbath commandment (Exod 20:11 and Deut 5:15, respectively). For Christians, Christ opens a way into God's Sabbath rest. For "a sabbath rest still remains for the people of God" (Heb 4:9).

Sabbath practice is not solitary. It is a community affair. It touches all our relations. Sabbath rest is for the whole community: "you, or your son or your daughter, or your male or female slave, or your ox or your donkey, or any of your livestock, or the resident alien in your towns, so that your male and female slave may rest as well as you" (Deut 5:14).

It is not rest purchased at the expense of others' work, suffering, or deprivation. It is rest shared by all. And this rest extends to the land itself. Every seventh year was to be a Sabbath year for the land itself (Exod 23:10-12; Lev 25:1-7). Every fiftieth year was to be a jubilee year, the Sabbath's Sabbath: a time of liberation and rectification of social relations (Lev 25:8-55). "What would be a world without Sabbath? It would be a world that knew only itself . . . a world without the vision of a window in eternity that opens into time."[34] We would lose any sense of the fullness of the banquet. In keeping the Sabbath, we are invited, in real time and space, in living community and in continuity with our ancestors in the faith, to celebrate in anticipation the fulfillment of creation and God's project of liberation and rest at one with God, neighbor, and creation and taste the fullness of the banquet.

Yet how readily we distort the order of things. We set the sisters Mary and Martha in opposition to each other. We mistake the means for the goal. How often we separate things of the spirit, holy matters, Sabbath time from things of the body, human needs, work time. Leisure, rest, and time to not work become the goal. Work becomes a necessary evil. We work harder and harder to not work, and our moments of rest cost others their rest. But to set aside one day in seven as Sabbath time is not to make time holy. All of time, work time included, is to be consecrated and shaped by the Sabbath. The Sabbath is time to get in sync with the rhythm of Jesus' walk. Or as the psalmist has written:

> Unless the LORD builds the house,
>   those who build it labor in vain.
> Unless the LORD guards the city,
>   the guard keeps watch in vain.
> It is in vain that you rise up early
>   and go late to rest,
> eating the bread of anxious toil;
>   for he gives sleep to his beloved (Ps 127:1-2).

Wendell Berry's contemporary reading of the inner heart of this Psalm captures the tandem quality of the life and work of the Spirit and of human work:

---

[34] Abraham J. Heschel, *The Sabbath: Its Meaning for Modern Man* (New York: Farrar, Straus & Co., 1952) 16.

Whatever is forseen in joy
Must be lived out from day to day.
Vision held open in the dark
By our ten thousand days of work.
Harvest will fill the barn; for that
The hand must ache, the face must sweat.

And yet no leaf or grain is filled
By work of ours; the field is tilled
And left to grace. That we may reap,
Great work is done while we're asleep.

When we work well, a Sabbath mood
Rests on our day, and finds it good.[35]

The rest of the Sabbath is all about good work, the redemption of work, work done in sync with the Spirit's "great work." Making time holy includes making our work holy. It means returning work to its original purposes in the service of the garden. It means humanizing work not only in its goals, but in its details.[36] It is not just about setting aside time to be holy, or escaping time, it is about consecrating time, all of it. It is the vision of the Sabbath in the service of human needs and the needs of all of creation (Mark 2:27).

In that first garden the original people worked, tilling, cultivating, nurturing, taking care of the garden. Yet, outside of the garden, having fallen out of step with God, our needs are met only through "toil," or as other translations read: "painful work":

In toil you shall eat of it [the earth]. . . .
By the sweat of your face you shall eat bread
until you return to the ground" (Gen 3:17b, 19a).

But this curse of work is not the final word. Christ's resurrection in which matter/energy itself is transformed and released from decay

---

[35] Wendell Berry, "1979#X 'Whatever is forseen in joy,'" *Sabbaths* (San Francisco: North Point Press, 1987) 19. See also Dorothy C. Bass, "Keeping Sabbath," *Practicing Our Faith: A Way of Life for a Searching People*, ed. Dorothy C. Bass (San Francisco: Jossey-Bass, 1997) 75–89.

[36] See Miroslav Volf, *Work in the Spirit: Toward a Theology of Work* (New York: Oxford University Press, 1991).

happened on the "first day of the week," after the Sabbath. This is the eighth day of creation, the time when the new creation is filled with the fullness of the One who fills all in all (Eph 1:23). It is Sabbath seen in a different horizon: not at the end of creation and therefore a day of rest, rest after work, the goal of the journey; but Sabbath as a holy time of waiting, in anticipation, in preparation for the full fruits of the first day of the week, of the new creation, the coming kingdom, the transformation of all work, all time, into the service of the banquet.

Just as our food needs keep us focused on the day to day, gardening keeps us attentive to the change of seasons, and agriculture teaches us what it takes to be fruitful over the years, so Sabbath practice is time to savor, to anticipate and to re-root in the fullness of the eternal banquet in the present. It is time for the cultivation of patience, food for pondering, for "carrying the tension of the present without giving in to premature resolution."[37] It is time in which we rest in, and are at one with, God. It is time to remember our history, to retell the story of salvation. It is time to link our experience of "God in history with the messianic hope in God for history."[38] It is time to reorder our priorities, to rectify our relationships, to delight in our kin and be with the community of life. It is a time of refreshment, a time indeed to drink in joy from the wells of our salvation (Isa 12:3). It is time to sing our praises to the Lord of history. It is *kairos* time, a foretaste of the banquet.

---

[37] Rolheiser, *The Holy Longing*, 223.

[38] Jurgen Moltmann, "Liberating and Anticipating the Future," *Liberating Eschatology: Essays in Honor of Letty M. Russell*, ed. Margaret A. Farley and Serene Jones (Louisville, Ky.: Westminster John Knox Press, 1999) 198.

Station 13 Litany: "Your Kingdom Come"

Voices 1: For your Word made known in the breaking of bread;
Voices 2: For the companionship of the Stranger;
All: **For the One who meets us in the gap between an ending and a beginning,**
Opening the past to understanding and the future to new directions;
We give thanks and pray: Come, Lord Jesus.

Voices 1: For your promise of restoration and healing, justice and peace,
Challenging us to live boldly into question marks of our times;
Voices 2: For the sharp spotlight your promised judgment
Casts on the tangled issues of our day;
All: **For the light of your presence coming toward us in love,**
We give thanks and pray: Come, Lord Jesus.

One: Let us bring all of who we are to You,
Voices 1: Open the treasures of our history to us, heal the fissures of our memory;
Teach us to trust the truth to set us free and the power of love to reconcile.

One: Help us to live in the present with all its ambiguity and tension,
Voices 2: Without rushing into a future of our own making,
Or accepting a future of someone else's design.

One: Free us from the tyranny of clocks and calendars, pagers and telephones,
Voices 1: To meet you in the here and now; to hear your voice and the beat of your heart,
To keep the Sabbath holy and to order our work to your purposes.

One: Ready us for the day of your coming.

Voices 2:   Teach us to read the signs of the times, the recipes of the banquet;

Enroll us in the school of kairos, instruct us in the tempo of your walk.

One: For all time is yours:

Voices 1:   You are the Beginning and the End, the Alpha and Omega, yet as present as our breath;

Voices 2:   You are our heart's desire and home;

In You all creation finds rest, completion, and replenishment.

Voices 1:   We wait for you;

We hold the present open for your redemption;

Voices 2:   We trust in the justice and mercy of your judgment,

In your plan for the fullness of time revealed in the Word;

Voices 1:   Song of the Universe, Rhythm of Life, and Pregnant Interruption;

Voices 2:   Host of the Banquet, Bread of Life, Kitchen Fire;

All: **Hallowed be your Name,**

All praise and glory is Yours,

As it was in the beginning, is now, and will be forever.

Amen.

Visual Focus: A clock, calendar, and day timer.

Station 14

ENDNOTE:
THE EIGHTH DAY OF CREATION

Voice 1: Spirit who plumbs the very depths of God (1 Cor 2:10),
Speak to us of the new creation, of the new Jerusalem.
Give us a plan, a recipe, a map.

Voice 2: No, it is for you and your kin to sing.
"Do you not know that you are God's temple,
that God's Spirit dwells in you?
For God's temple is holy, and you are that temple"
    (1 Cor 3:16, 17b).
For "you are no longer strangers and aliens, . . .
You are citizens with the saints and also members of the
    household of God,
Built upon the foundations of the apostles and prophets,
With Christ Jesus himself as the cornerstone.
In him the whole structure is joined together and
Grows into a holy temple in the Lord;
In whom you also are built together spiritually
Into a dwelling place for God" (Eph 2:19-22).
You are the song of the new creation,
So, "sing to the Lord a new song" (Psalms 95; 96; 98; 100).

For "it is now the moment for you to wake from sleep.
The night is far gone, the day is near" (Rom 13:11b, 12a).
The bright morning star is shining (Rev 22:16; 2 Pet 1:19).

Voice 1:   Throw open the windows, open the door.
Awake, my soul! Awake, O harp and lyre!
I will awake the dawn (Ps 57:8).
For, "my soul longs, indeed it faints
   for the courts of the LORD;
My heart and my flesh sing for joy
   to the living God.
Even the sparrow finds a home
   and the swallow a nest for herself,
   where she may lay her young
at your altars, O LORD of hosts,
   my . . . God" (Ps 84:2-3).
So, "Yes," I sing! "Yes," I shout to your invitation!

All: **"Come and have breakfast," you say (John 21:12).**
"Yes," we respond.
Yes, to the Banquet of the Holy One!
Yes, to the path of abundant life for all—
   Every last sheep, every lost child, every fragment of
      creation.
Yes, your kin(g)dom come!"

Voice 3:   For the nations *will* come to the light,
And kings to the brightness of the dawn (Isa 60:3).
We will each understand each other in our own native
   language (Acts 2:6b),
And there will be no need for swords or spears (Isa 2:4).

Voice 4:   The earth will bear fruit abundantly (Psalms 65; 104),
Each will gather as much as each needs,
And there will be enough for all (Exod 16:4, 18; Acts 2:45).
All will eat and be satisfied, with baskets left over (Matt
   14:20; Mark 6:42; Luke 9:17; John 6:12).

Voice 5:   The blind will see, the oppressed go free,
the poor will hear good news, and the captives be released
   (Luke 4:18; Isa 61:1).

Voice 6:   The Lord God will wipe away the tears from all faces
   (Isa 25:8; Rev 21:4a).

And each will hear: "You are my beloved, with whom I am
well pleased" (see Matt 3:17; Mark 1:11; Luke 2:22b).

Voice 7: The earth will be full of the knowledge of the Lord,
As the waters cover the sea (Isa 11:9),
And the people will dance and sing, "My home is here!"
(Ps 87:6 IECL).

Voice 8: The hills will sing together for joy,
All the earth will make a joyful noise to the Lord
(Ps 95; 96; 98; 100).
And the glory of God will fill the earth.

Voice 1: BUT—but, Lord, we do not know the way! (John 14:5).

Voice 2: "Do not let your hearts be troubled, do not let them be
afraid.
I will not leave you orphaned.
The Spirit will teach you everything" (John 14:18, 25, 27b).
"The Spirit helps us in our weakness,
For we do not know how to pray as we ought,
But that very Spirit intercedes with sighs too deep for
words" (Rom 8:26).
For "we know that all things work together for good
For those who love God, who are called according to God's
purpose" (Rom 8:28).
And we know that nothing—
"Neither death nor life, nor angels nor rulers,
Nor things present, nor things to come,
Nor powers, nor height, nor depth, nor anything else in all
creation
Will be able to separate us from the love of God"
(Rom 8:38-39).

All: **So in the perfect love which casts out all fear** (1 John 4:18),
We clothe ourselves in the light and love of Christ
And gather for the wedding feast (Rev 19:9; Matt 22:1-14;
Luke 14:16-24);
The banquet of joy for which we are created.

Joining with all who have gone before us,
We sing with all our hearts, souls, minds, and bodies,
The song of the universe from before time:
The goodness, justice, peace, and abundance of the new
    creation.
All shout "Glory" in your temple, O God (Ps 29:9b).
"Amen! Blessing and glory and wisdom and thanksgiving
And honor and power and might be to our God forever
    and ever!" (Rev 7:12).
Amen. Alleluia! Amen. Alleluia!

Visual focus: Picture of an open door with light on the other side.

Appendix 1

THE "STATIONS" AS COMMUNAL PRAYER

It is one thing to talk about our relationship with God and each other, and it is another to enact those relationships. The litanies in each station are for us to use a different voice and engage a different part of ourselves together. Much like the psalms, they are for personal and corporate prayer and reflection.

Although each litany can stand on its own for use in study groups or occasions for which a short prayer form is useful, the original intention is that the fourteen litanies serve as the backbone for a communal prayer event, quiet day, or retreat. An outline for such an event is provided as a starting point for the creation of a Stations of the Banquet event. Building on experience with the traditional Stations of the Cross, Stations of the Banquet include prayer (the litanies at the end of each Station), time for reflection on Scripture, a visual focus, and a sense of progression or movement on a journey.

- Scripture readings are suggested for Stations 2 through 13, although a group who has studied each station may want to substitute others. For Stations 1 and 14, the readings are incorporated into the station itself.

- Two short musical refrains are included to provide continuity between the stations and to include our breath, bodies, and emotions in our prayer. Each of the litanies for Stations 2 through 13 include an opening section of thanksgiving and conclude with praise. The first refrain, "Source of All Blessing," was written to contribute to the spirit of thanksgiving. It also has a rhythm to give a gentle sense of movement or journey. The second refrain, "Holy Is Your Name," is to allow a full expression of our praise. Together they allow a tempo to be set for the event as a whole. In addition, a gong or chime is useful for marking reflection times.

- The suggestions for a visual focus for each station can be elaborated as is helpful and the time and creativity of the group permits. They can also become participatory: fruit eaten, bread broken, stones taken up and put down, water poured, yeast and mustard seeds passed from hand to hand, etc. Such involvement invites engagement and encourages the translation of words into action. It also provides time for reflection. If stations are set up around a room and participants move from one station to another, the journey metaphor is accented. Alternatively, as at a banquet table, changing stations can be marked by changing the visual focus at the center of a circle or front of a room.

- If the Stations are to be one continuous event, it is important to take time before beginning to assign readers for each station, and to familiarize the group with the music. If the Stations are to be used over a quiet day or weekend, logical break moments have been indicated.

- The variation in voices suggested in each litany can be taken as parts of the group: by seating, by gender, by birth year, etc.; or as single voices. The "one" voice can help to set a prayerful pace to the litany.

Although the Stations of the Banquet with music, Scripture, and prayers can be accomplished in seventy-five to eighty minutes, it is not recommended. It is not fast food. Like a rich meal, time taken to savor each course increases its value. Rushed prayer keeps us in our heads and in action mode. It reduces our openness to the movement of the Spirit and inhibits that subtle shift to simply being in the presence of the Holy. Many people have little experience of praying and reading simultaneously. A slower pace can help. Pauses or breaks for reflection can enhance the enjoyment of the feast and keep the tone prayerful.

OUTLINE OF STATIONS OF THE BANQUET PRAYER EVENT

Station 1:
Prologue: The Song of the Universe [pp. 1–4]

> Refrain: Source of All Blessing

Station 2:
In the Beginning . . . Food

> Reading: Genesis 2:9, 16, 17; 3:1-9
> pause
> Refrain: "Source of All Blessing"
> Litany: pp. 20–1
> Refrain: "Holy Is Your Name"
> pause then move to next station

Station 3:
Hear "The Cries of My People"

> Reading: Luke 16:19-24a, 26-29
> pause
> Refrain: "Source of All Blessing"
> Litany: pp. 39–40
> Refrain: "Holy Is Your Name"
> pause then move to next station

Station 4:
"I Am the Bread of Life"

> Readings: Isaiah 55:1-2; Mark 14:22-24
> pause
> Refrain: "Source of All Blessing"
> Litany: pp. 57–8
> Refrain: "Holy Is Your Name"
> pause then move to next station

[Possible Break]

Station 5:
Table Etiquette 1: Love—"I Was Hungry and You Gave Me Bread"

> Reading: John 13:1-5, 12-17
> pause

Refrain: "Source of All Blessing"
Litany: pp. 78–9
Refrain: "Holy Is Your Name"
pause then move to next station

Station 6:
Table Etiquette 2:
Hospitality—"Invite Everyone You Find to the Banquet"

Reading: Acts 11:1-12
pause
Refrain: "Source of All Blessing"
Litany: pp. 100–1
Refrain: "Holy Is Your Name"
pause then move to next station

Station 7:
Table Etiquette 3:
Economics—"Where Your Treasure Is, There Your Heart Will Be Also"

Reading: Revelation 3:14a, 15-18, 20
pause
Refrain: "Source of All Blessing"
Litany: pp. 121–2
Refrain: "Holy Is Your Name"
pause then move to next station

[Possible Break]

Station 8:
"It Is Impossible"

Readings: Mark 10:17-27 and Matthew 17:20b or Mark 9:17-29
pause
Refrain: "Source of All Blessing"
Litany: pp. 142–3
Refrain: "Holy Is Your Name"
pause then move to next station

Station 9:
"My Cup Overflows"

Reading: Mark 8:14-21

pause
Refrain: "Source of All Blessing"
Litany: pp. 167–8
Refrain: "Holy Is Your Name"
pause then move to next station

Station 10:
"Let Justice Roll Down Like Water"

Readings: Isaiah 58:6-7, 9b-10; John 8: 2-11
pause
Refrain: "Source of All Blessing"
Litany: pp. 196–7
Refrain: "Holy Is Your Name"
pause then move to next station

[Possible Break]

Station 11:
"Abide in Me, As I Abide in You"

Readings: Luke 10:38-42; John 15:4-5
pause
Refrain: "Source of All Blessing"
Litany: pp. 218–9
Refrain: "Holy Is Your Name"
pause then move to next station

Station 12:
The Banquet

Readings: Isaiah 25:6-9 and Luke 4:18-21
pause
Refrain: "Source of All Blessing"
Litany: pp. 243–4
Refrain: "Holy Is Your Name"
pause then move to next station

Station 13:
"Your Kingdom Come!"

Reading: Matthew 24:3 and Luke 24:13-21a, 28-35
pause

Refrain: "Source of All Blessing"
Litany: pp. 271–2
Refrain: "Holy Is Your Name"
pause then move to next station

Station 14:
Endnote: The Eighth Day of Creation

Refrain: "Source of All Blessing"
Litany: pp. 275–8
Refrain: "Allelulia! Amen," *see* "Holy Is Your Name"

SOURCE OF ALL BLESSING

Words: Cathy Campbell
Music: Maureen Hollins

HOLY, HOLY IS YOUR NAME

Words: Cathy Campbell
Music: Maureen Hollins

Appendix 2

COMMUNITY FOOD SECURITY

In secular circles, food security is the most inclusive umbrella name for banquet work.[1] Most simply, food security is access by all people at all times to enough food for an active, healthy life. The simplicity of the concept belies the complexity of its achievement.

There are three dimensions of food security work and each dimension must be in place for food security to be a reality:

1. Assured access to food over time requires an ecologically and economically sustainable agriculture system. Farmers and the food industry must not only be able to cultivate, process, and transport sufficient food for everyone, but must do that with enough ecological wisdom and equity to be sustainable over the generations. In addition, the food-related component (both organic matter and packaging) of waste, recycling, and garbage disposal work is an ancillary issue that is growing in significance in urban areas in particular.

2. Access to food requires adequate money to purchase either food or what is needed to grow, gather, fish, or hunt one's own food. This dimension of food security work, therefore, involves issues of employment opportunities and wage levels, support for those unable to work, as well as housing, health, and education costs

---

[1] Other terms include hunger work, food justice, food sustainability, food democracy.

287

that often directly compete for household food dollars. Also, the availability and quality of food outlets can limit food security in some communities. A strictly economic approach to this dimension can obscure two other access issues. One is the distribution of available food within a household and the second is the dignity and choice that is afforded to people who do not get their food through grocery stores and restaurants.

3. The quality of the food that is acquired is the third dimension of food security concern. Here the issues are the nutritional value of the food for health, the quantity of food relative to activity levels, the personal and cultural acceptability of the available food, its safety and the regulations necessary to ensure food quality. Related concerns are the food literacy levels of consumers, labeling concerns, and the availability of food information and educational opportunities to enhance consumer understanding and skill levels.

In addition, issues of war, peace, violence and instability, justice, human rights, and governance, as well as personal health and safety and ecosystem integrity, critically affect the level of food security experienced and thus the work that is possible on these issues.

There are extraordinary networks of people working on each of these clusters of issues. They range from highly technical professionals working as scientists, economists, policy analysts, anthropologists, and health care practitioners to small groups of concerned people who provide food for children, seniors, the vulnerable and lonely in their neighborhoods, and/or who organize community gardens, kitchens, food cooperatives, and buying clubs. Food security work happens in church basements, farms, government offices and businesses, and nongovernmental organizations of all sorts. The scope of any one endeavor can involve people in a neighborhood or municipality, or can happen at regional, national, or international levels of organization. The networks are rich, diverse, and interconnected. There are many points of view of most issues and more than enough for everyone to do. Coalitions and partnerships are critical in this work as no one person or group could be expected to address all of the issues or really any one issue in all its dimensions. Together this work builds food security around the globe so that day by day, place by place, people taste the banquet intended for all.

Over time an amazing array of resources have been developed to support this work. The web sites listed below are one way to begin to explore the work of the banquet and to expand your personal networks and coalitions. Another way is simply to begin to talk with the people involved in food work who live nearest to you. Those conversations are the heart of the journey of the banquet.

CHRISTIAN FOOD AND FAITH LINKS

www.bread.org: Bread for the World is a Christian citizens' movement seeking justice for the world's hungry people. It includes an excellent set of links to other anti-hunger and poverty organizations.

www.christianfarmers.org: Christian Farmers Federation of Ontario links together faith, agriculture, and public policy work.

www.kairoscanada.org: Kairos brings together the work of ten Canadian ecumenical justice coalitions and initiatives.

www.pcusa.org/hunger: The Presbyterian (USA) Hunger Program broadly addresses hunger and its underlying causes.

www.ncrlc.com: National Catholic Rural Life Conference works on a variety of agriculture, rural community, and food issues, including the "eating is a moral act" campaign.

www.wcc-coe.org: World Council of Churches site includes a good set of ecumenical links.

FOOD SECURITY LINKS

www.brown.edu/Departments/World_Hunger_Program: Brown University's HungerWeb is an extensive listing of hunger-related links categorized by research, fieldwork, advocacy and policy, and education and training.

www.cafb-acba.ca: Canadian Association of Food Banks coordinates food donations and transportation and is a liaison among food banks in Canada and with food industries and the government.

www.cityfarmer.org: City Farmer provides links on local to international urban agriculture work.

www.cspinet.org: Center for Science in the Public Interest focuses on the safety and nutritional quality of our food supply; see also www.cspinet.org/canada for Canadian links.

www.feedingminds.org: "Feeding Minds, Fighting Hunger" is a school curriculum developed by broad based national and international agencies to support World Food Day October 16 (although it is useful at any time).

www.foodfirst.org: Institute for Food and Development Policy is a member-supported, nonprofit people's think tank and education for action center.

www.foodroutes.org: Foodroutes supports "on-the-ground" advocates of sustainable farming and local food systems. It provides an excellent set of links to relevant information and resources as well as other relevant community-based organizations.

www.foodsecurity.org: Community Food Security Coalition highlights community-based solutions to hunger, poor nutrition, and the globalization of the food system. It includes links to many other community-based food security programs.

www.frac.org: Food Research and Action Center focuses primarily on childhood hunger and school nutrition issues.

www.nal.usda.gov/fnic: Food and Nutrition Information Center of the U.S. Department of Agriculture provides extensive information on a broad range of issues. Links under "community food systems" (accessed through the directory or www.nal.usda.gov/fnic/etext/000061.html) are particularly relevant.

www.ryerson.ca/~foodsec: Ryerson University's Centre for Studies in Food Security; includes links to online courses on food security.

www.secondharvest.org: Second Harvest is the largest hunger relief organization in the United States. Site includes links to other hunger organizations and to relevant public policy work.

www.sustainweb.org: Sustain is a British-based alliance for better food and farming with excellent resources, programming ideas, and links.

www.worldfooddayusa.org: This site provides resource material and support for World Food Day (October 16) activities all year round.

FOOD SECURITY ORGANIZATIONS WITH GOOD PROGRAMMING IDEAS FOR LOCAL WORK

www.ffcf.bc.ca: Farm Folk/City Folk is a Vancouver-based food and agriculture organization.

www.foodshare.net: Foodshare is a Toronto-based food advocacy and program development and support organization.

www.hartford.food.org: Hartford Food System implements a variety of programs to promote a sustainable and equitable food system in Connecticut.

www.nsnc.ca: Nova Scotia Nutrition Council is a coalition of professionals and community activists working on food security. It provides links to relevant Canadian work.

ORGANIZATIONS WITH A MORE INTERNATIONAL FOCUS

www.dietforasmallplanet.com: Provides links to eleven domains of constructive action on food issues from around the globe that are highlighted in Anna Lappé and Frances Moore Lappé's book *Hope's Edge: The New Diet for a Small Planet.*

www.fian.org: FIAN is an international human rights organization dedicated to the promotion of the right to feed oneself.

www.foodgrainsbank.ca: Canadian Foodgrains Bank is a Christian-based food aid and development organization that collects donations of grain, cash, and other agricultural commodities for distribution to the world's hungry.

www.ifpri.org: International Food Policy Research Institute concentrates on economic growth and poverty alleviation in low-income countries, improvement of the well-being of poor people, and sound management of the natural resource base that supports agriculture.

www.iatp.org: The Institute for Agriculture and Trade Policy promotes resilient family farms, rural communities, and ecosystems around the world.

UNITED NATIONS AGENCIES WITH RELEVANT INFORMATION AND DATA

www.wfp.org: The World Food Programme is the frontline agency addressing food crises around the globe.

www.fao.org: Food and Agriculture Organization of the United Nations works on systemic food security issues.

www.undp.org: United Nations Development Programme focuses on development issues holistically.

www.unicef.org: UNICEF provides information on maternal and child nutrition.

These websites represent a tiny proportion of those that are relevant, but they will connect you through their "links" to hundreds of additional sites, and to a whole variety of good resource material for ways to participate in food security work.

BIBLIOGRAPHY

Ammerman, Nancy T. "Golden Rule Christianity." *Lived Religion in America: Toward a History of Practice.* Ed. David D. Hall. Princeton, N.J.: Princeton University Press, 1997.

Bailie, Gil. *Violence Unveiled: Humanity at the Crossroads.* New York: Crossroad, 1995.

Bane, Mary Jo, and Brent Coffin. "Introduction." *Who Will Provide? The Changing Role of Religion in American Social Welfare.* Ed. Mary Jo Bane, Brent Coffin, Ronald Thiemann. Boulder, Colo.: Westview Press, 2000.

Barnhart, Bruno. *The Good Wine: Reading John from the Center.* New York: Paulist Press, 1993.

Bass, Dorothy C. "Keeping Sabbath." *Practicing Our Faith: A Way of Life for a Searching People.* Ed. Dorothy C. Bass. San Francisco: Jossey-Bass, 1997.

Berry, Wendell. "The Pleasures of Eating." *Simpler Living, Compassionate Life: A Christian Perspective.* Ed. Michael Schut. Denver, Colo.: Living the Good News/Moorhouse Group, 1999.

_____. "1979#X 'Whatever is forseen in joy.'" *Sabbaths.* San Francisco: North Point Press, 1987.

Blake, William. "Eternity." *The Complete Poetry and Prose of William Blake.* Rev. ed. Ed. David V. Erdman. Berkeley: University of California Press, 1982.

Bondi, Roberta. *To Love as God Loves: Conversations with the Early Church.* Philadelphia: Fortress Press, 1987.

Borg, Marcus J. *Conflict, Holiness, and Politics in the Teachings of Jesus.* 2d ed. Harrisburg, Pa.: Trinity Press International, 1998.

Bourgeault, Cynthia. "Centering Prayer as Radical Consent." *Sewanee Theological Review* 40:1 (1996) 46–54.

Brown, Robert McAfee. *Kairos: Three Prophetic Challenges to the Church.* Grand Rapids, Mich.: Eerdmans, 1990.

Brueggemann, Walter. "The Daily Voice of Faith: The Covenanted Self." *The Covenanted Self: Explorations in Law and Covenant.* Minneapolis: Fortress Press, 1999.

293

_____. "Four Indispensable Conversations Among Exiles." *Deep Memory, Exuberant Hope: Contested Truth in a Post-Christian World.* Minneapolis: Fortress Press, 2000.

_____. "The Liturgy of Abundance, the Myth of Scarcity." *Deep Memory, Exuberant Hope: Contested Truth in a Post-Christian World.* Ed. Patrick D. Miller. Minneapolis: Fortress Press, 2000.

_____. *The Prophetic Imagination.* Philadelphia: Fortress Press, 1978.

_____. "The Truth of Abundance: Relearning Dayenu." *The Covenanted Self: Explorations in Law and Covenant.* Ed. Patrick D. Miller. Minneapolis: Fortress Press, 1999.

Buber, Martin. *I and Thou.* Trans. Walter Kaufmann. New York: Charles Scribner's Sons, 1970.

Coakley, Sarah. "Deepening Practices: Perspectives from Ascetical and Mystical Theology." *Practicing Theology: Beliefs and Practices in Christian Life.* Ed. Miroslav Volf and Dorothy C. Bass. Grand Rapids, Mich.: Eerdmans, 2002.

Cobb, John B., Jr. "Liberation Theology and the Global Economy." *Liberating the Future: God, Mammon and Theology.* Ed. Joerg Rieger. Minneapolis: Augsburg Fortress, 1998.

Coffin, William Sloan. "Who Is There Big Enough to Love the Whole Planet?" *The Future of Prophetic Christianity: Essays in Honor of Robert McAfee Brown.* Ed. Denise Lardner Carmody and John Tully Carmody. Maryknoll, N.Y.: Orbis Books, 1993.

Cohen, Stanley. *States of Denial: Knowing about Atrocities and Suffering.* Malden, Mass.: Blackwell, 2001.

Crosson, John Dominic. *The Historical Jesus: The Life of a Mediterranean Jewish Peasant.* San Francisco: HarperSanFrancisco, 1992.

Daly, H. E., and John B. Cobb. *For the Common Good: Redirecting the Economy Toward Community, the Environment and a Sustainable Future.* Boston: Beacon Press, 1989.

Douglas, Mary. *Leviticus as Literature.* New York: Oxford University Press, 1999.

Dreze, Jean, and Amartya Sen. *Hunger and Public Action.* Oxford: Clarendon Press, 1989.

Eliot, T. S. "Little Gidding." *The Complete Poems and Plays.* New York: Harcourt, Brace and Co., 1972.

Elsbernd, Mary, and Reimund Bieringer. *When Love Is Not Enough: A Theo-Ethic of Justice.* Collegeville: The Liturgical Press, 2002.

Esquival, Julia. *Threatened with Resurrection: Prayers and Poems from an Exiled Guatemalan.* 2d ed. Elgin, Ill.: Brethren Press, 1994.

Fischer, Norman, and others. *Benedict's Dharma: Buddhists Reflect on the Rule of Saint Benedict.* Ed. Patrick Henry. New York: Riverhead Books, 1991.

Flinders, Carol Lee. *At the Root of This Longing: Reconciling a Spiritual Hunger and a Feminist Thirst.* New York: HarperCollins, 1999.

Frank, Arthur. *The Wounded Storyteller: Body, Illness and Ethics.* Chicago: University of Chicago Press, 1995.

Grassi, Joseph A. *Broken Bread and Broken Bodies: The Lord's Supper and World Hunger.* Maryknoll, N.Y.: Orbis Books, 1985.

Griffin, Susan. *A Chorus of Stones: The Private Life of War.* New York: Doubleday, 1992.

Haan, Roelf. The *Economics of Honour: Biblical Reflections on Money and Property.* Trans. Nancy Forest-Flier. Geneva: World Council of Churches, 1988.

Habermas, Jurgen. *Legitimation Crisis.* Boston: Beacon Press, 1973.

Hellwig, Monika. *The Eucharist and the Hunger of the World.* 2d ed. Franklin, Wis.: Sheed and Ward, 1999.

Herzog, Frederick. *God-Walk: Liberation Shaping Dogmatics.* Maryknoll, N.Y.: Orbis Books, 1988.

Heschel, Abraham. *The Prophets.* New York: HarperCollins, 1962; Perennial Classics edition, 2001.

_____. *The Sabbath: Its Meaning for Modern Man.* New York: Farrar, Straus & Co., 1952.

Human Development Report 1998. New York: Oxford University Press, 1998.

Hyde, Lewis. *The Gift: Imagination and the Erotic Life of Property.* New York: Vintage Books, 1979.

Isasi-Diaz, Ada Maria. "Solidarity: Love of Neighbor in the 1980s." *Feminist Theological Ethics: A Reader.* Ed. Lois K. Daly. Louisville, Ky.: Westminster John Knox Press, 1994.

Johnson, Luke T. *Sharing Possessions: Mandate and Symbol of Faith.* Philadelphia: Fortress Press, 1981.

Keck, Leander E. *Paul and His Letters.* 2nd ed. Philadelphia: Fortress Press, 1988.

_____. *Who Is Jesus? History in Perfect Tense.* Columbia: University of South Carolina Press, 2000.

Kleinman, Arthur, and Joan Kleinman. "The Appeal of Experience; The Dismay of Images: Cultural Appropriations of Suffering in Our Times." *Social Suffering.* Ed. Arthur Kleinman, Veena Das, and Margaret Lock. Berkeley: University of California Press, 1997.

LaCugna, Catherine Mowry. *God for Us: The Trinity and Christian Life.* New York: HarperCollins, 1991.

Lebacqz, Karen. "Bridging the Gap: Pain and Compassion." *The Future of Prophetic Christianity: Essays in Honor of Robert McAfee Brown.* Ed. Denise Lardner Carmody and John Tully Carmody. Maryknoll, N.Y.: Orbis Books, 1993.

Leddy, Mary Jo. *Radical Gratitude*. Maryknoll, N.Y.: Orbis Books, 2002.

_____. *Say to the Darkness, We Beg to Differ*. Toronto: Lester and Orpen Dennys, 1990.

McFague, Sallie. *Life Abundant: Rethinking Theology and Economy for a Planet in Peril*. Minneapolis: Fortress Press, 2001.

McNeill, Donald P., and others. *Compassion: A Reflection on the Christian Life*. Garden City, N.Y.: Double Day and Co., 1983.

Maimon, Moses ben (1135–1204). "Book Seven: Seeds." *A Maimonides Reader*. Ed. Isadore Twersky. New York: Behrman House, 1972.

May, Gerald. *Will and Spirit: A Contemplative Psychology*. San Francisco: Harper & Row, 1982.

Meeks, M. Douglas. "Economy and the Future of Liberation Theology in North America." *Liberating the Future: God, Mammon and Theology*. Ed. Joerg Rieger. Minneapolis: Fortress Press, 1998.

_____. *God the Economist: The Doctrine of God and Political Economy*. Minneapolis: Fortress Press, 1989.

Moltmann, Jurgen. *The Coming of God: Christian Eschatology*. Minneapolis: Fortress Press, 1996.

_____. *God in Creation: An Ecological Doctrine of Creation*. London: SCM Press, 1985.

_____. "God's Kenosis in the Creation and Consummation of the World." *The Work of Love: Creation as Kenosis*. Ed. John Polkinghorne. Grand Rapids, Mich.: Eerdmans, 2001.

_____. "Liberating and Anticipating the Future." *Liberating Eschatology: Essays in Honor of Letty M. Russell*. Ed. Margaret A. Farley and Serene Jones. Louisville: Westminster John Knox Press, 1999.

_____. "Political Theology and Theology of Liberation." *Liberating the Future: God, Mammon and Theology*. Ed. Joerg Rieger. Minneapolis: Fortress Press, 1998.

Morrill, Bruce T. *Anamnesis as Dangerous Memory: Political and Liturgical Theology in Dialogue*. Collegeville: The Liturgical Press, 2000.

Morris, Bruce. "About Suffering: Voice, Genre, and Moral Community." *Social Suffering*. Ed. Arthur Kleinman, Veena Das and Margaret Lock. Berkeley: University of California Press, 1997.

Nouwen, Henri. *Lifesigns: Intimacy, Fecundity and Ecstasy in Christian Perspective*. Garden City, N.Y.: Doubleday & Co., 1986.

_____. *Reaching Out: The Three Movements of the Spiritual Life*. Garden City, N.Y.: Doubleday, 1975.

O'Connor, Kathleen. *Lamentations and the Tears of the World*. Maryknoll, N.Y.: Orbis Books, 2002.

Phan, Peter C. *Eternity in Time: A Study of Karl Rahner's Eschatology*. Cranbury, N.J.: Associated University Presses, 1988.

Pieris, Aloysius. *An Asian Theology of Liberation*. Maryknoll, N.Y.: Orbis Books, 1988.

Poynor, Rick. "First Things Next." *Adbusters* (July/August 2001).

Rahner, Karl. *Every Day Faith*. Trans. W. J. O'Hara. New York: Herder and Herder, 1968.

Reiser, Konrad. "Utopia and Responsibility." *The Jubilee Challenge: Utopia or Possibility? Jewish and Christian Insights*. Ed. Hans Ucko. Geneva: World Council of Churches Publications, 1997.

Ricoeur, Paul. "The Logic of Jesus, the Logic of God." *Christianity and Crisis* (1979) 324–7.

Rohr, Richard. *Jesus' Plan for a New World: The Sermon on the Mount*. Cincinnati: St. Anthony Messenger Press, 1996.

Rolheiser, Ronald. *The Holy Longing: The Search for a Christian Spirituality*. New York: Doubleday, 1999.

Sample, Tex. *Hard Living People and Mainstream Christians*. Nashville: Abingdon Press, 1993.

Schmidt, Leigh Eric. "Practices of Exchange: From Market Culture to Gift Economy in the Interpretation of American Religion." *Lived Religion in America: Toward a History of Practice*. Ed. David D. Hall. Princeton, N.J.: Princeton University Press, 1998.

Schneiders, Sandra M. *Finding the Treasure: Locating Catholic Religious Life in a New Ecclesial and Cultural Context*. Mahwah, N.J.: Paulist Press, 2000.

_____. "The Resurrection of Jesus and Christian Spirituality." *Christian Resources of Hope*. Collegeville: The Liturgical Press, 1995.

_____. *The Revelatory Text: Interpreting the New Testament as Sacred Scripture*. New York: Harper SanFrancisco, 1991.

_____. *Written That You May Believe: Encountering Jesus in the Fourth Gospel*. New York: Crossroad, 1999.

Schwartz, Regina M. *The Curse of Cain: The Violent Legacy of Monotheism*. Chicago: University of Chicago Press, 1997.

Sen, Amartya. *Poverty and Famines: An Essay on Entitlement and Deprivation*. Oxford: Clarendon Press, 1981.

_____. "Property and Hunger." *Economics and Philosophy* 4 (1988) 57–68.

Sider, Ron. *Rich Christians in an Age of Hunger*. 2d ed. Dallas: Word Publishing, 1997.

Soelle, Dorothee. *The Strength of the Weak: Toward a Christian Feminist Identity*. Trans. Robert and Rita Kimber. Philadelphia: Westminster Press, 1984.

Stendahl, Krister. "Christ's Lordship and Religious Pluralism." *Meanings: The Bible as Document and as Guide*. Minneapolis: Fortress Press, 1984.

Suchocki, Marjorie Hewitt. *The Fall to Violence: Original Sin in Relational Theology*. New York: Continuum, 1999.

Swimme, Brian, and Thomas Berry. *The Universe Story: From the Primordial Flaring Forth to the Ecozoic Era, a Celebration of the Unfolding of the Cosmos*. New York: HarperCollins, 1992.

Tanner, Kathryn. "Theological Reflection and Christian Practices." *Practicing Theology: Beliefs and Practices in Christian Life*. Ed. Miroslav Volf and Dorothy C. Bass. Grand Rapids, Mich.: Eerdmans, 2002.

Taylor, Barbara Brown. *The Luminous Web: Essays on Science and Religion*. Cambridge, Mass.: Cowley Publications, 2000.

_____. *Speaking of Sin: The Lost Language of Salvation*. Cambridge, Mass.: Cowley Publications, 2000.

Trible, Phyllis. *God and the Rhetoric of Sexuality*. Philadelphia: Fortress Press, 1978.

_____. *Texts of Terror: Literary-Feminist Readings of Biblical Narratives*. Philadelphia: Fortress Press, 1984.

Tronto, Joan C. *Moral Boundaries: A Political Argument for an Ethic of Care*. New York: Routledge, 1993.

Volf, Miroslav. *Exclusion and Embrace: A Theological Exploration of Identity, Otherness and Reconciliation*. Nashville: Abingdon Press, 1996.

_____. "In the Cage of Vanities: Christian Faith and the Dynamics of Economic Progress." *Rethinking Materialism: Perspectives on the Spiritual Dimension of Economic Behavior*. Ed. Robert Wuthnow. Grand Rapids, Mich.: Eerdmans, 1995.

_____. *Work in the Spirit: Toward a Theology of Work*. New York: Oxford University Press, 1991.

Weiskel, T. C. "Some Notes from Belshaz'zar's Feast." *Simpler Living Compassionate Life: A Christian Perspective*. Ed. M. Schut. Denver: Living the Good News/Moorhouse Group, 1999.

Welch, Sharon. *A Feminist Ethic of Risk*. Rev. ed. Minneapolis: Fortress Press, 2000.

Welker, Michael. *God the Spirit*. Trans. John T. Hoffmeyer. Minneapolis: Fortress Press, 1994.

Wink, Walter. *Engaging the Powers: Discernment and Resistance in a World of Domination*. Minneapolis: Fortress Press, 1992.

Young, Frances M. *Sacrifice and the Death of Christ*. Philadelphia: Westminster Press, 1975.

SCRIPTURE INDEX